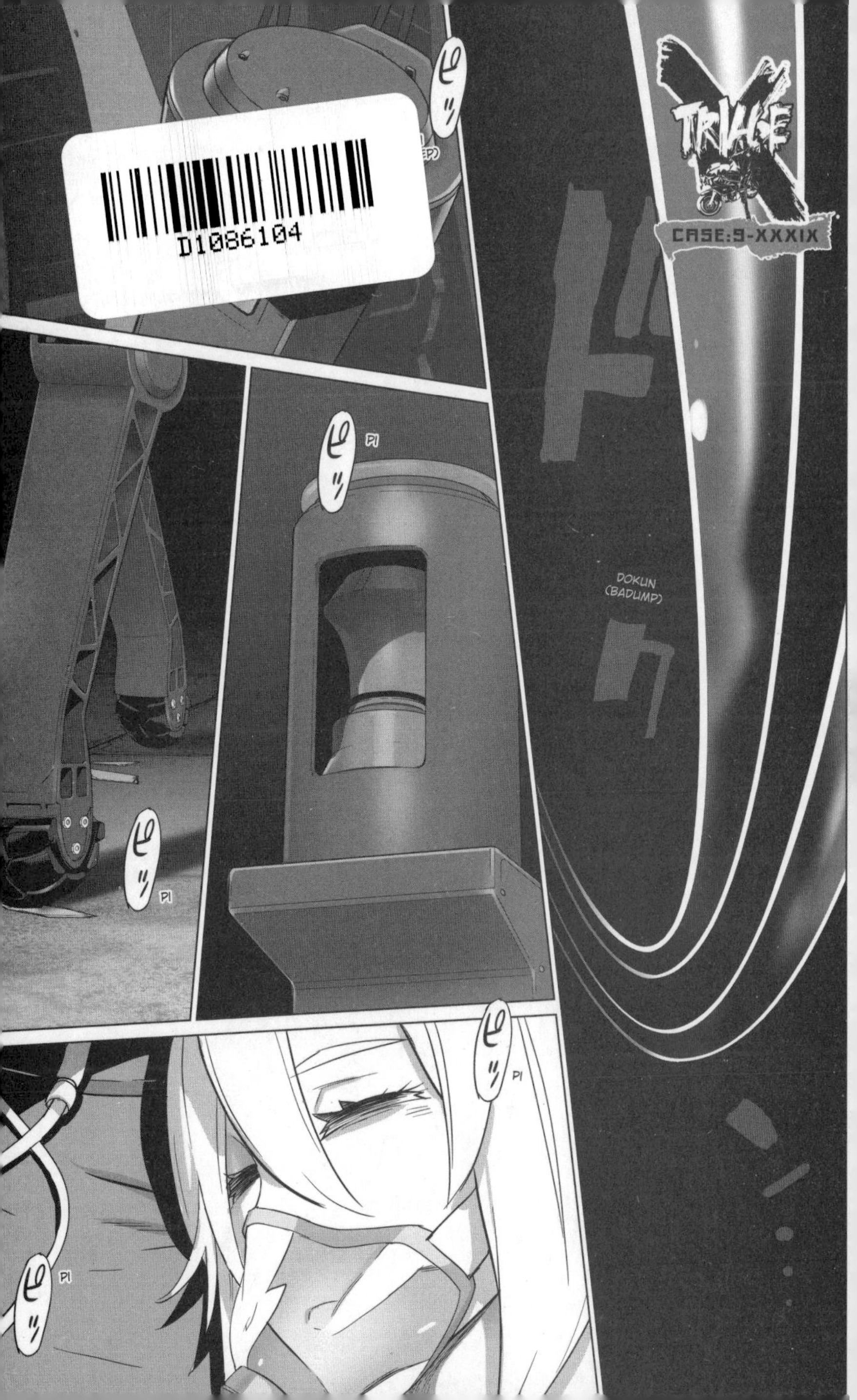

TRIAGE X
CASE:9-XXXIX
DOKUN
(BADUMP)
ピッ
ピッ
PI
ピッ
PI
ピッ
PI
ピッ
PI

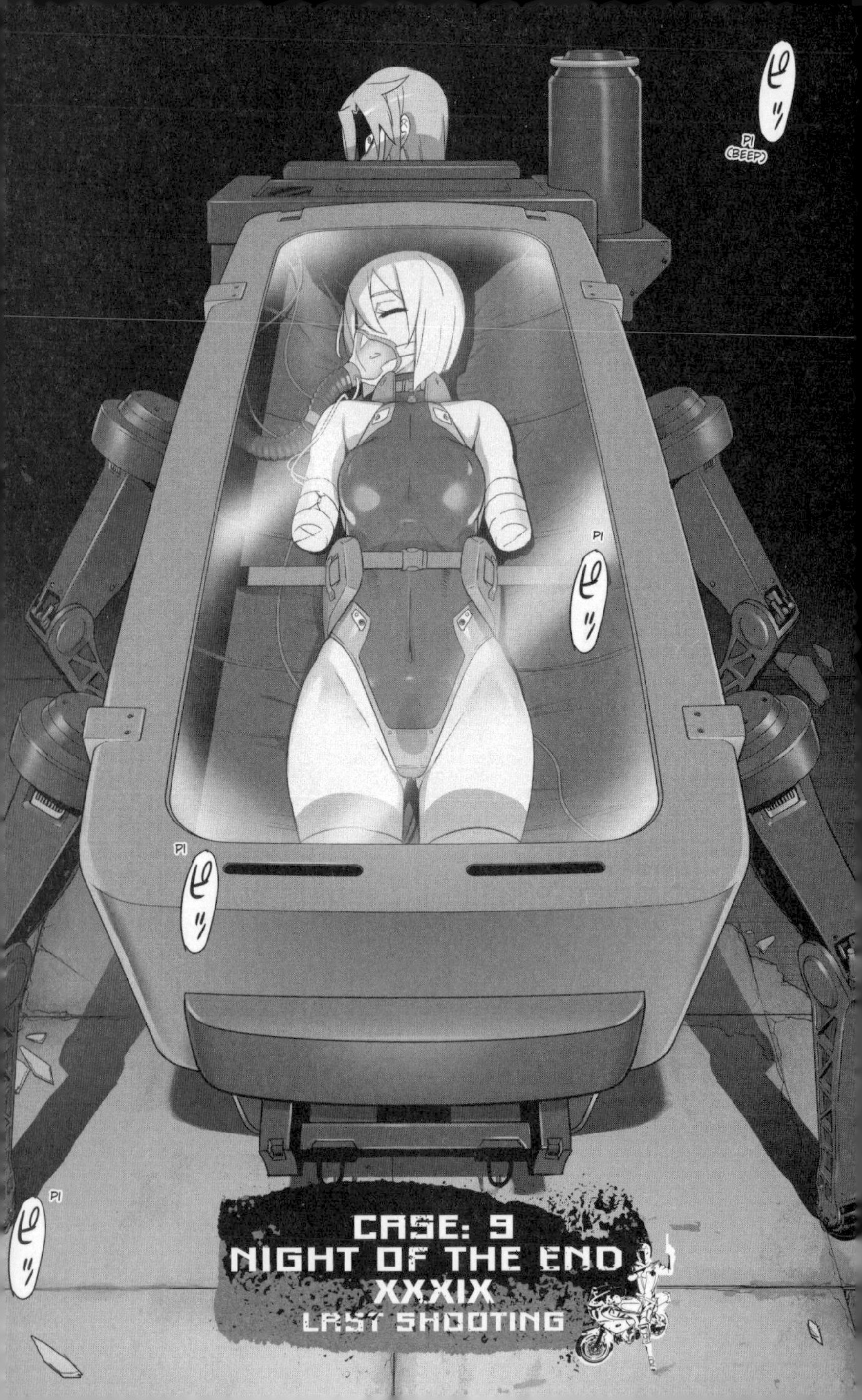

ピッ
PI (BEEP)
ピッ
PI
ピッ
PI
ピッ
PI
CASE: 9
NIGHT OF THE END
XXXIX
LAST SHOOTING

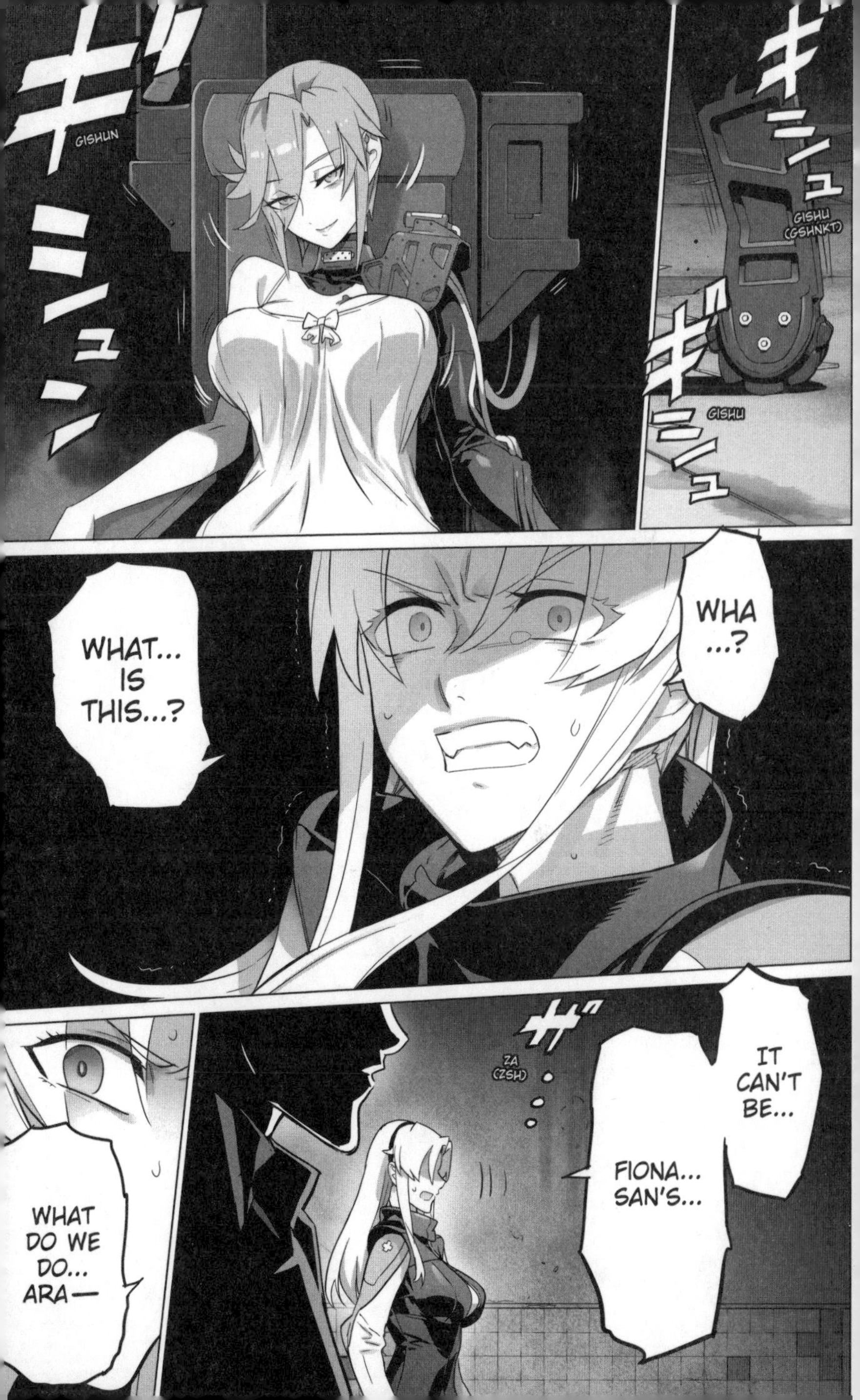
ギシュ
GISHU (GSHNKT)
ギシュ
GISHU
ギシュン
GISHUN
WHA ...?
WHAT... IS THIS...?
IT CAN'T BE...
ザ
ZA (ZSH)
FIONA... SAN'S...
WHAT DO WE DO... ARA—

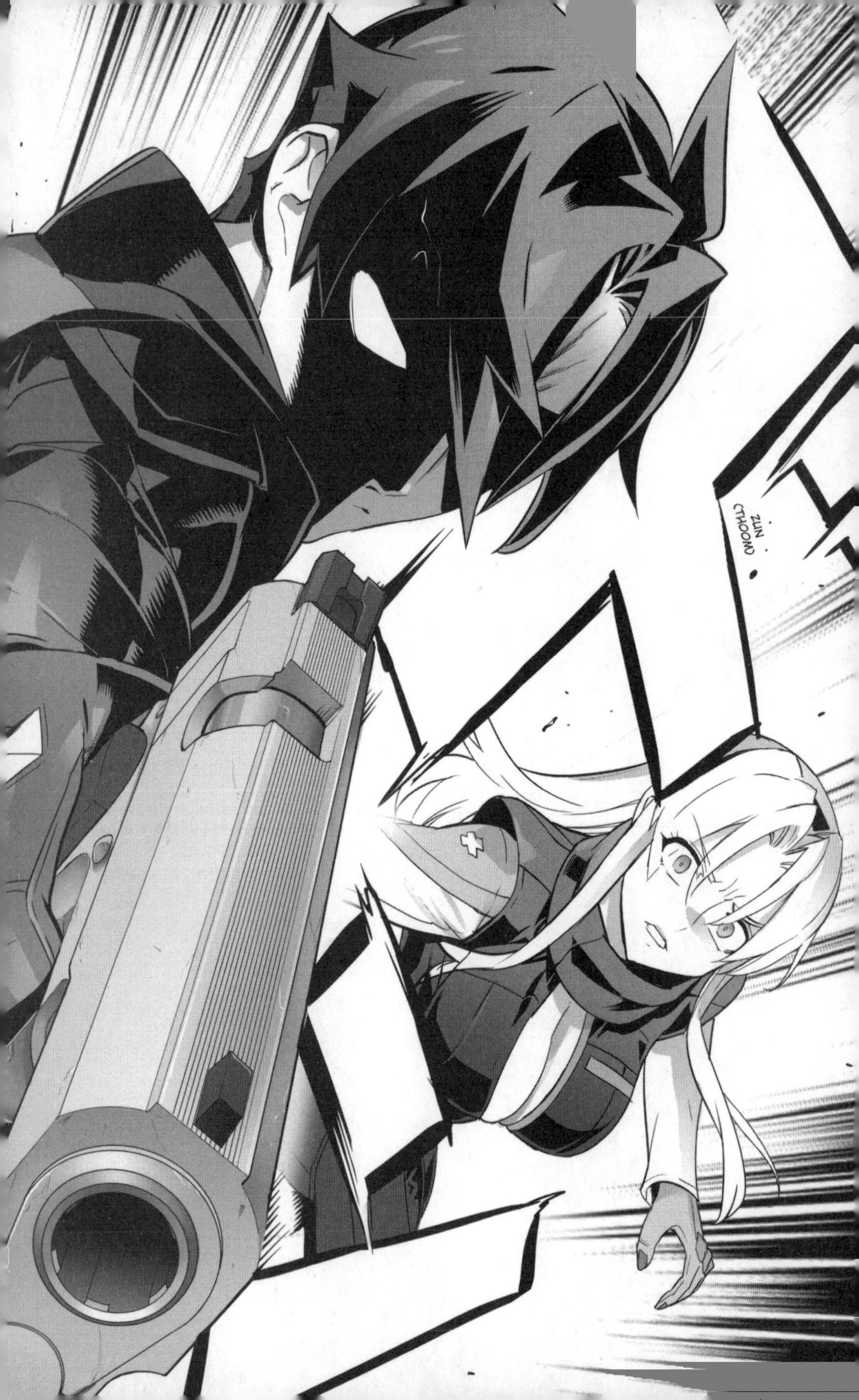
ZUN
(THOOM)

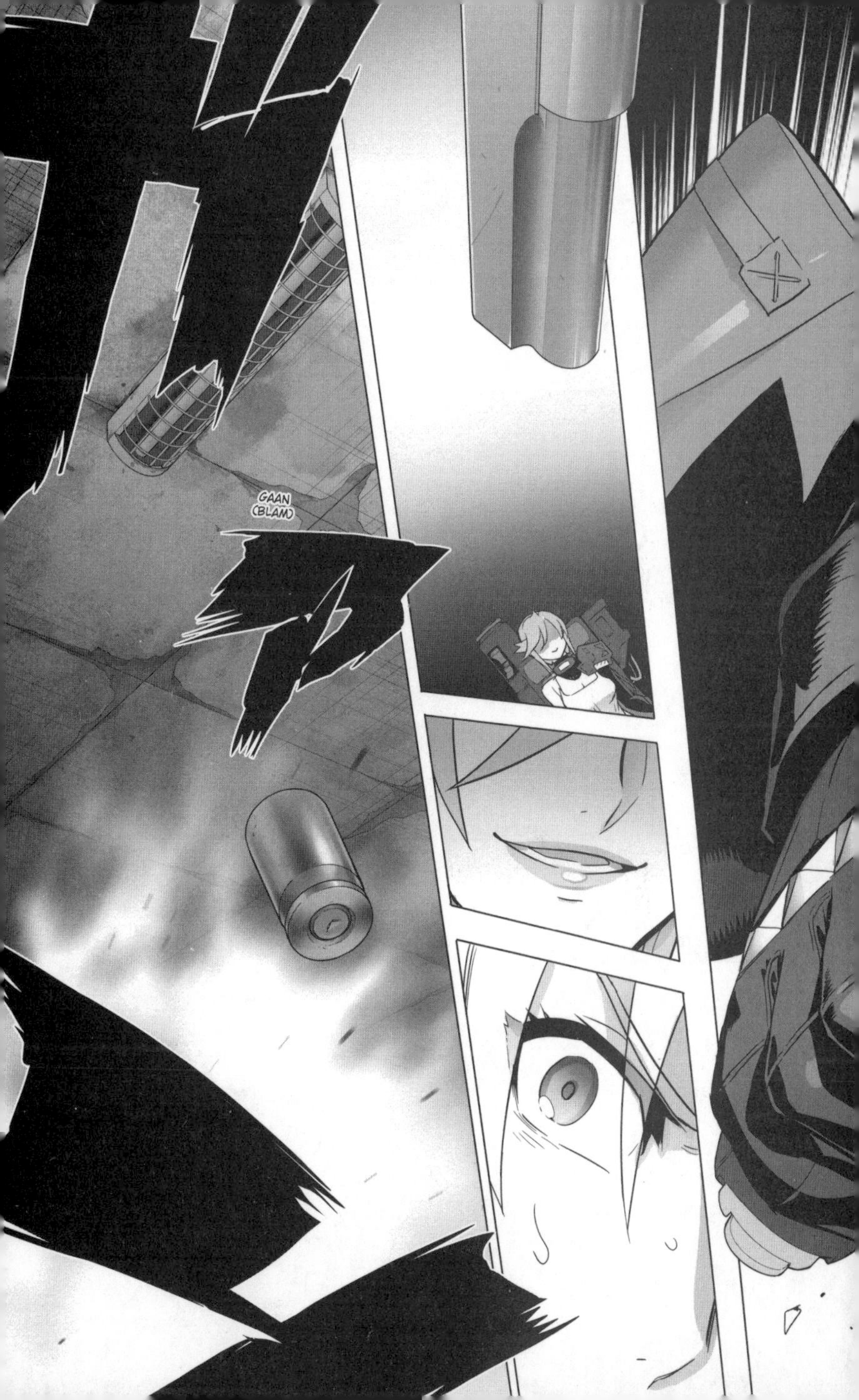
GAAN
(BLAM)

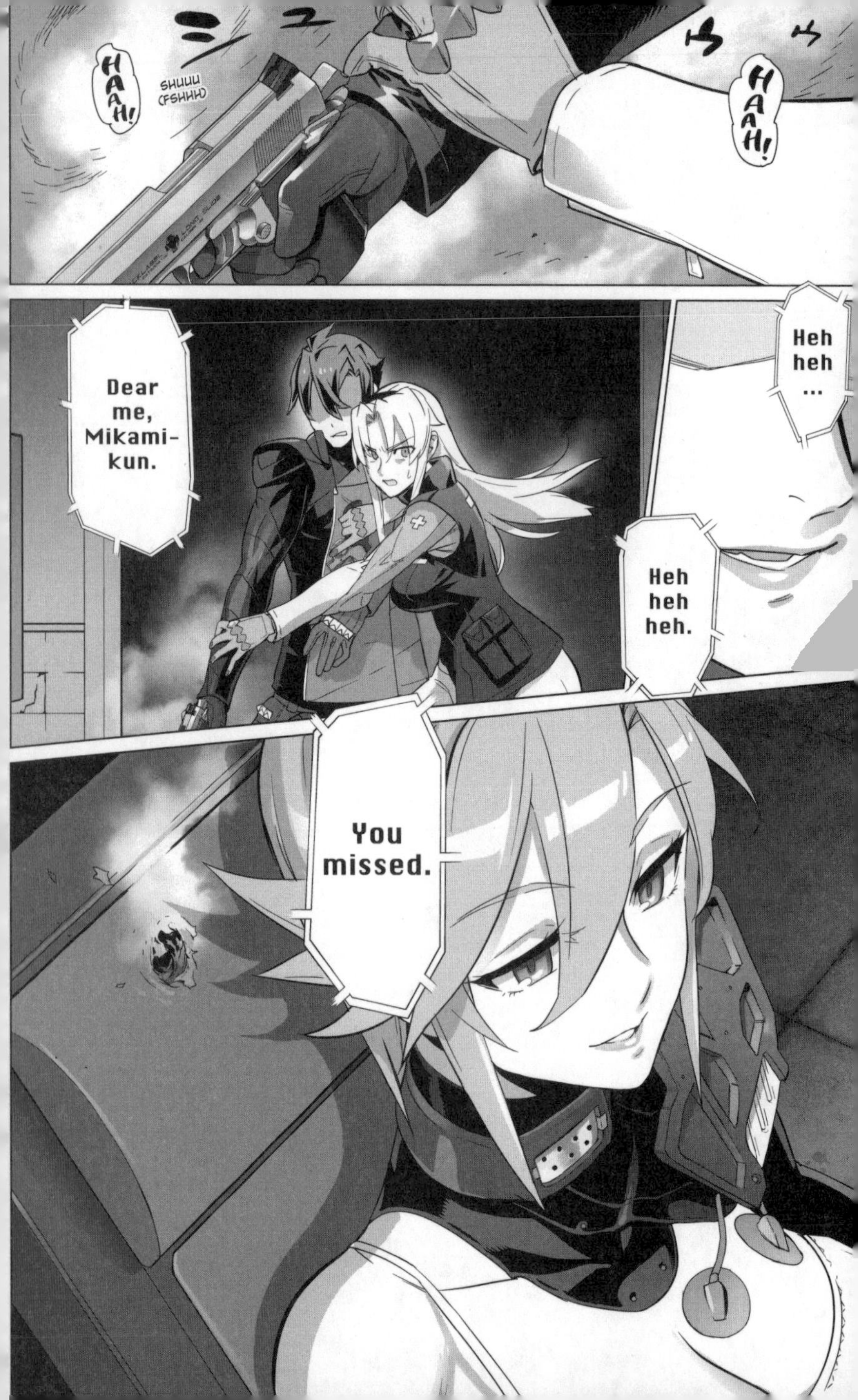
HAAH!
HAAH!
SHUUU (FSHHH)
Heh heh ...
Heh heh heh.
Dear me, Mikami-kun.
You missed.

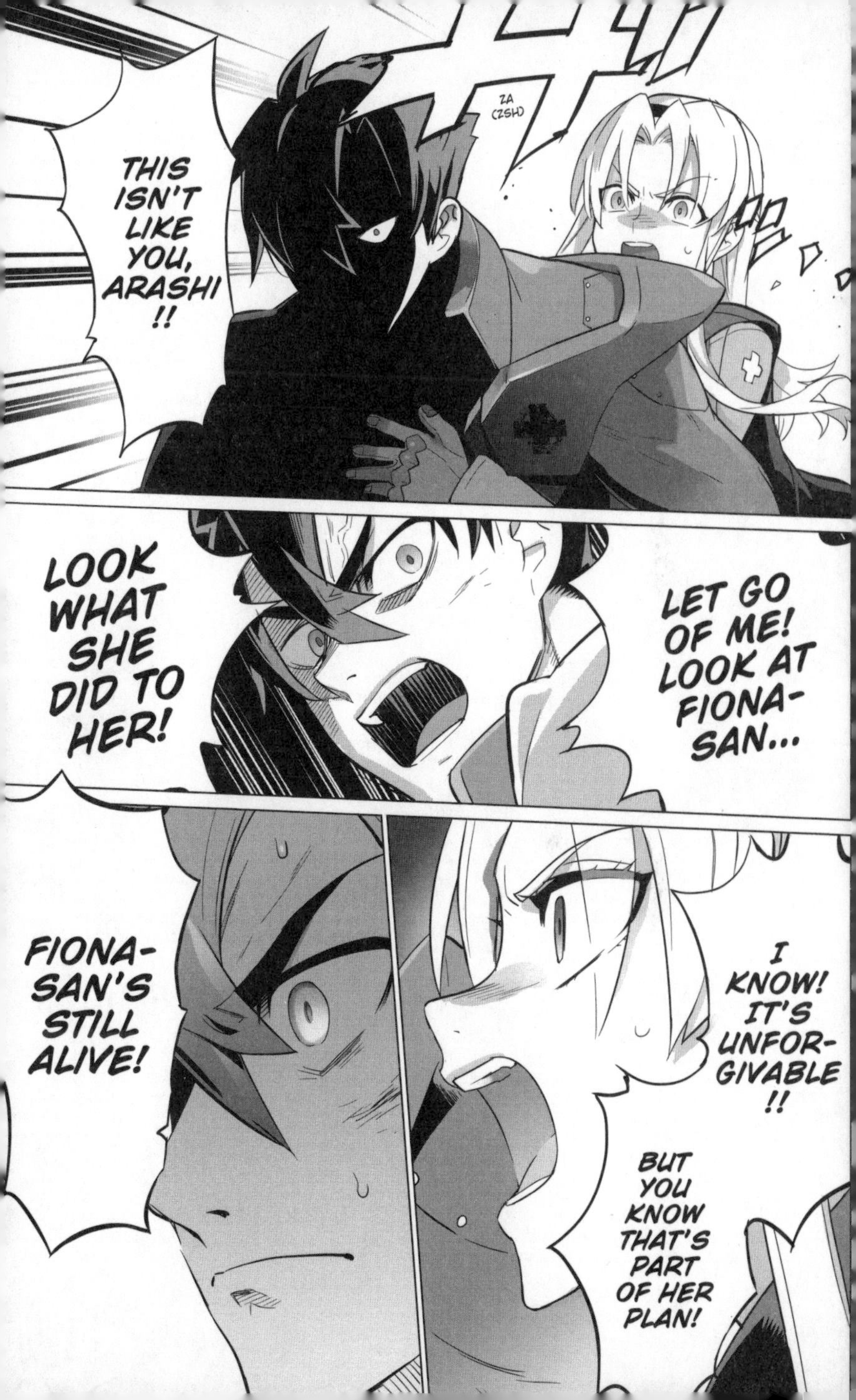
ZA (ZSH)
THIS ISN'T LIKE YOU, ARASHI!!
LET GO OF ME! LOOK AT FIONA-SAN...
LOOK WHAT SHE DID TO HER!
I KNOW! IT'S UNFORGIVABLE!!
BUT YOU KNOW THAT'S PART OF HER PLAN!
FIONA-SAN'S STILL ALIVE!

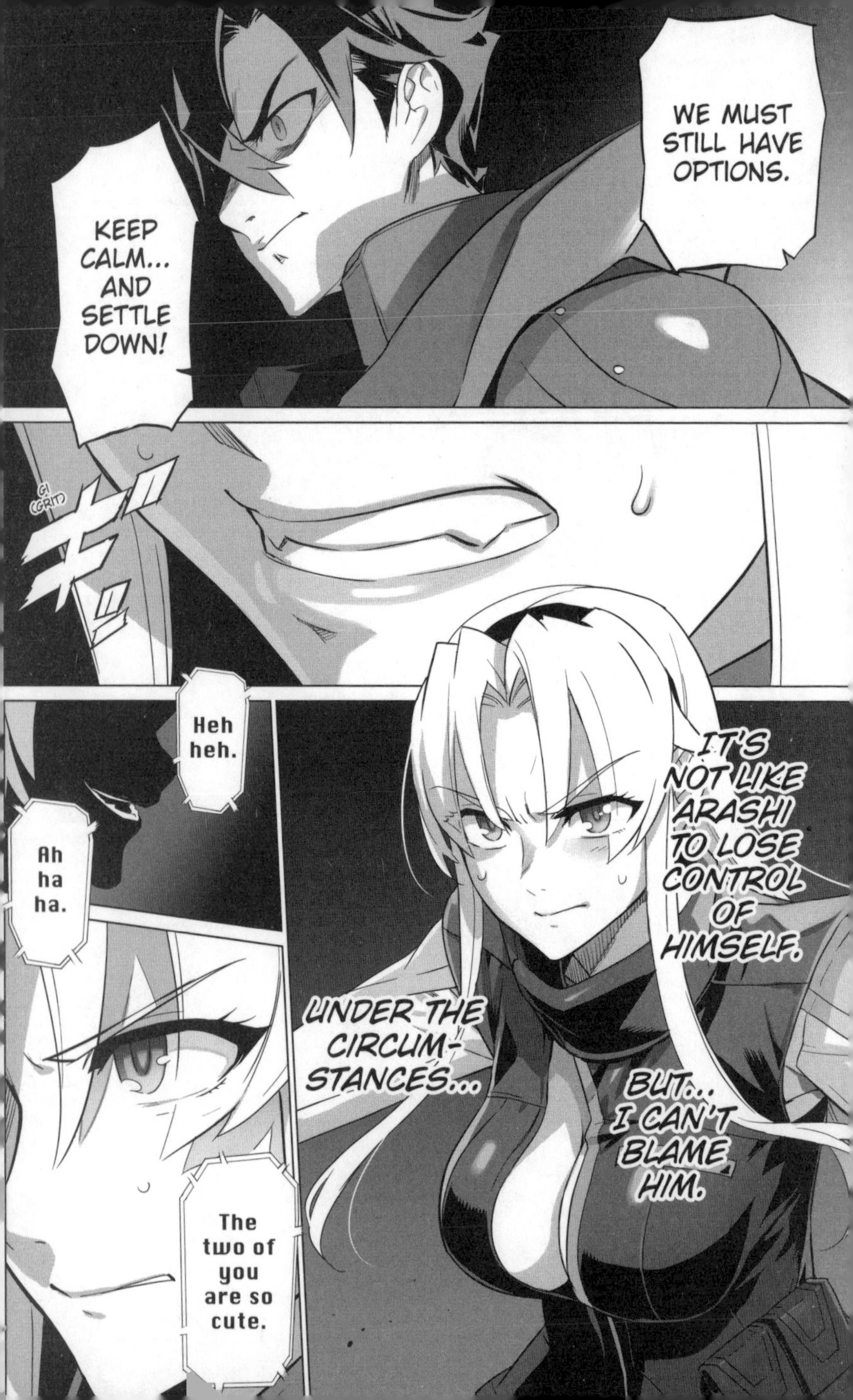
WE MUST STILL HAVE OPTIONS.
KEEP CALM... AND SETTLE DOWN!
GI (GRIT)
IT'S NOT LIKE ARASHI TO LOSE CONTROL OF HIMSELF.
UNDER THE CIRCUM-STANCES...
BUT... I CAN'T BLAME HIM.
Heh heh.
Ah ha ha.
The two of you are so cute.

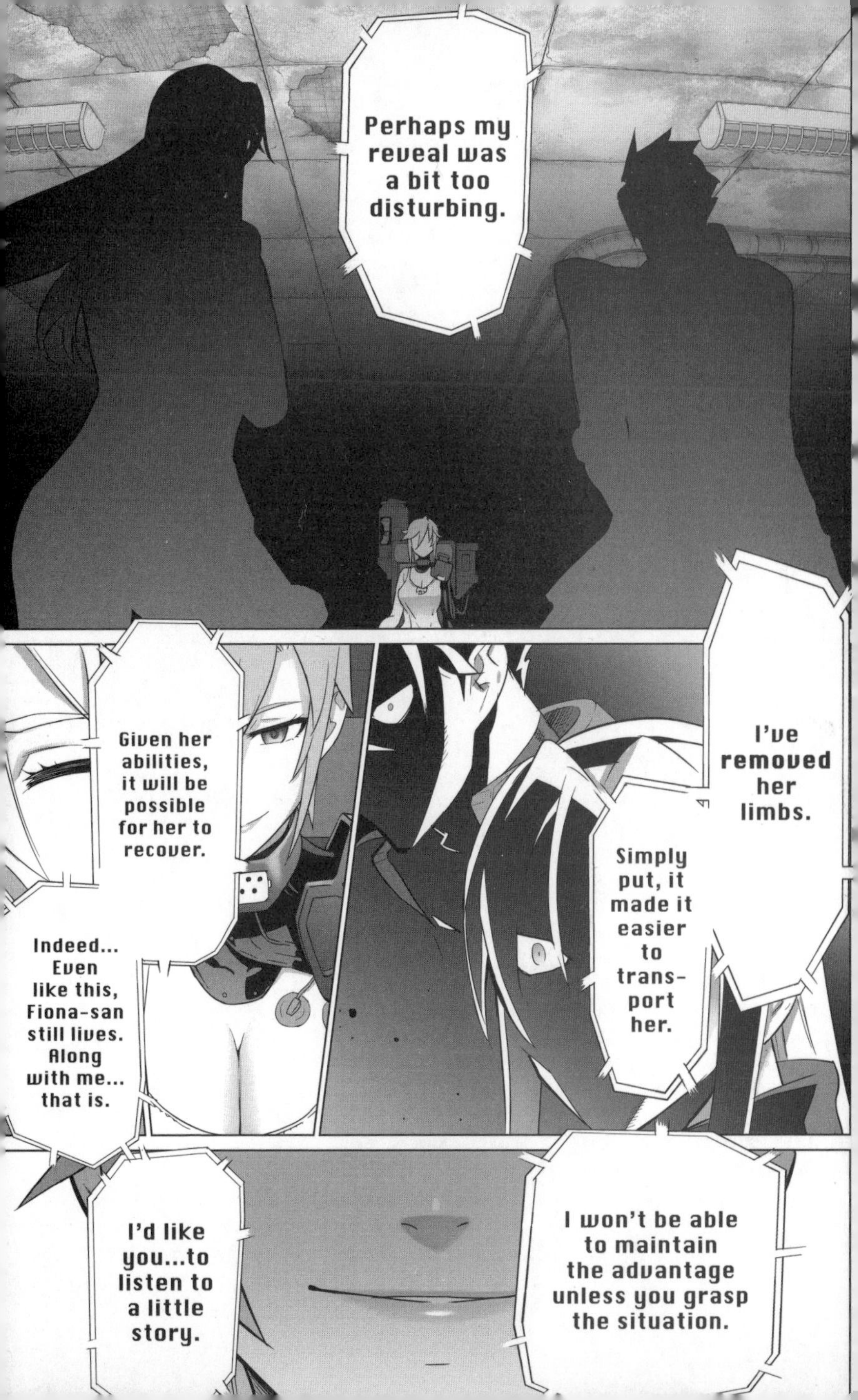
Perhaps my reveal was a bit too disturbing.
I've removed her limbs.
Simply put, it made it easier to transport her.
Given her abilities, it will be possible for her to recover.
Indeed... Even like this, Fiona-san still lives. Along with me... that is.
I won't be able to maintain the advantage unless you grasp the situation.
I'd like you...to listen to a little story.

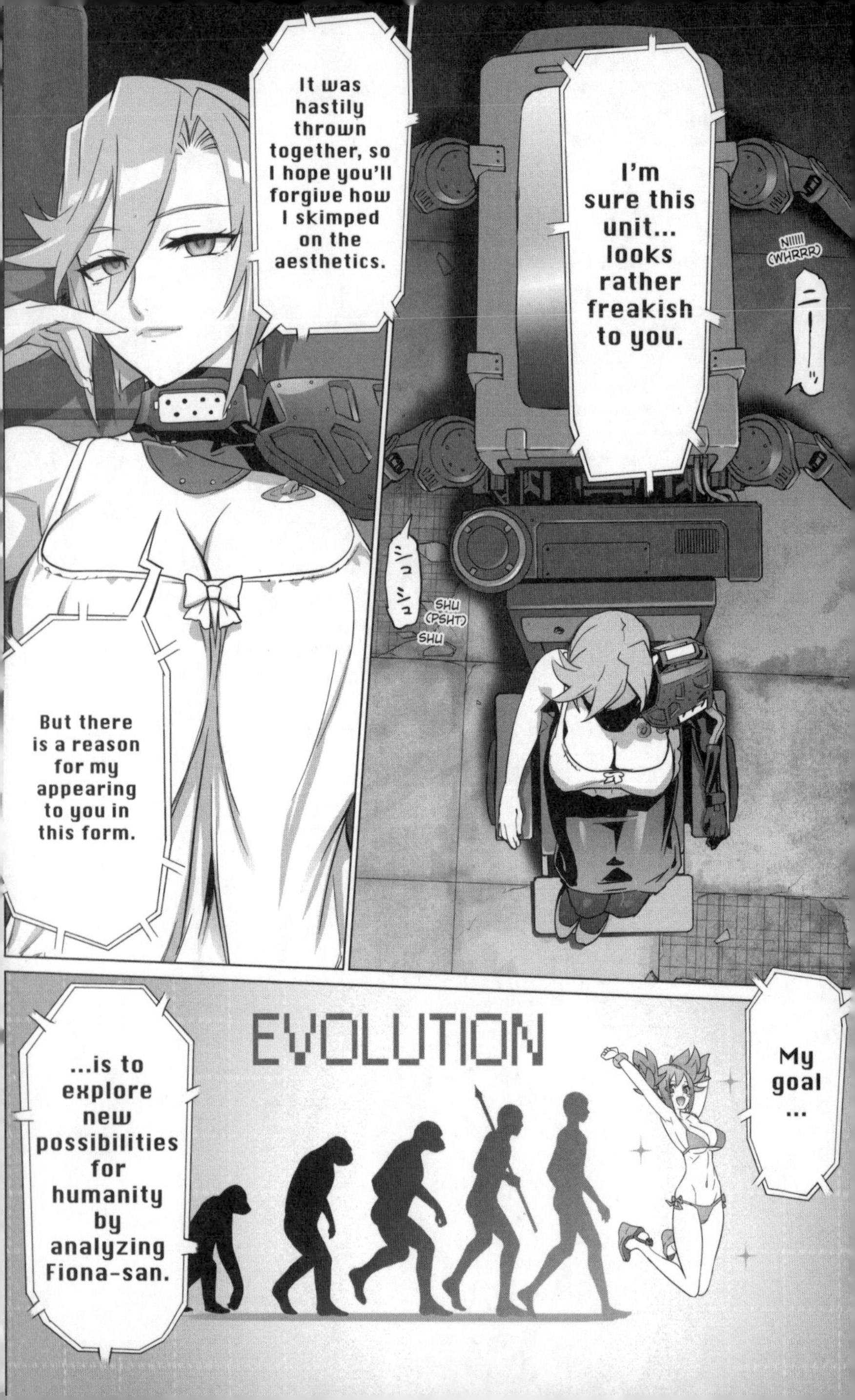
I'm sure this unit... looks rather freakish to you.
NIIIII (WHRRR)
SHU (PSHT) SHU
It was hastily thrown together, so I hope you'll forgive how I skimped on the aesthetics.
But there is a reason for my appearing to you in this form.
My goal...
EVOLUTION
...is to explore new possibilities for humanity by analyzing Fiona-san.

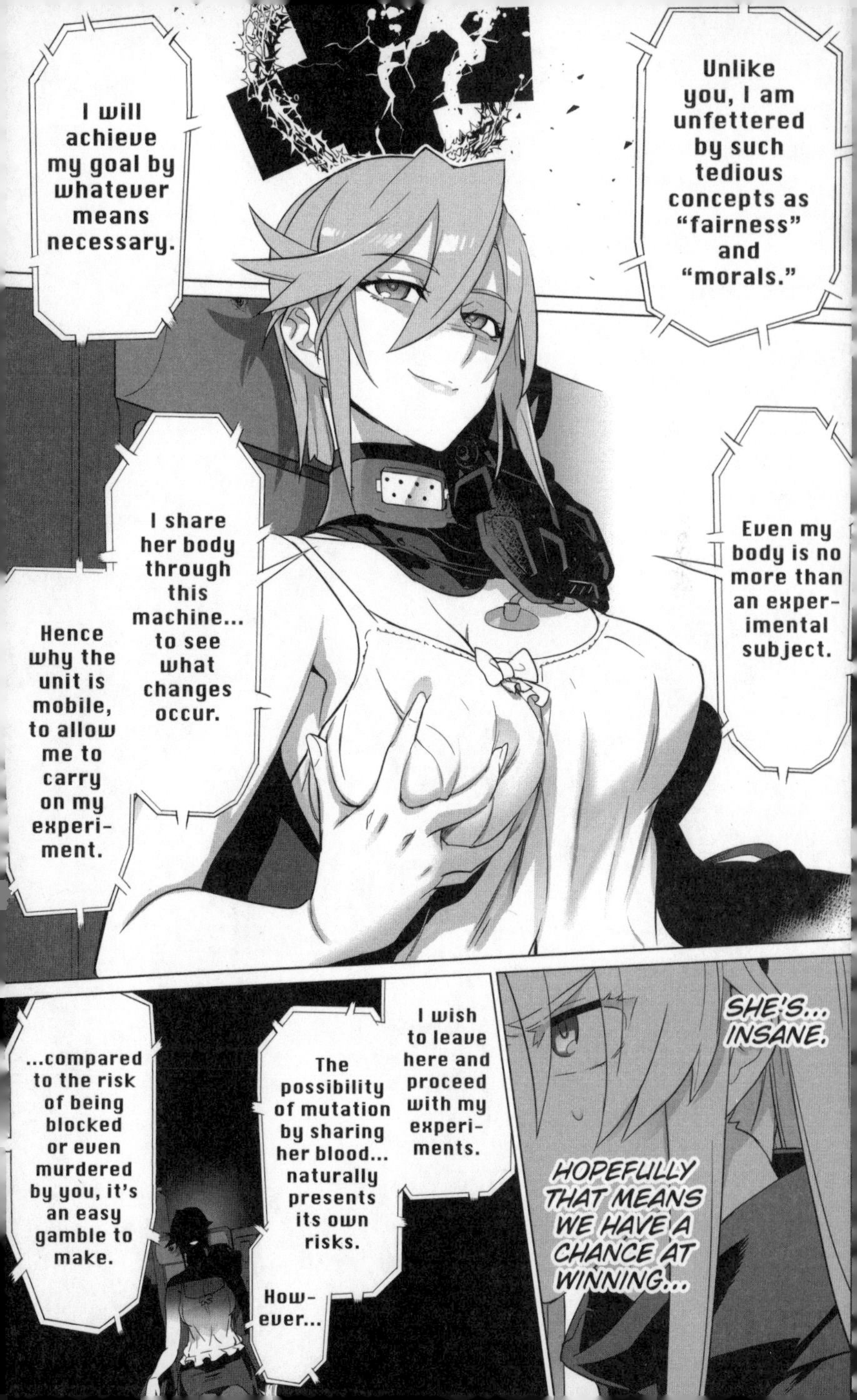
Unlike you, I am unfettered by such tedious concepts as "fairness" and "morals."
I will achieve my goal by whatever means necessary.
Even my body is no more than an exper-imental subject.
I share her body through this machine... to see what changes occur.
Hence why the unit is mobile, to allow me to carry on my experi-ment.
SHE'S... INSANE.
HOPEFULLY THAT MEANS WE HAVE A CHANCE AT WINNING...
I wish to leave here and proceed with my experi-ments.
The possibility of mutation by sharing her blood... naturally presents its own risks.
How-ever...
...compared to the risk of being blocked or even murdered by you, it's an easy gamble to make.

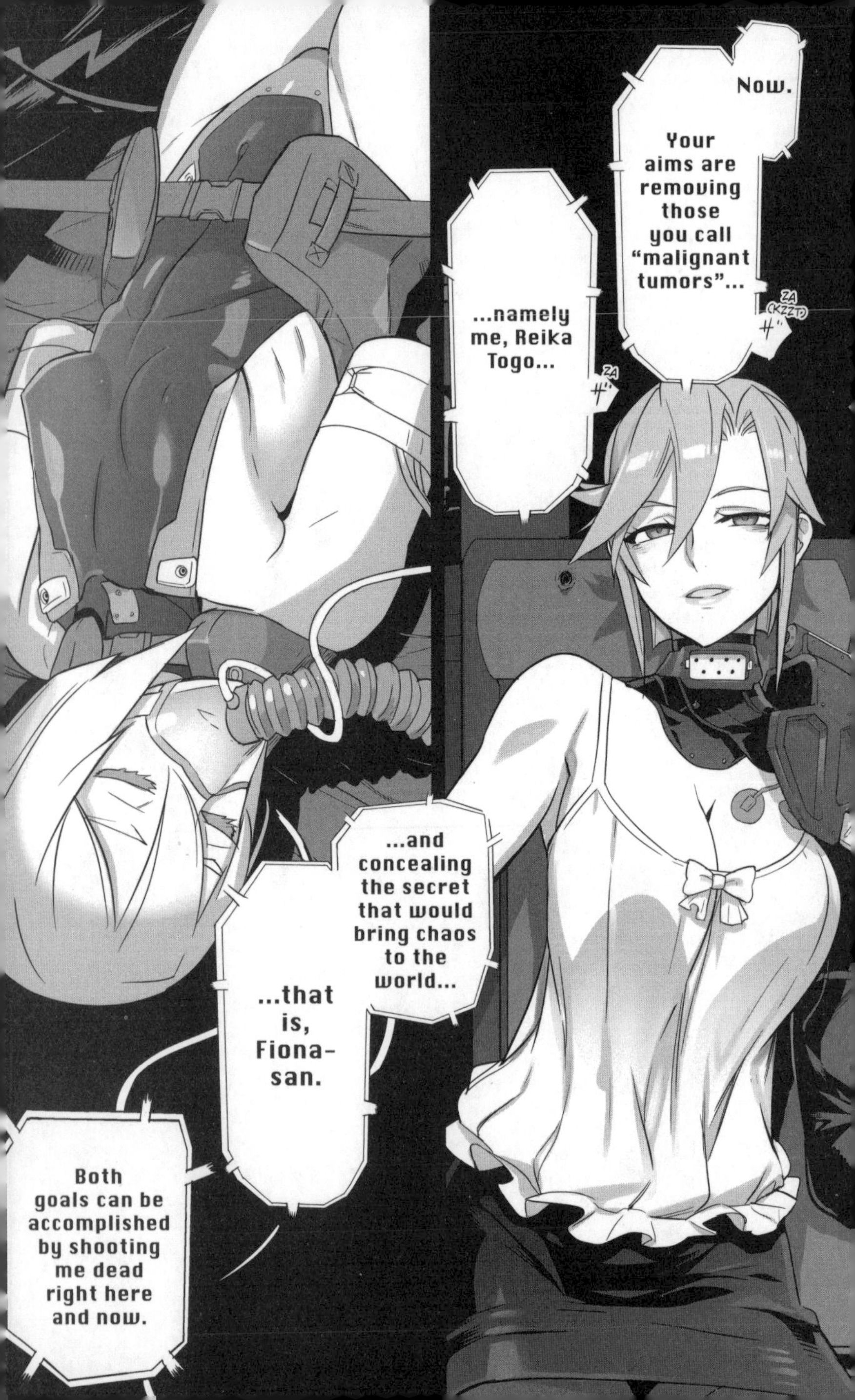
Now.
Your aims are removing those you call "malignant tumors"...
ZA (KZZT)
...namely me, Reika Togo...
ZA
...and concealing the secret that would bring chaos to the world...
...that is, Fiona-san.
Both goals can be accomplished by shooting me dead right here and now.

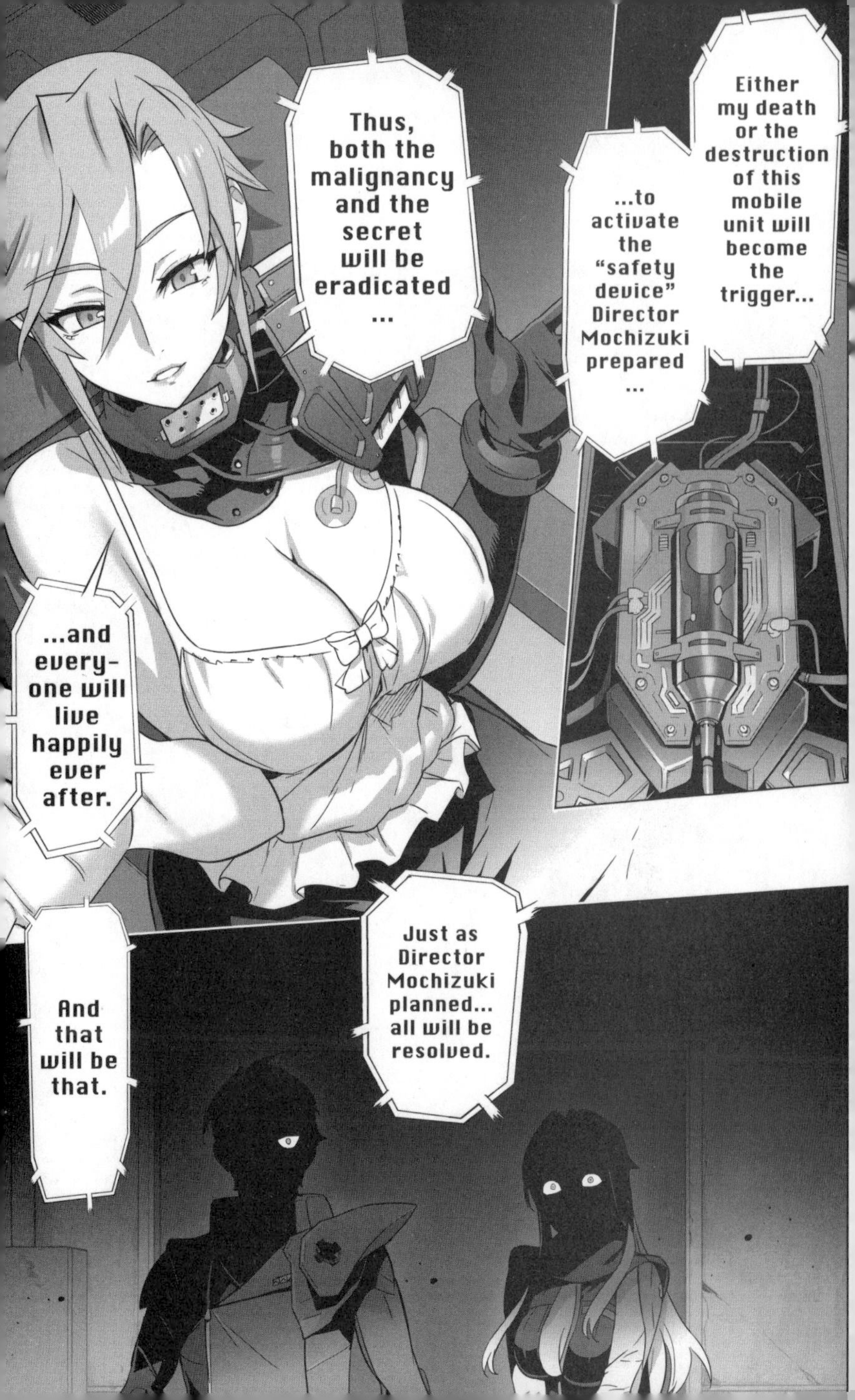
Either my death or the destruction of this mobile unit will become the trigger...
...to activate the "safety device" Director Mochizuki prepared...
Thus, both the malignancy and the secret will be eradicated...
...and every-one will live happily ever after.
Just as Director Mochizuki planned... all will be resolved.
And that will be that.

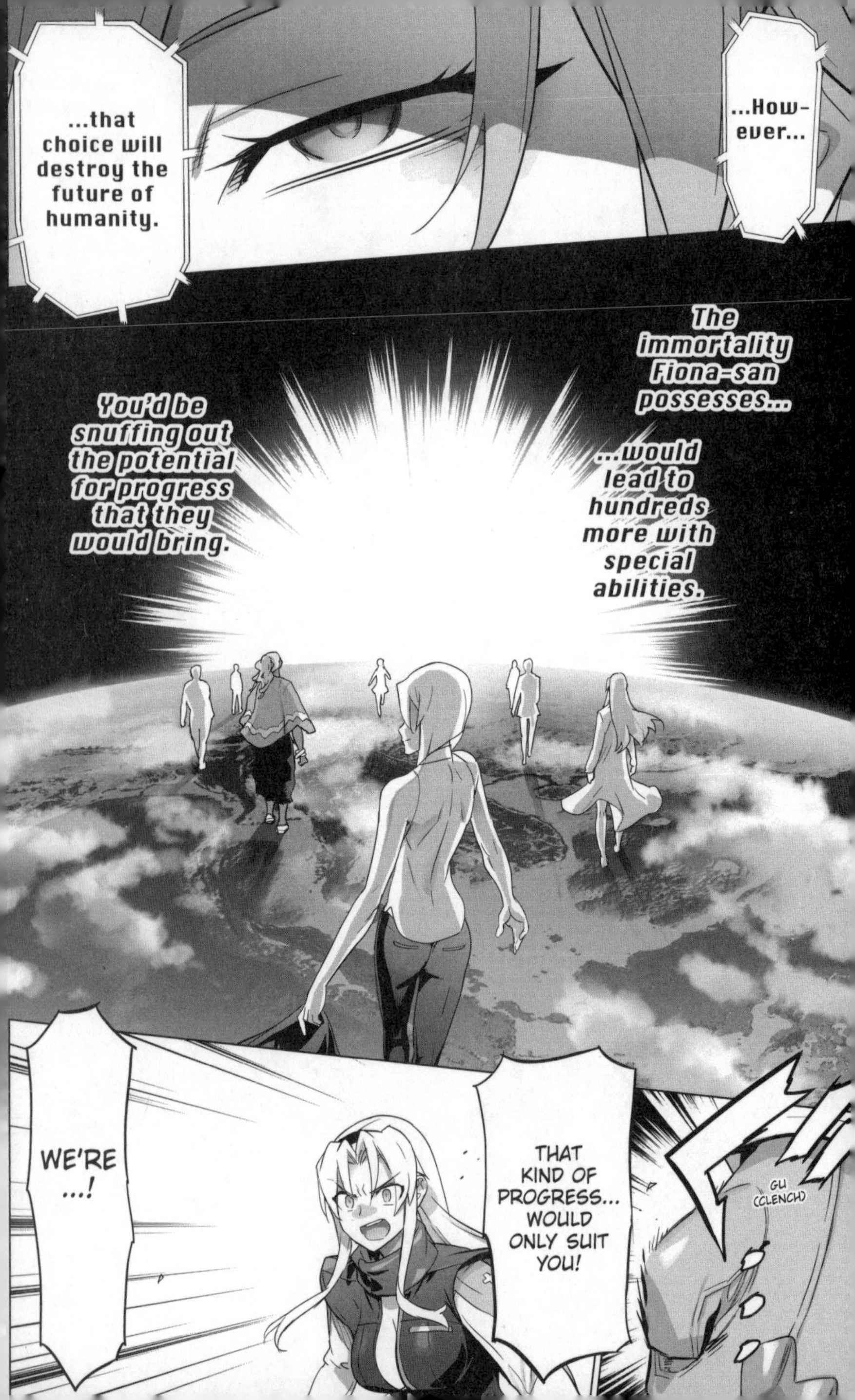
...However...
...that choice will destroy the future of humanity.
The immortality Fiona-san possesses...
...would lead to hundreds more with special abilities.
You'd be snuffing out the potential for progress that they would bring.
GU (CLENCH)
THAT KIND OF PROGRESS... WOULD ONLY SUIT YOU!
WE'RE ...!

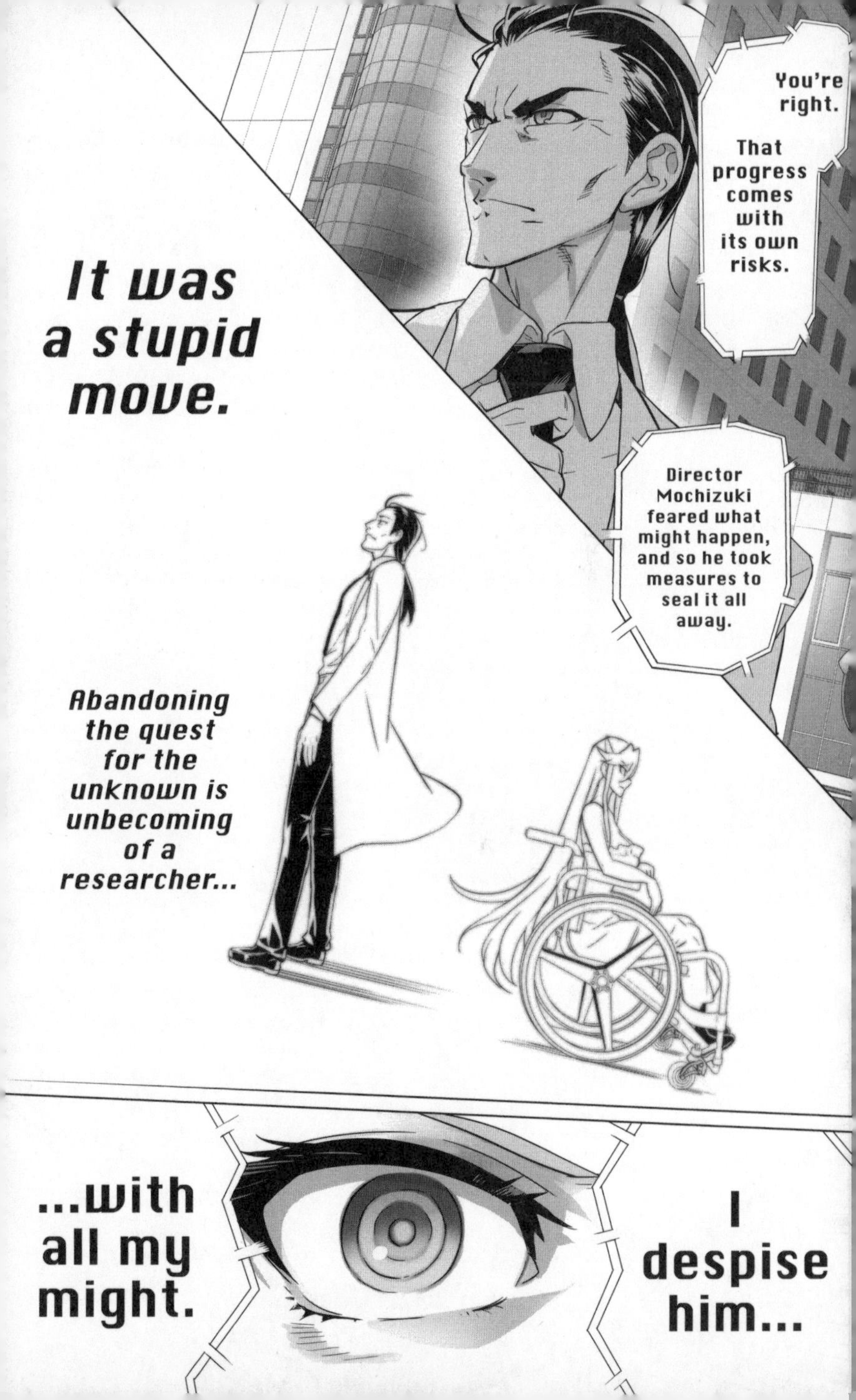
You're right.
That progress comes with its own risks.
Director Mochizuki feared what might happen, and so he took measures to seal it all away.
It was a stupid move.
Abandoning the quest for the unknown is unbecoming of a researcher...
I despise him...
...with all my might.

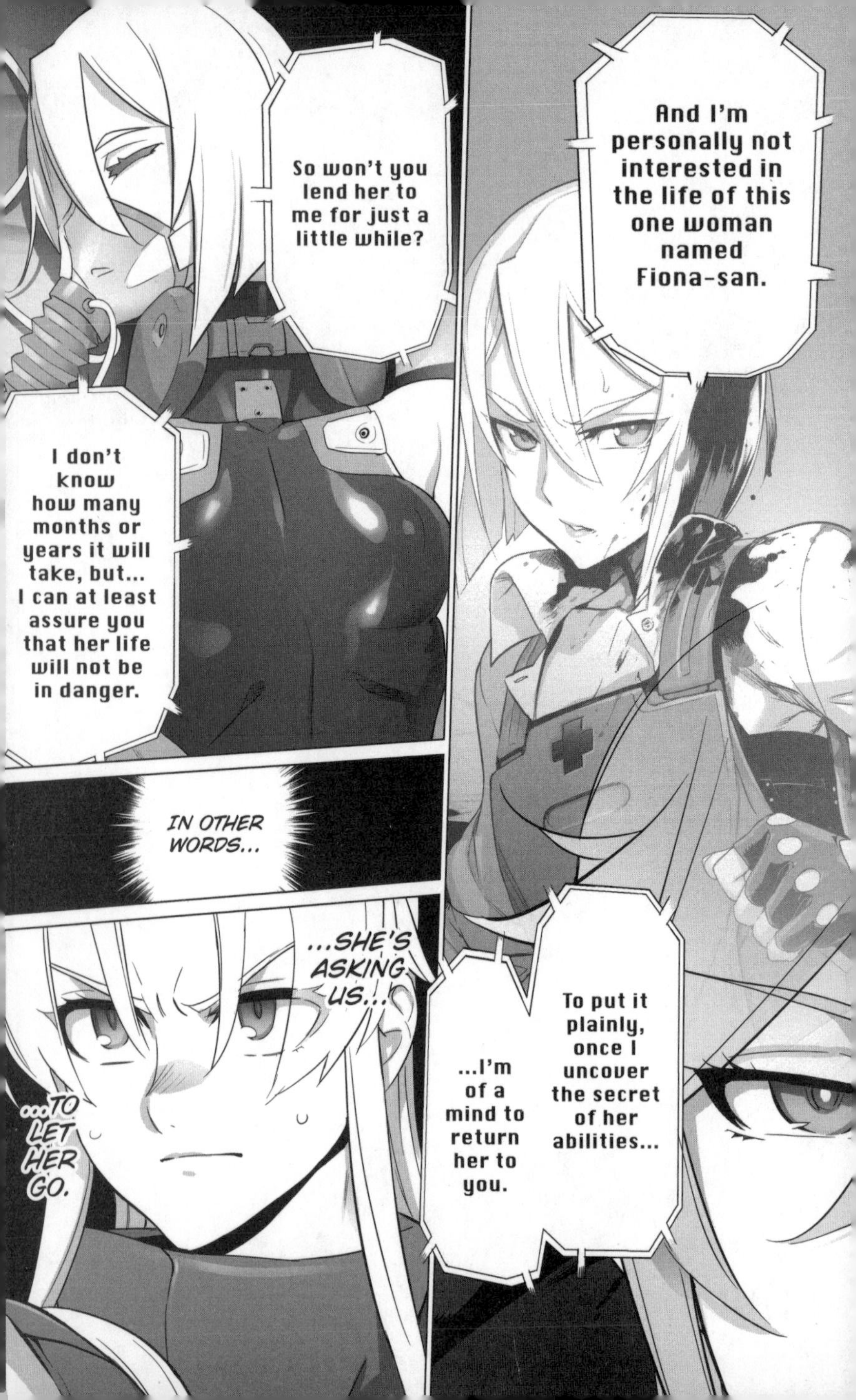
And I'm personally not interested in the life of this one woman named Fiona-san.
To put it plainly, once I uncover the secret of her abilities...
...I'm of a mind to return her to you.
So won't you lend her to me for just a little while?
I don't know how many months or years it will take, but... I can at least assure you that her life will not be in danger.
IN OTHER WORDS...
...SHE'S ASKING US...
...TO LET HER GO.

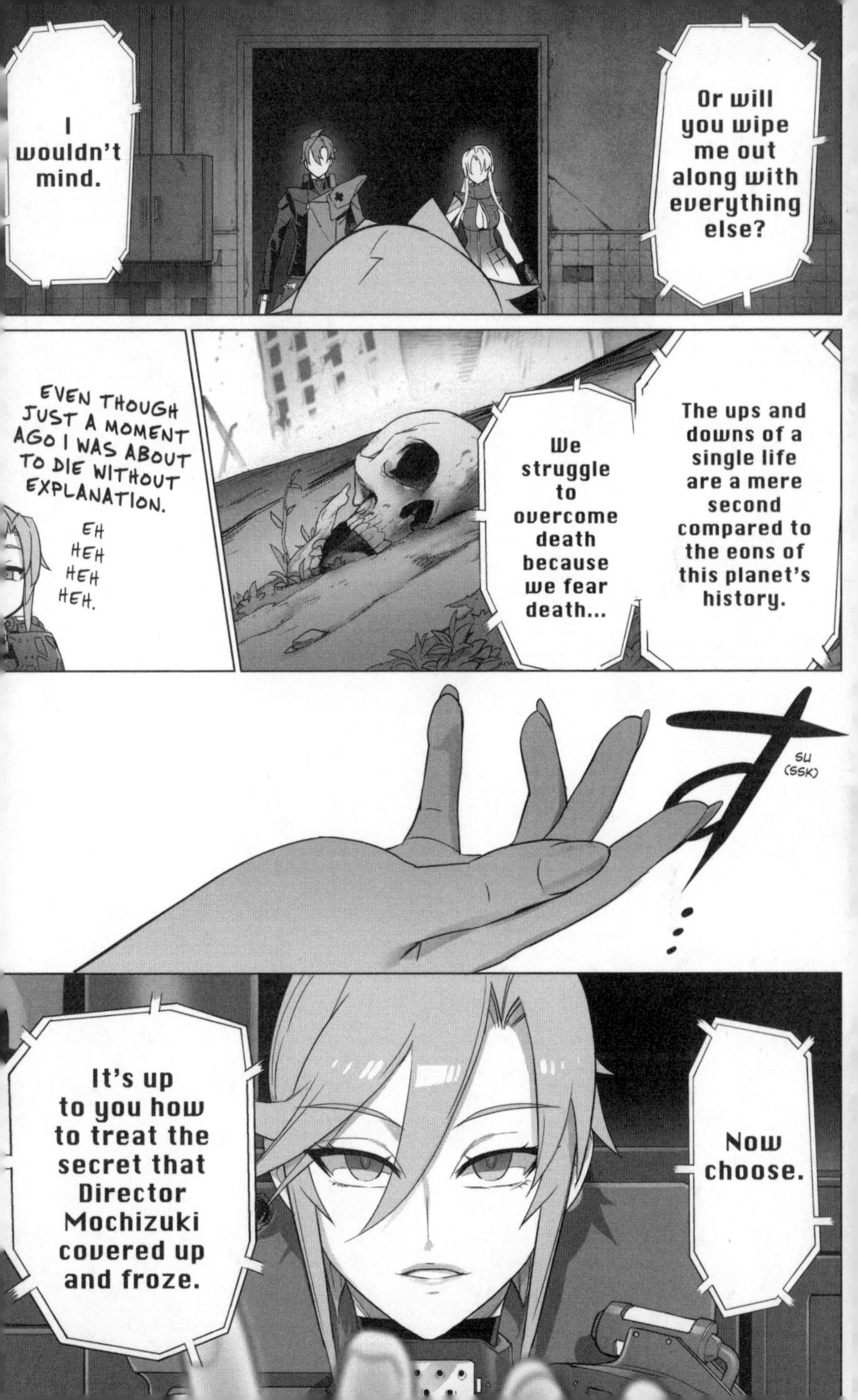

Or will you wipe me out along with everything else?
I wouldn't mind.
The ups and downs of a single life are a mere second compared to the eons of this planet's history.
We struggle to overcome death because we fear death...
EVEN THOUGH JUST A MOMENT AGO I WAS ABOUT TO DIE WITHOUT EXPLANATION.
EH HEH HEH HEH.
SU (SSK)
Now choose.
It's up to you how to treat the secret that Director Mochizuki covered up and froze.

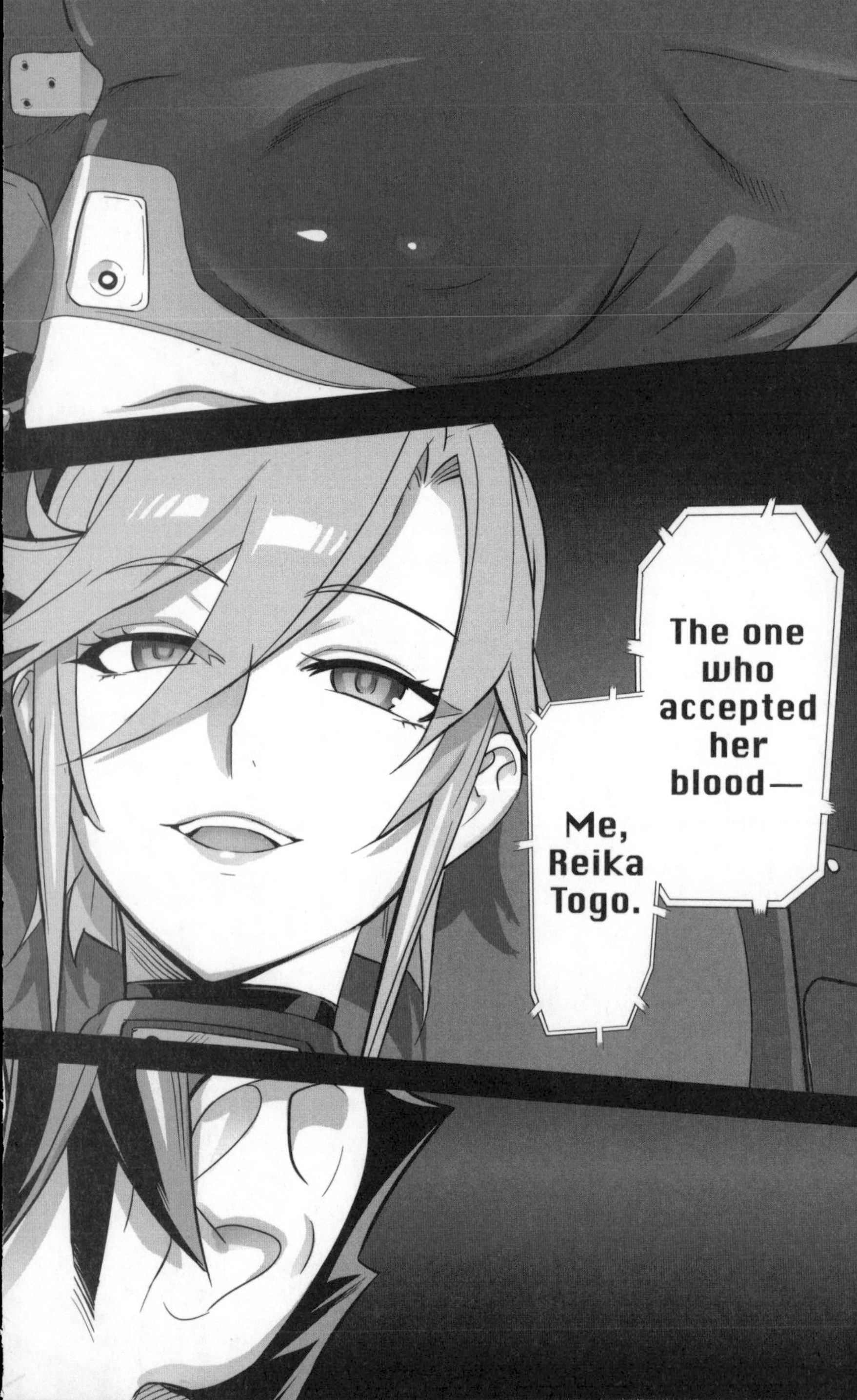
The one who accepted her blood—
Me, Reika Togo.

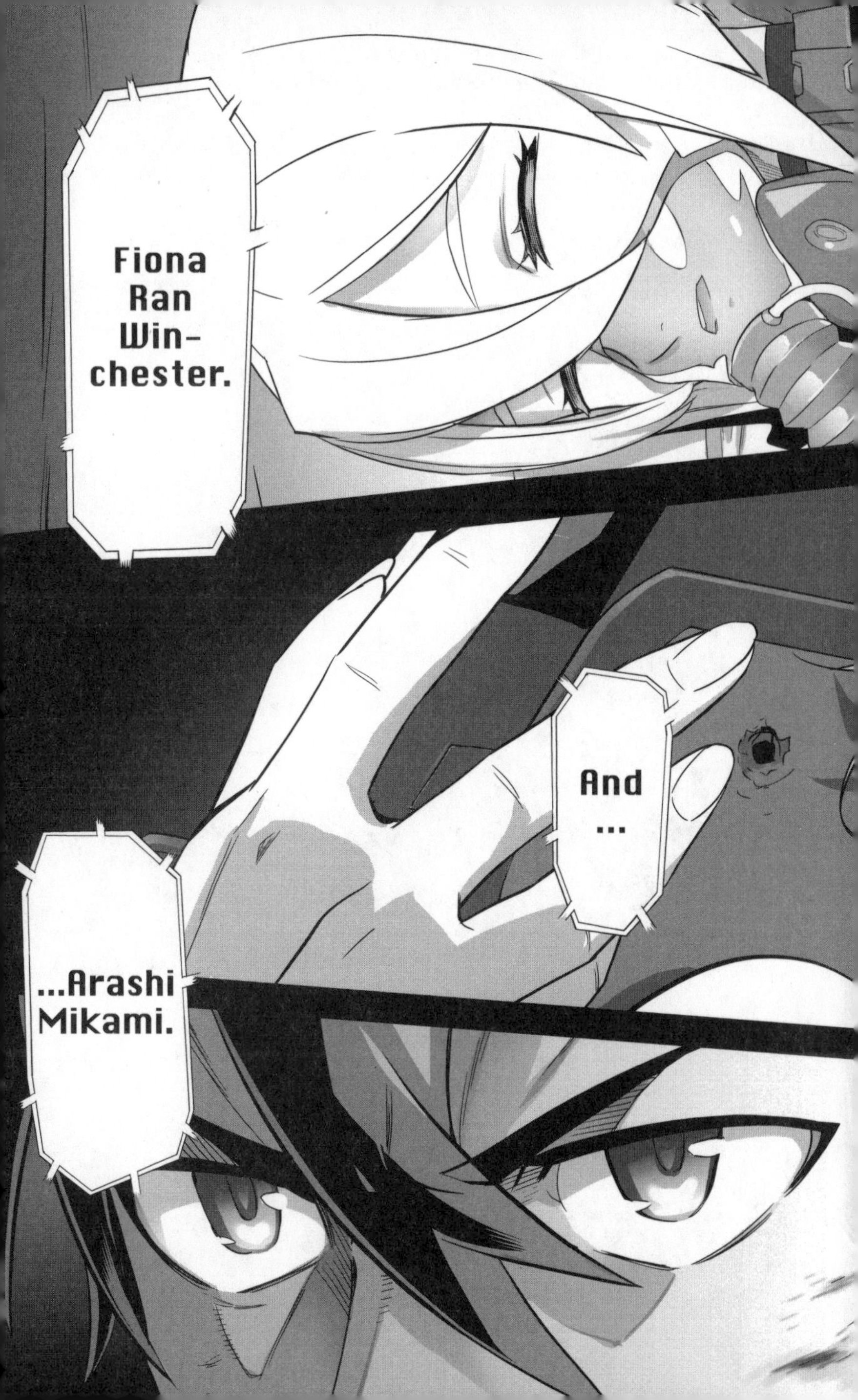
Fiona Ran Win-chester.
And ...
...Arashi Mikami.

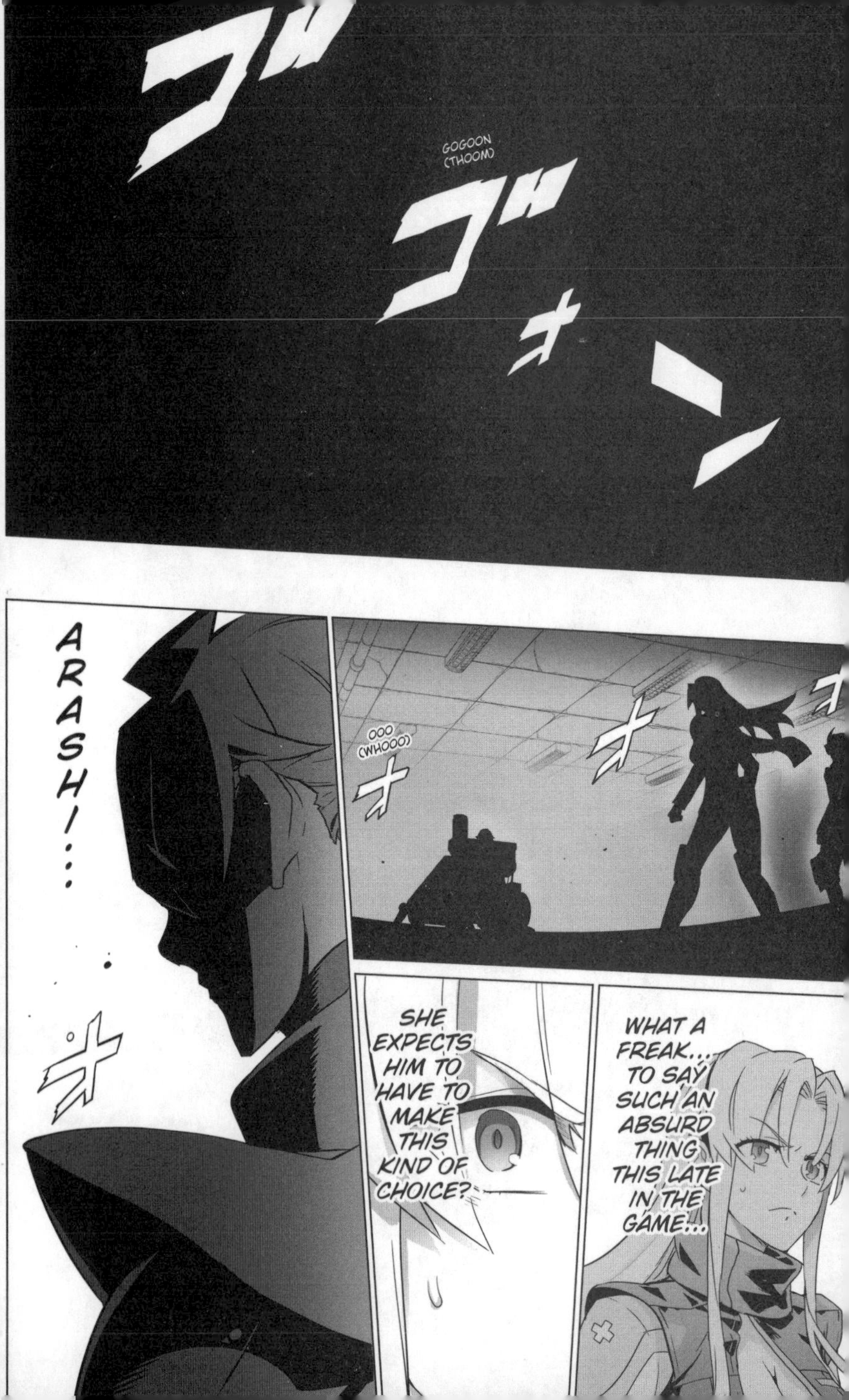
GOGOON (THOOM)
OOO (WHOOO)
WHAT A FREAK... TO SAY SUCH AN ABSURD THING THIS LATE IN THE GAME...
SHE EXPECTS HIM TO HAVE TO MAKE THIS KIND OF CHOICE?
ARASHI...

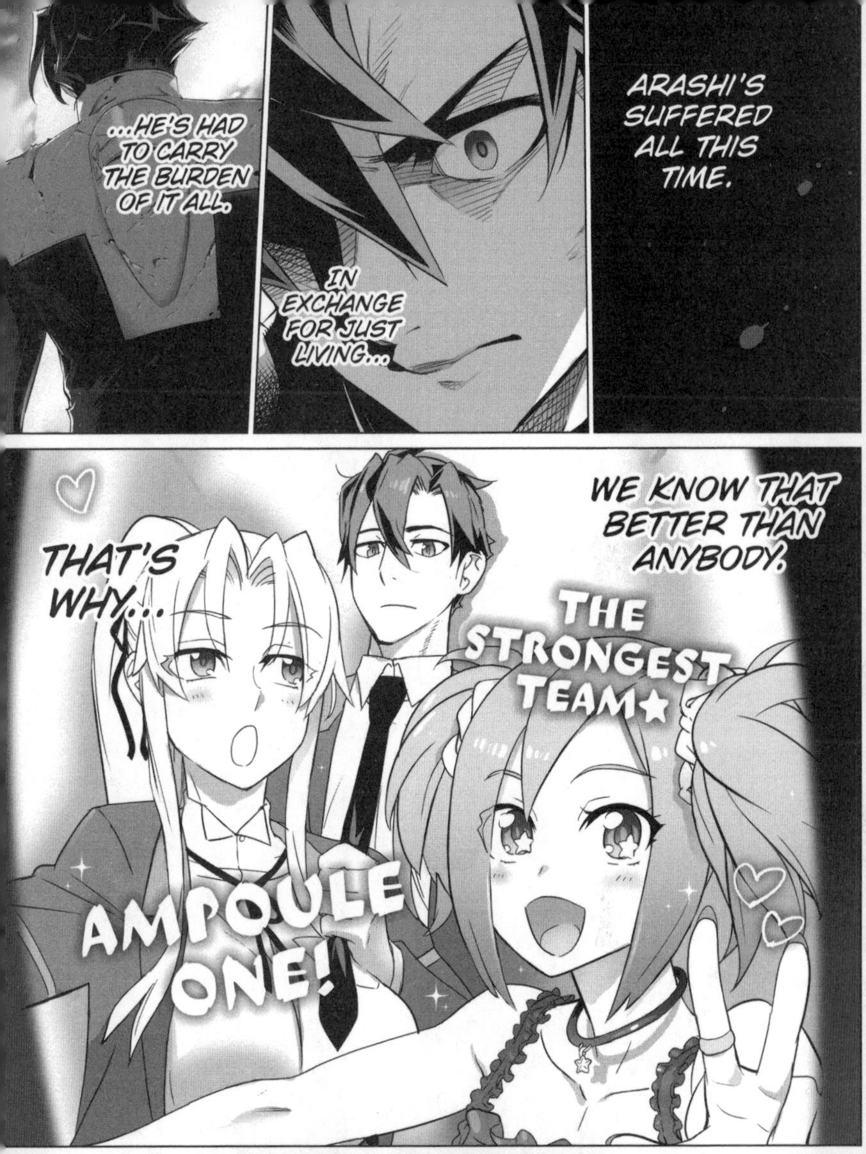
ARASHI'S SUFFERED ALL THIS TIME.
IN EXCHANGE FOR JUST LIVING...
...HE'S HAD TO CARRY THE BURDEN OF IT ALL.
WE KNOW THAT BETTER THAN ANYBODY.
THAT'S WHY...
THE STRONGEST TEAM★
AMPOULE ONE!

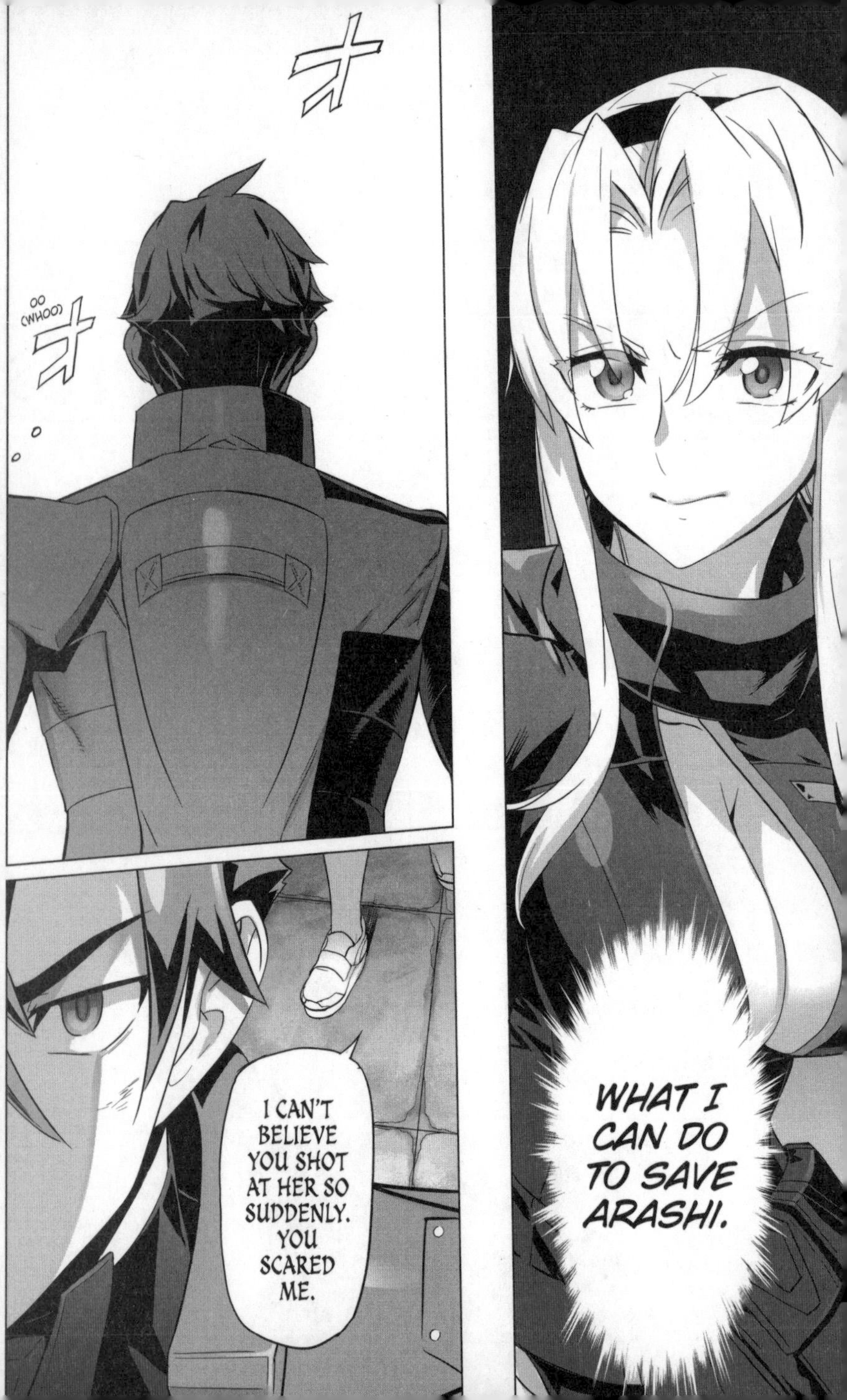
WHAT I CAN DO TO SAVE ARASHI.
OO (WHOO)
I CAN'T BELIEVE YOU SHOT AT HER SO SUDDENLY. YOU SCARED ME.

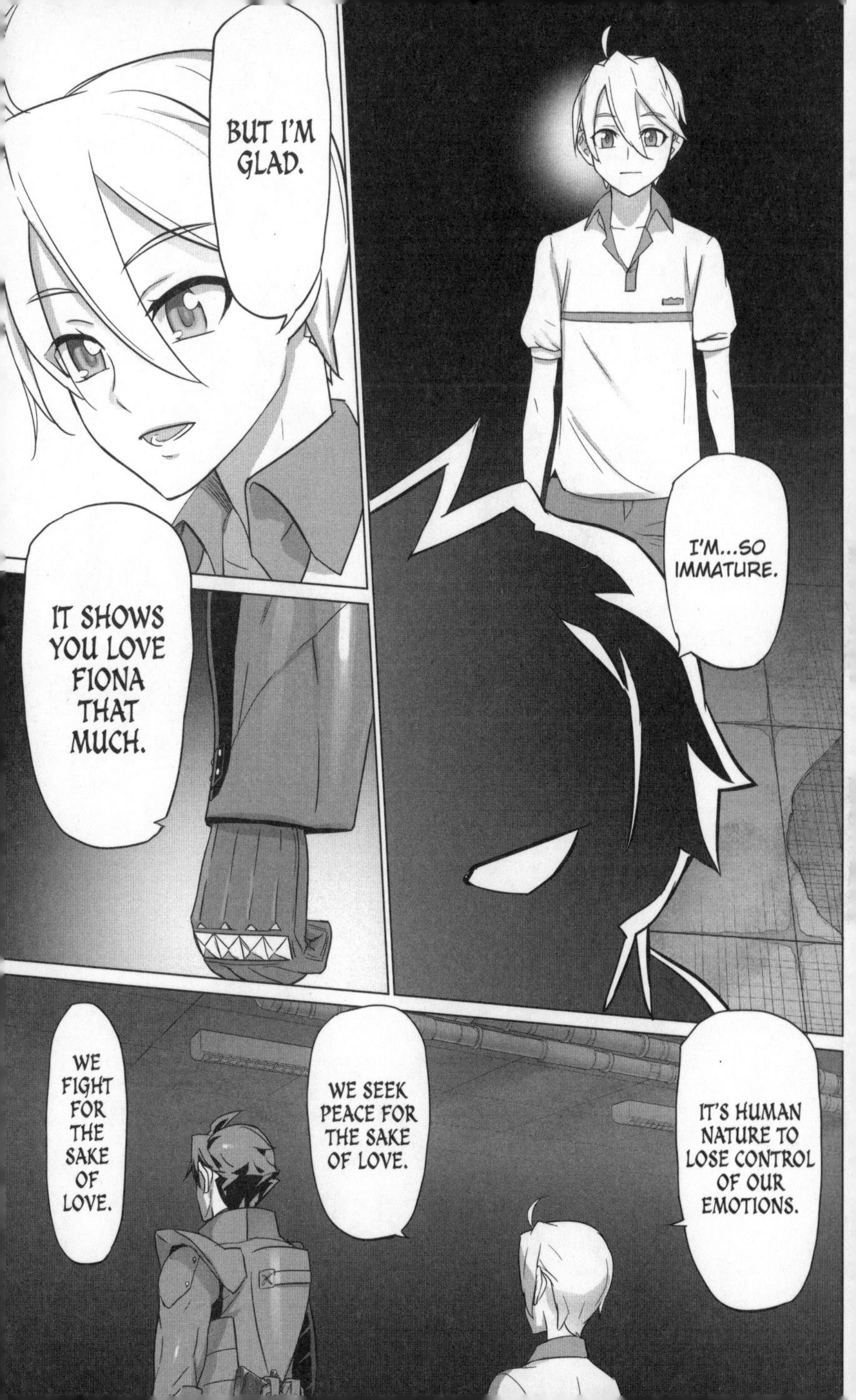
I'M...SO IMMATURE.
BUT I'M GLAD.
IT SHOWS YOU LOVE FIONA THAT MUCH.
IT'S HUMAN NATURE TO LOSE CONTROL OF OUR EMOTIONS.
WE SEEK PEACE FOR THE SAKE OF LOVE.
WE FIGHT FOR THE SAKE OF LOVE.

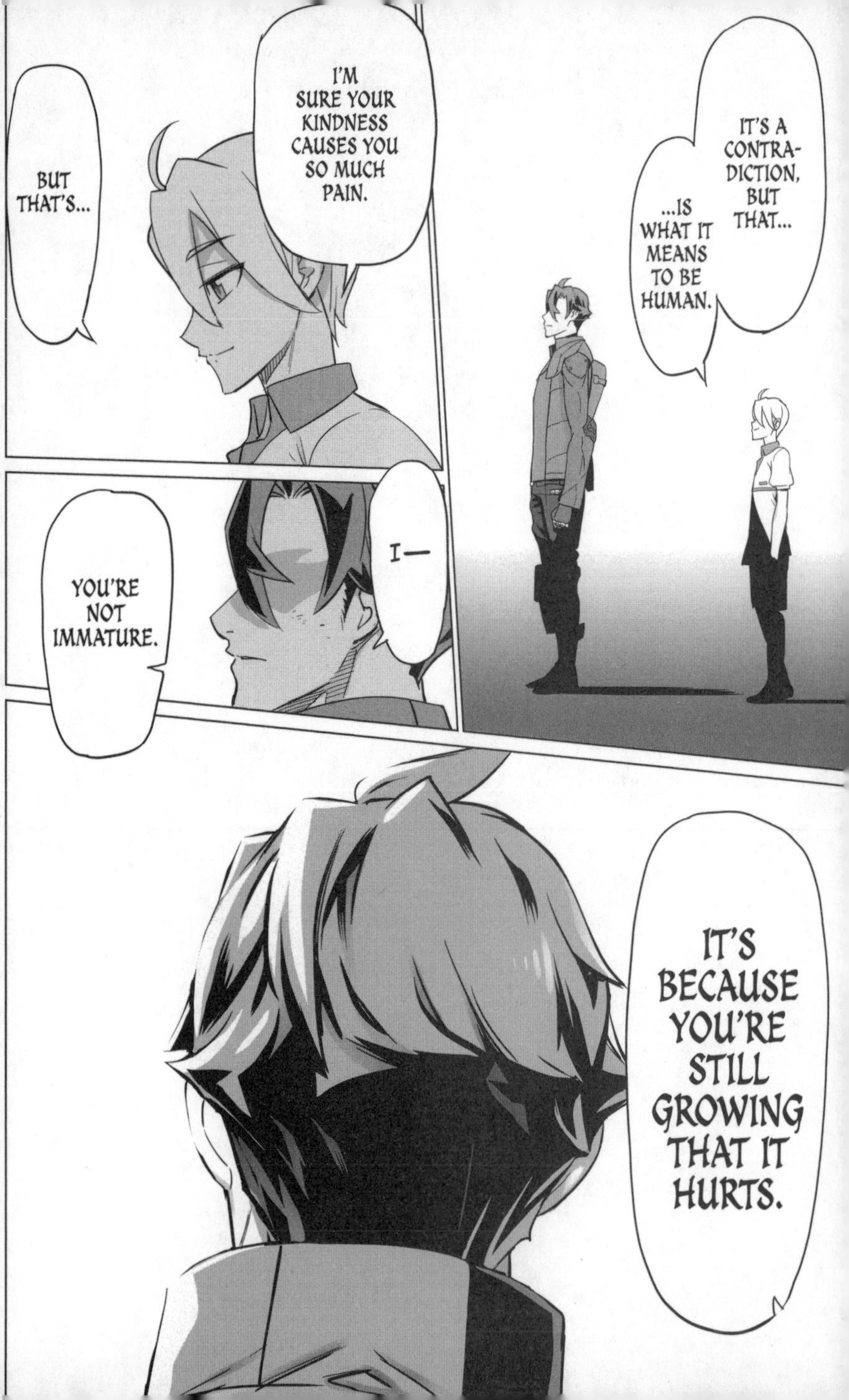
IT'S A CONTRA-DICTION, BUT THAT...
...IS WHAT IT MEANS TO BE HUMAN.
I'M SURE YOUR KINDNESS CAUSES YOU SO MUCH PAIN.
BUT THAT'S...
I—
YOU'RE NOT IMMATURE.
IT'S BECAUSE YOU'RE STILL GROWING THAT IT HURTS.

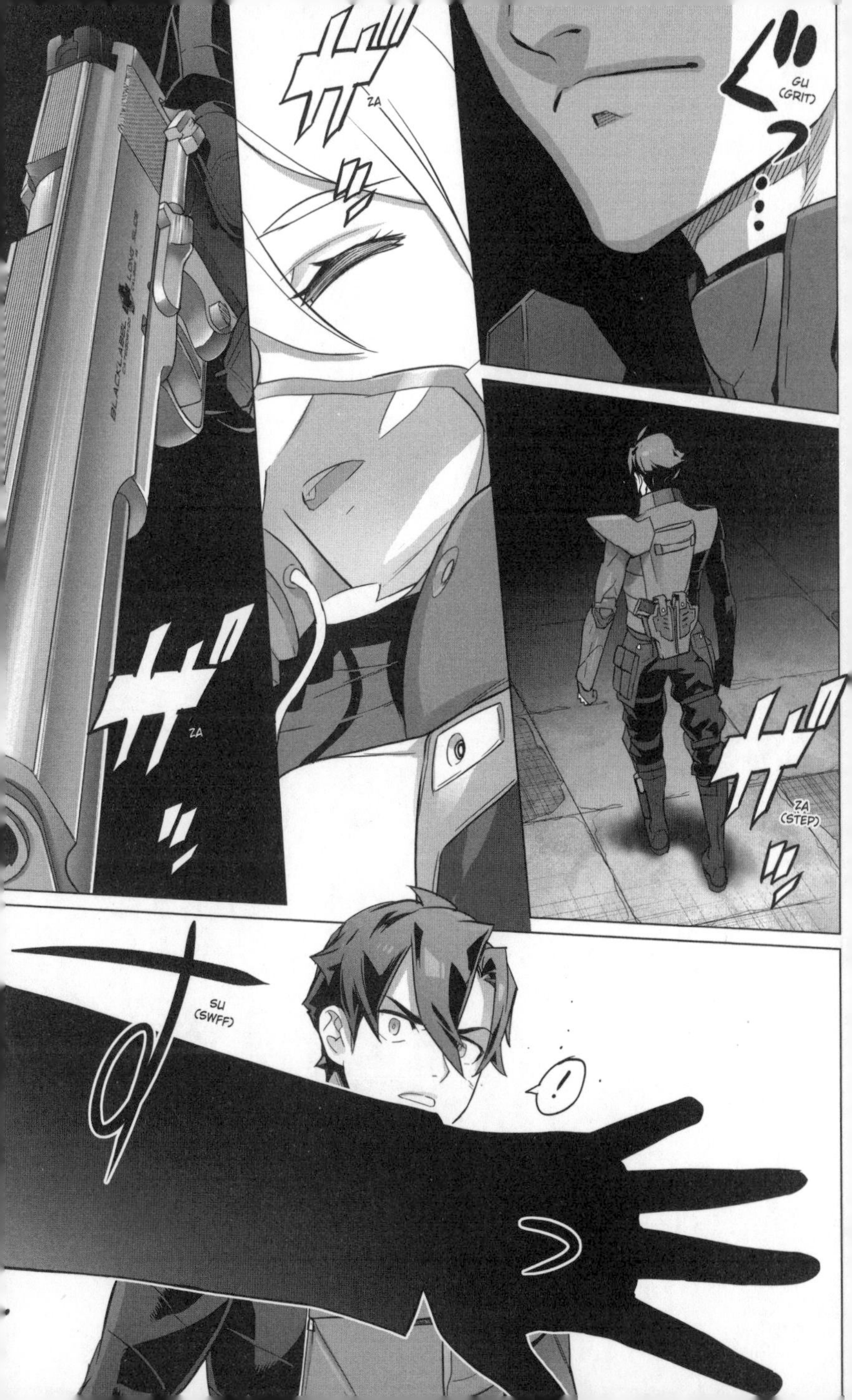
GU (GRIT)
ZA (STEP)
ZA
ZA
SU (SWFF)
!

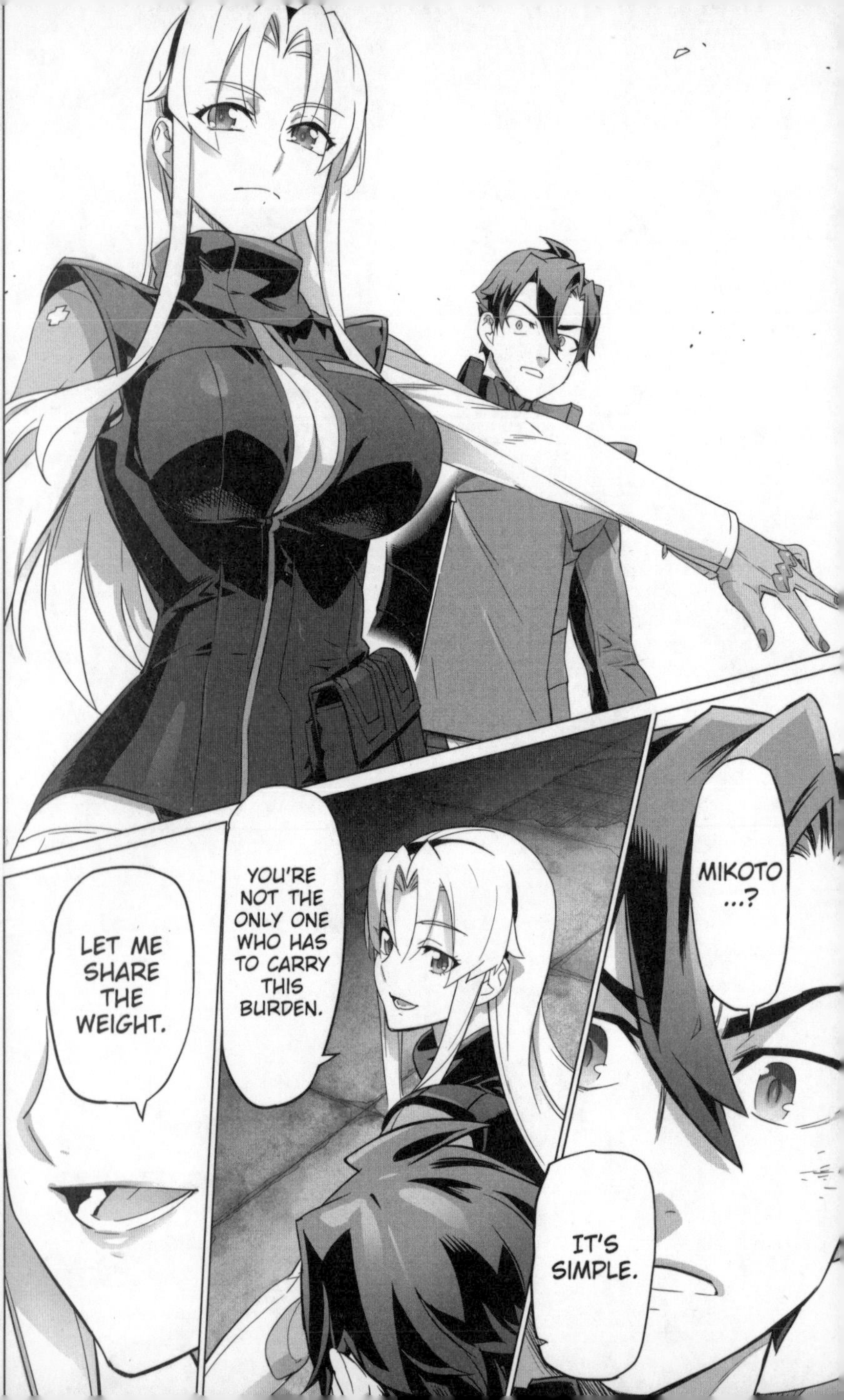
MIKOTO ...?
IT'S SIMPLE.
YOU'RE NOT THE ONLY ONE WHO HAS TO CARRY THIS BURDEN.
LET ME SHARE THE WEIGHT.

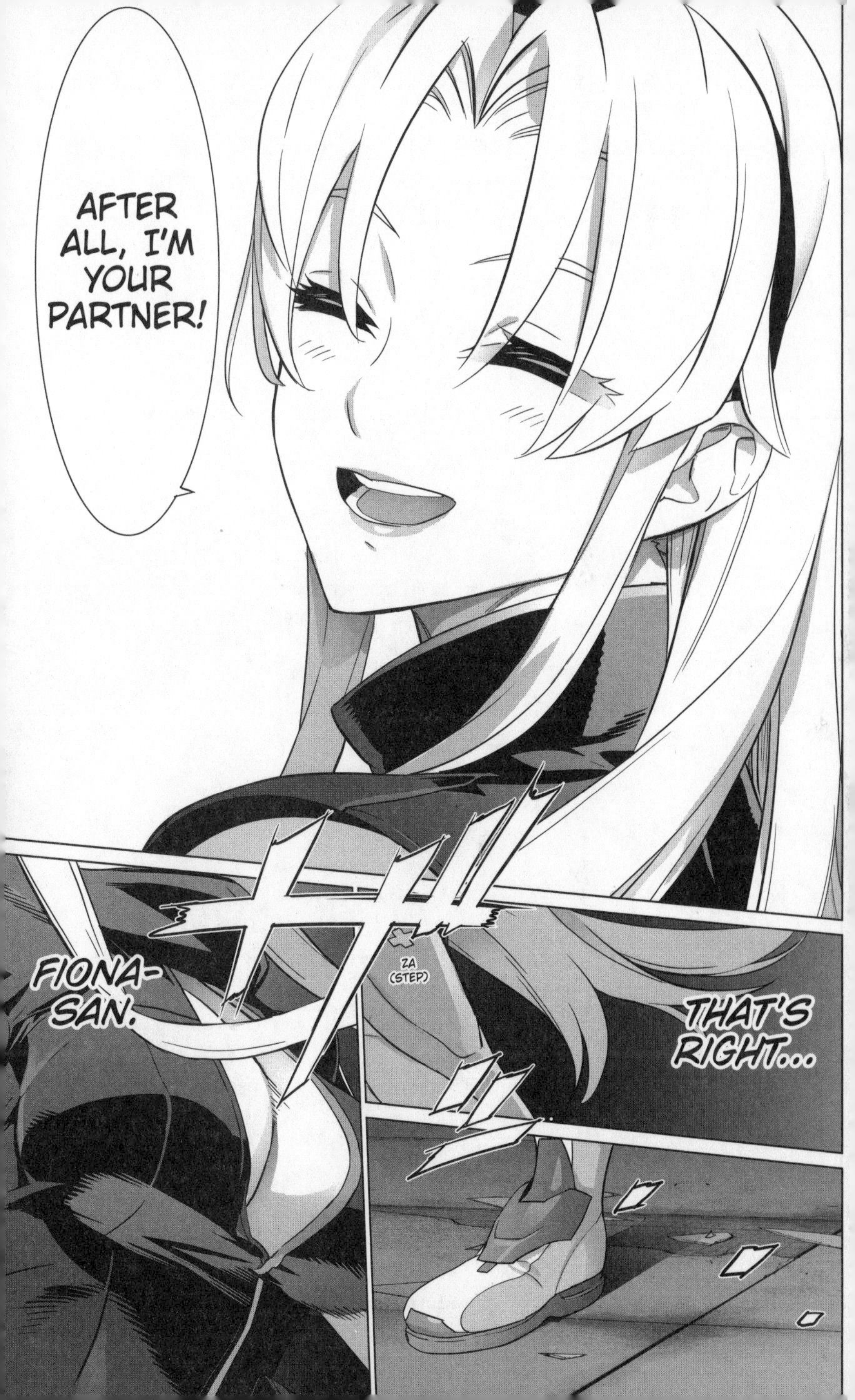
AFTER ALL, I'M YOUR PARTNER!
THAT'S RIGHT...
ZA (STEP)
FIONA-SAN.

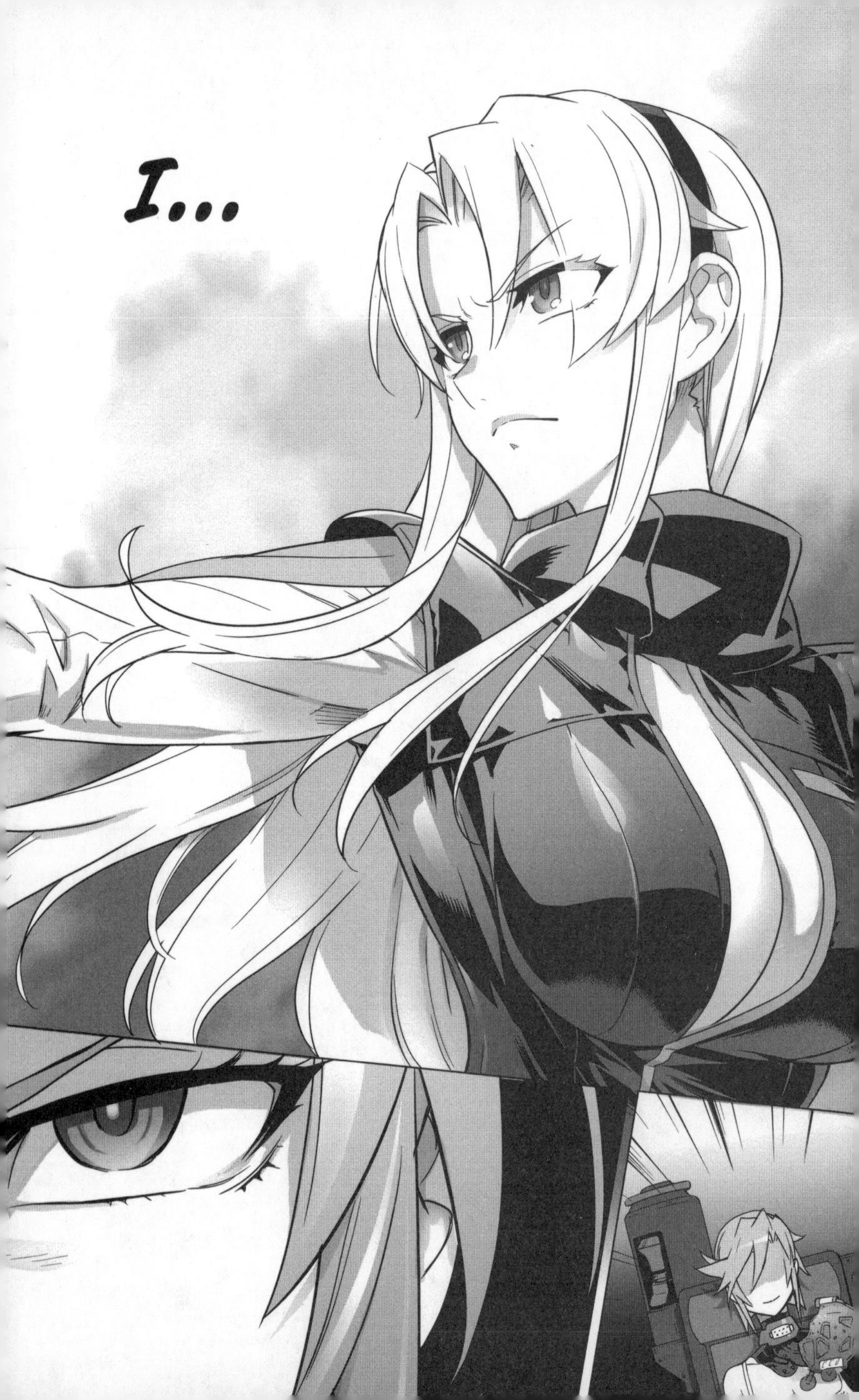
I...

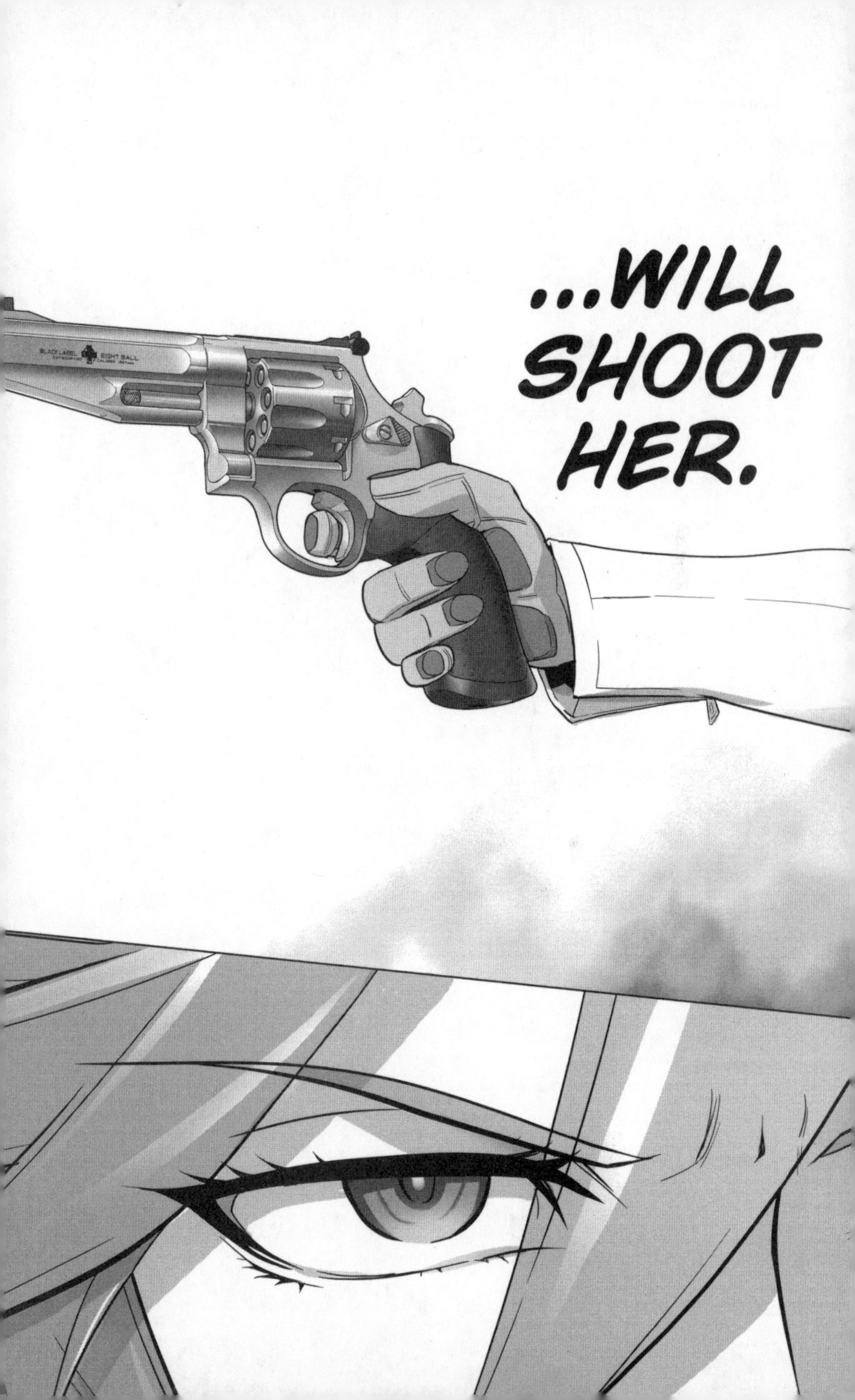
...WILL SHOOT HER.

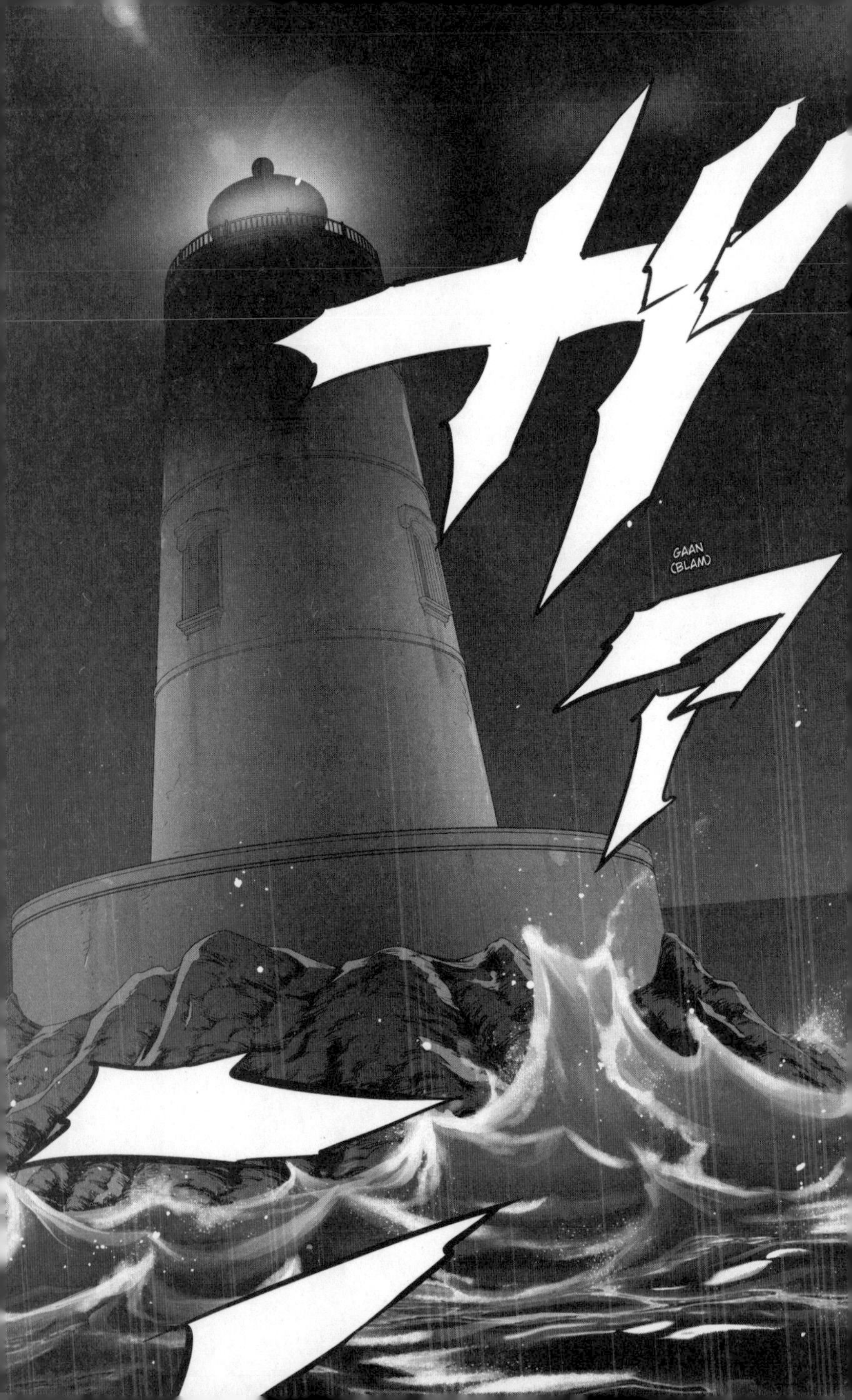
GAAN
(BLAM)

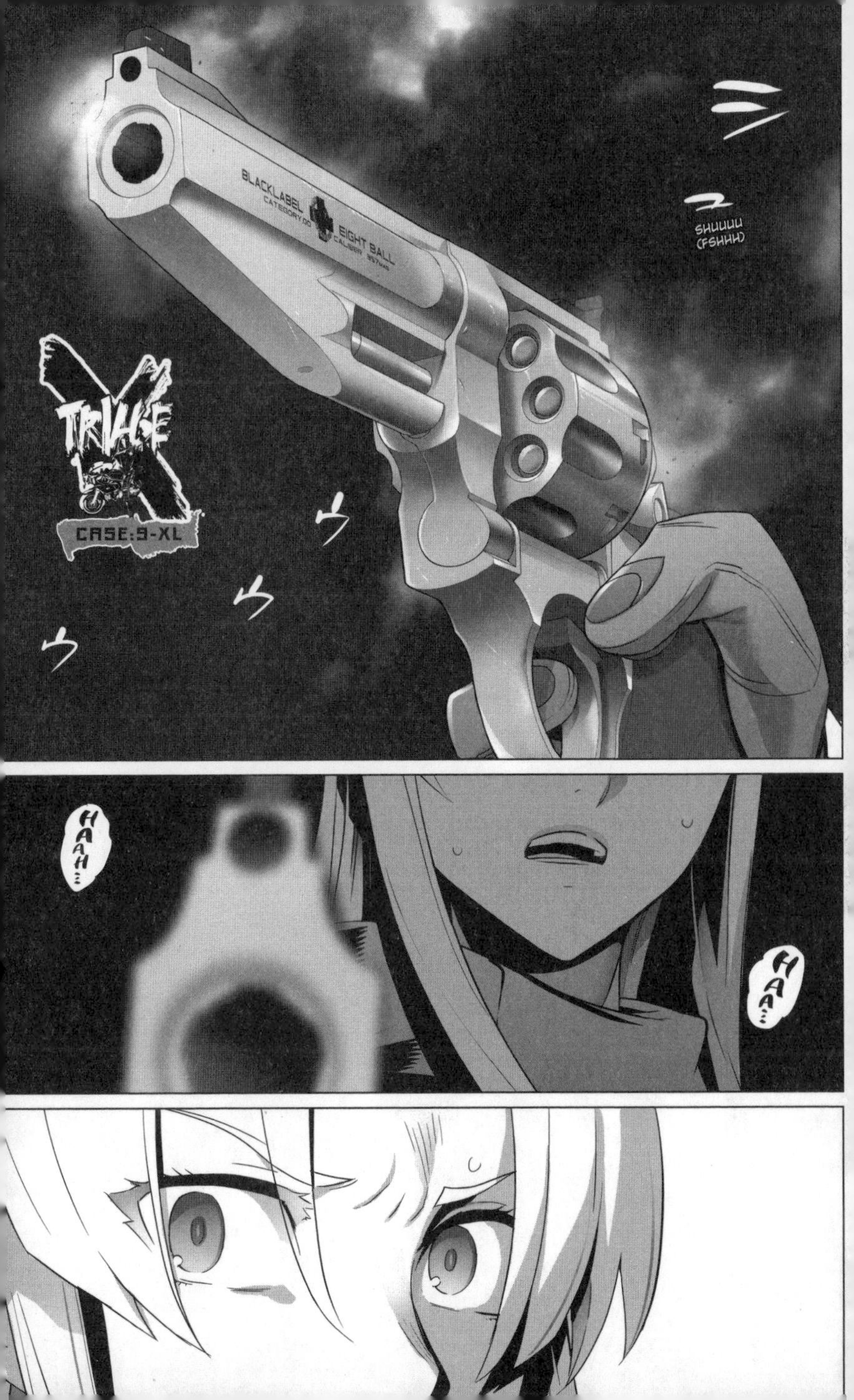
SHUUUU
(FSHHH)
BLACKLABEL
CATEGORY.00
EIGHT BALL
CALIBER .357MAG
TRIAGE X
CASE:9-XL
HAA...
HAAH...

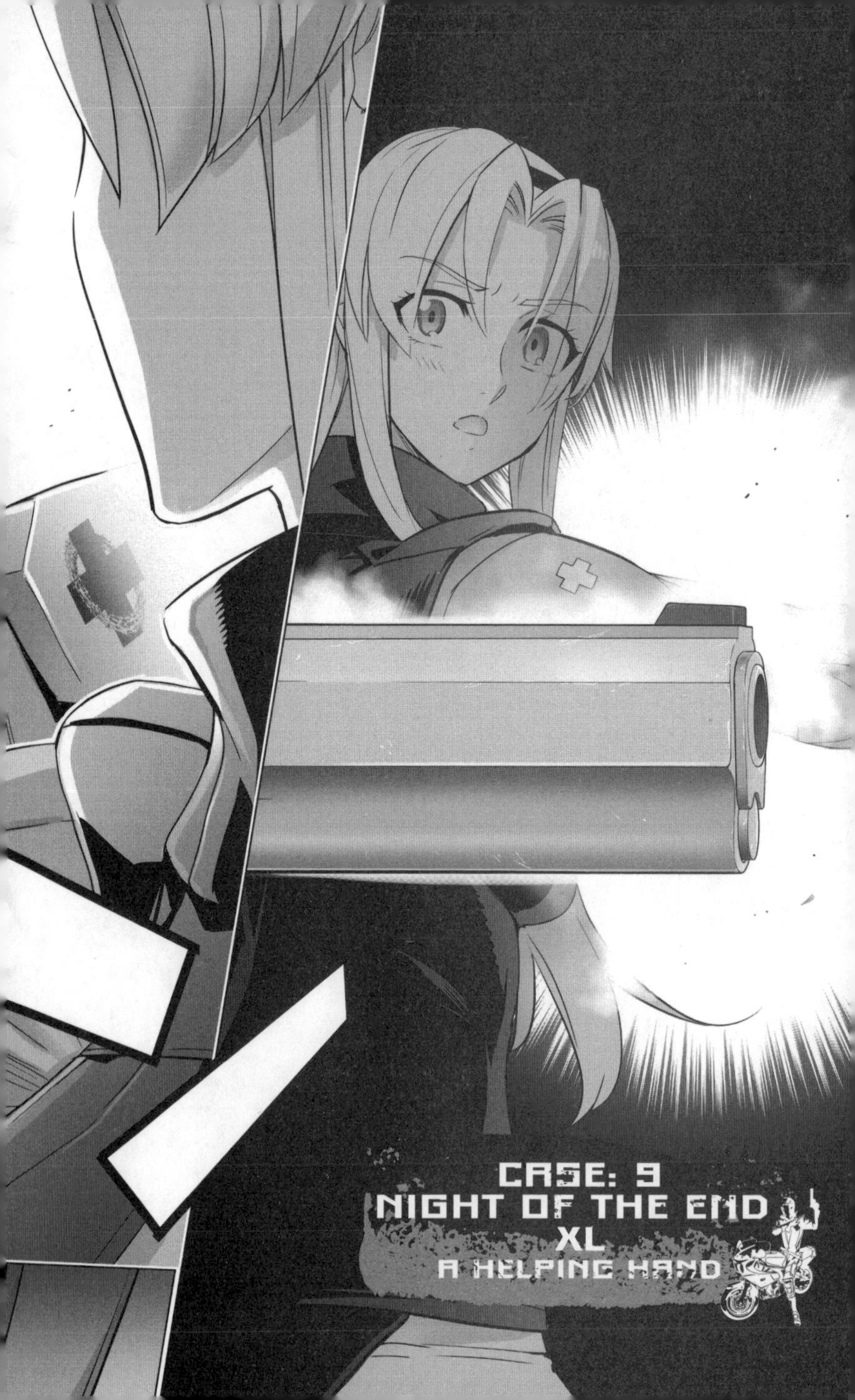
CASE: 9
NIGHT OF THE END
XL
A HELPING HAND

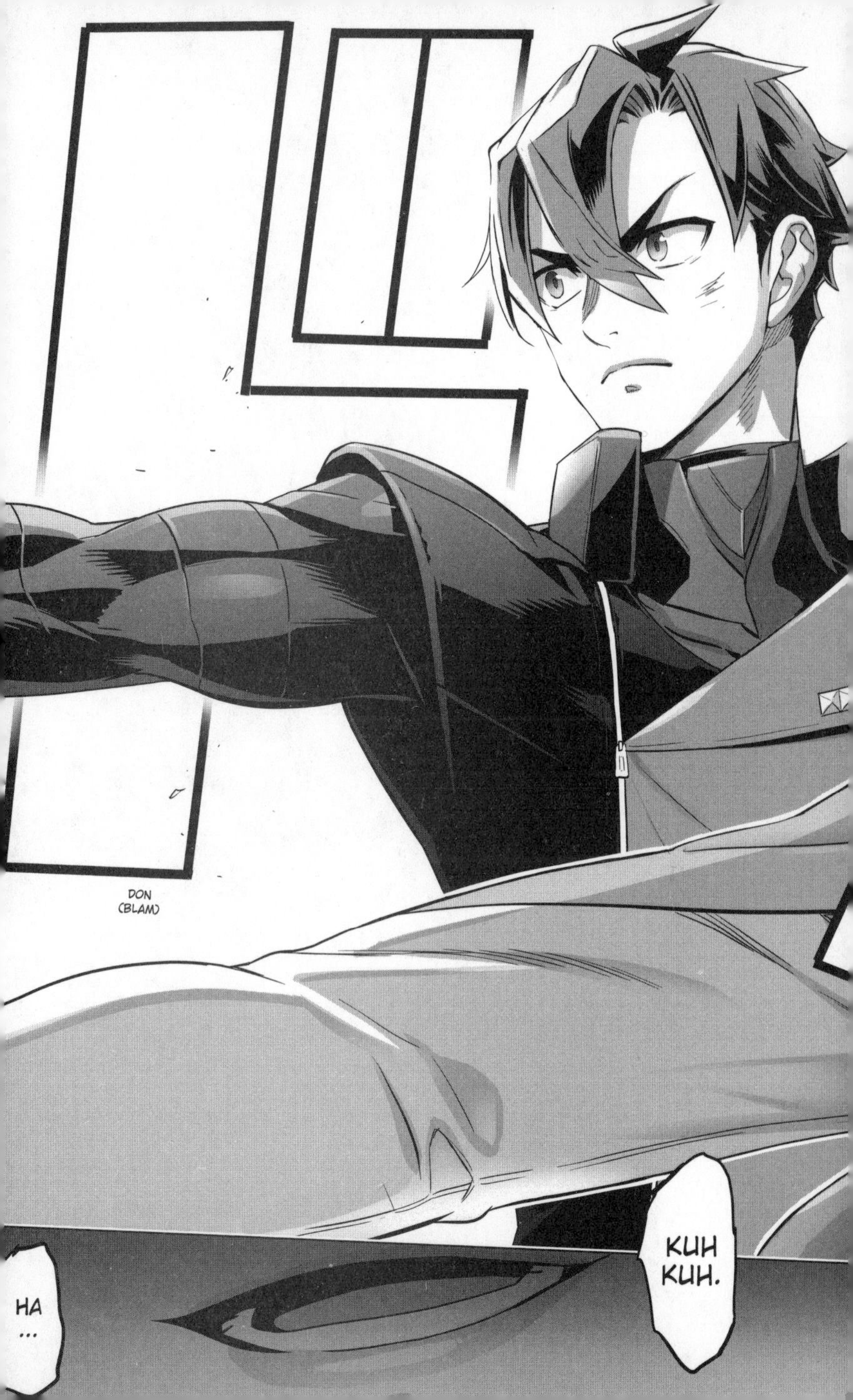
DON (BLAM)
KUH KUH.
HA ...

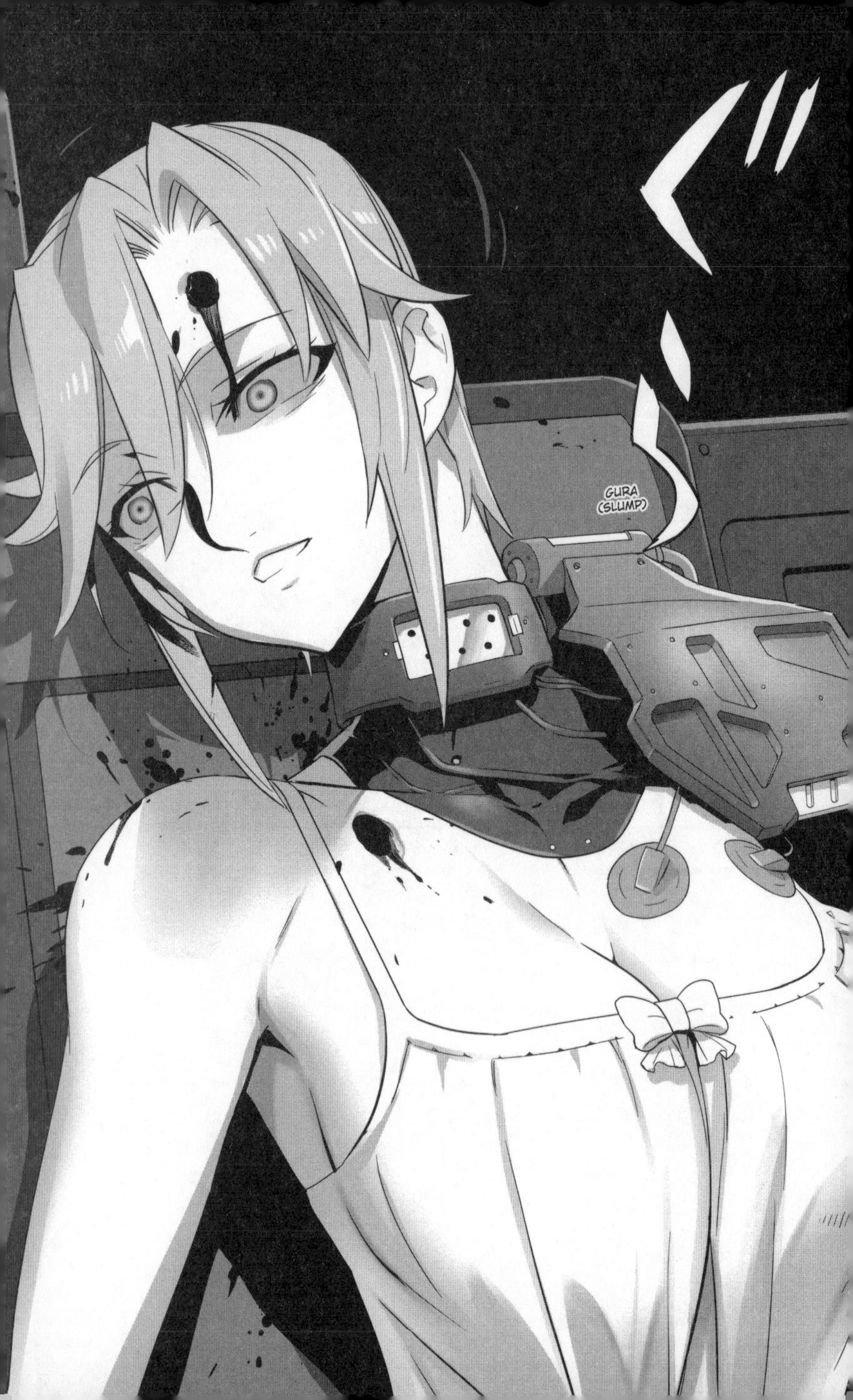
GURA
(SLUMP)

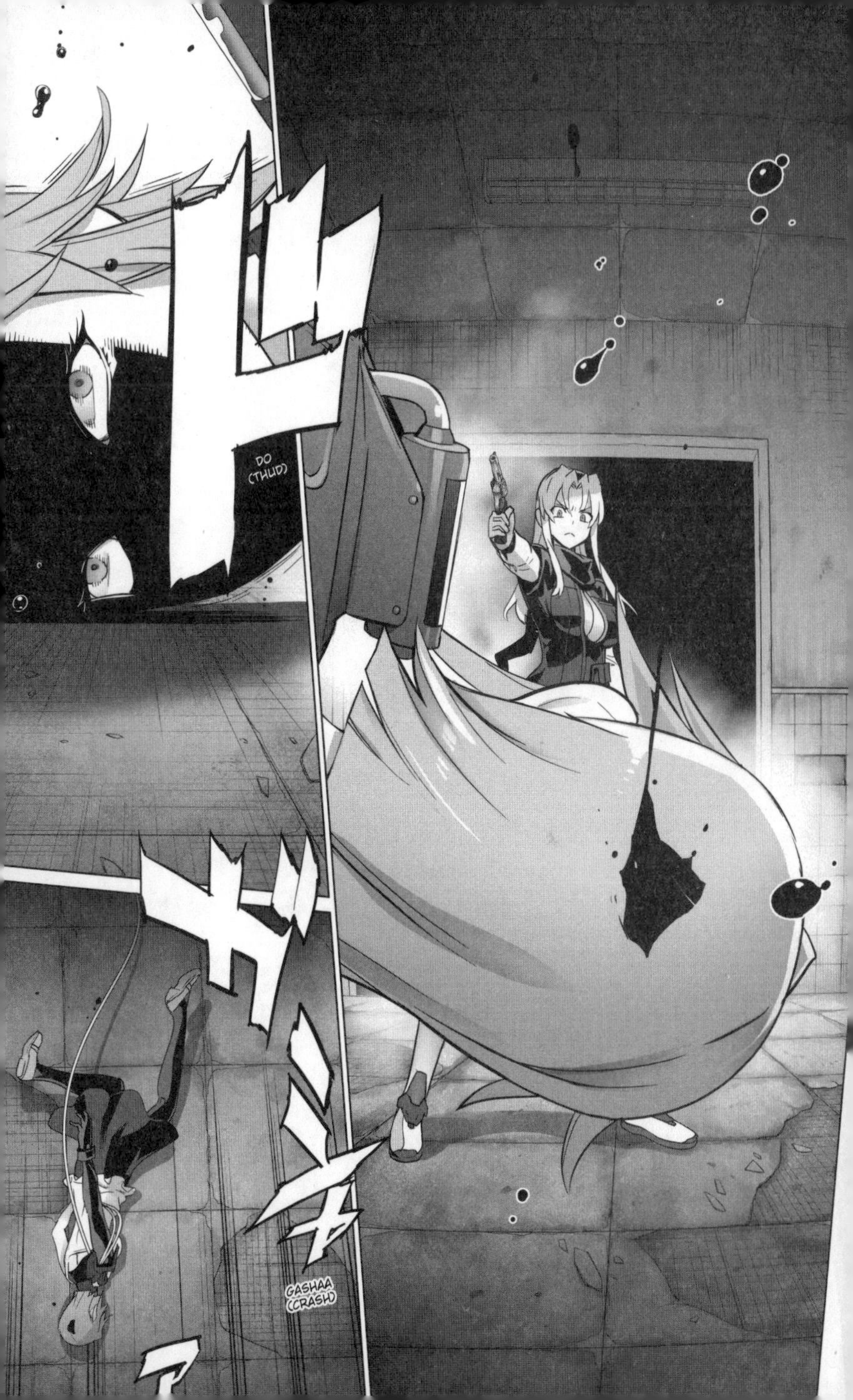
DO
(THUD)
GASHAA
(CRASH)

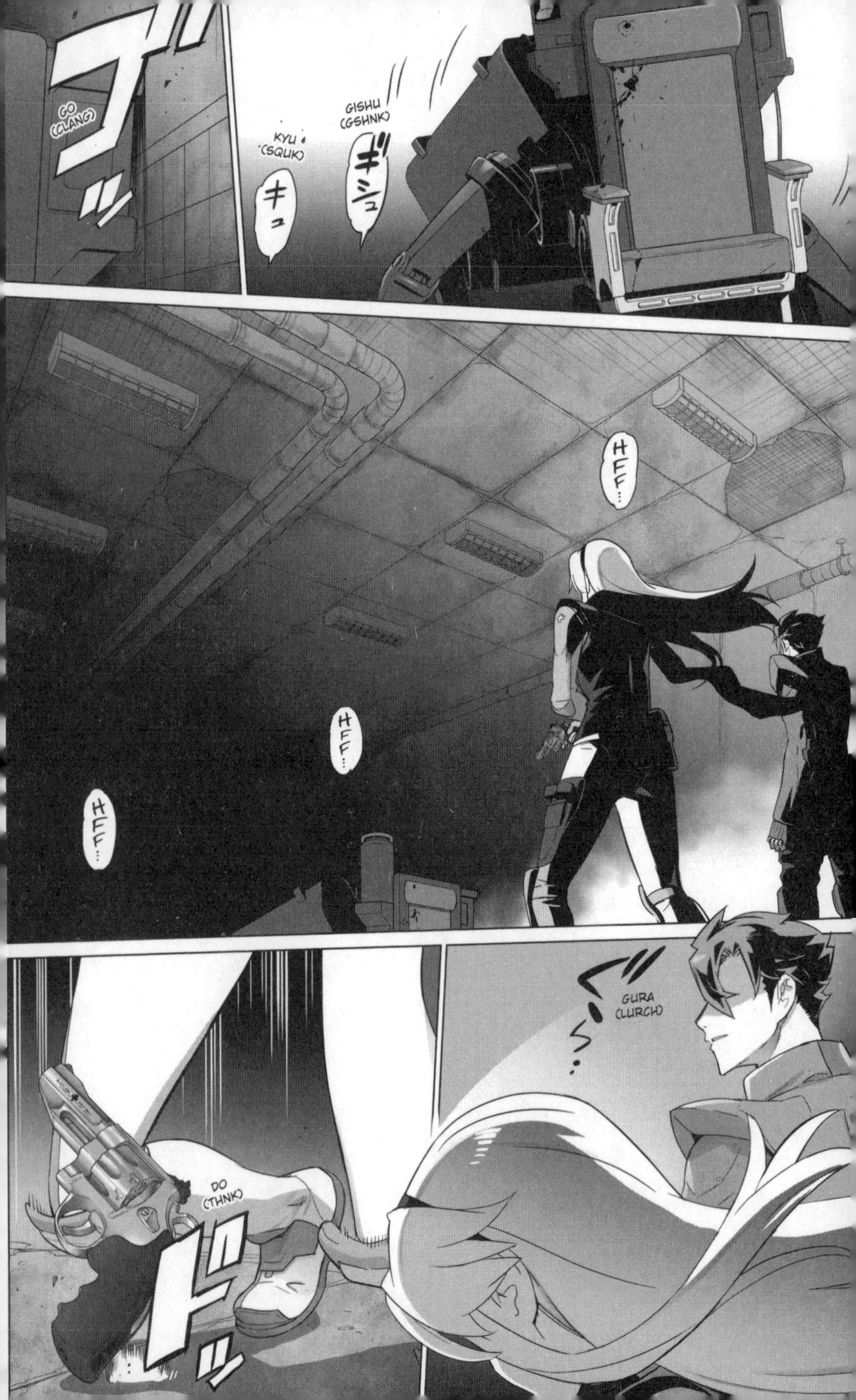
GISHU (GSHNK)
ギシュ
KYU (SQUK)
キュ
GO (CLANG)
HFF...
HFF...
HFF...
GURA (LURCH)
DO (THNK)

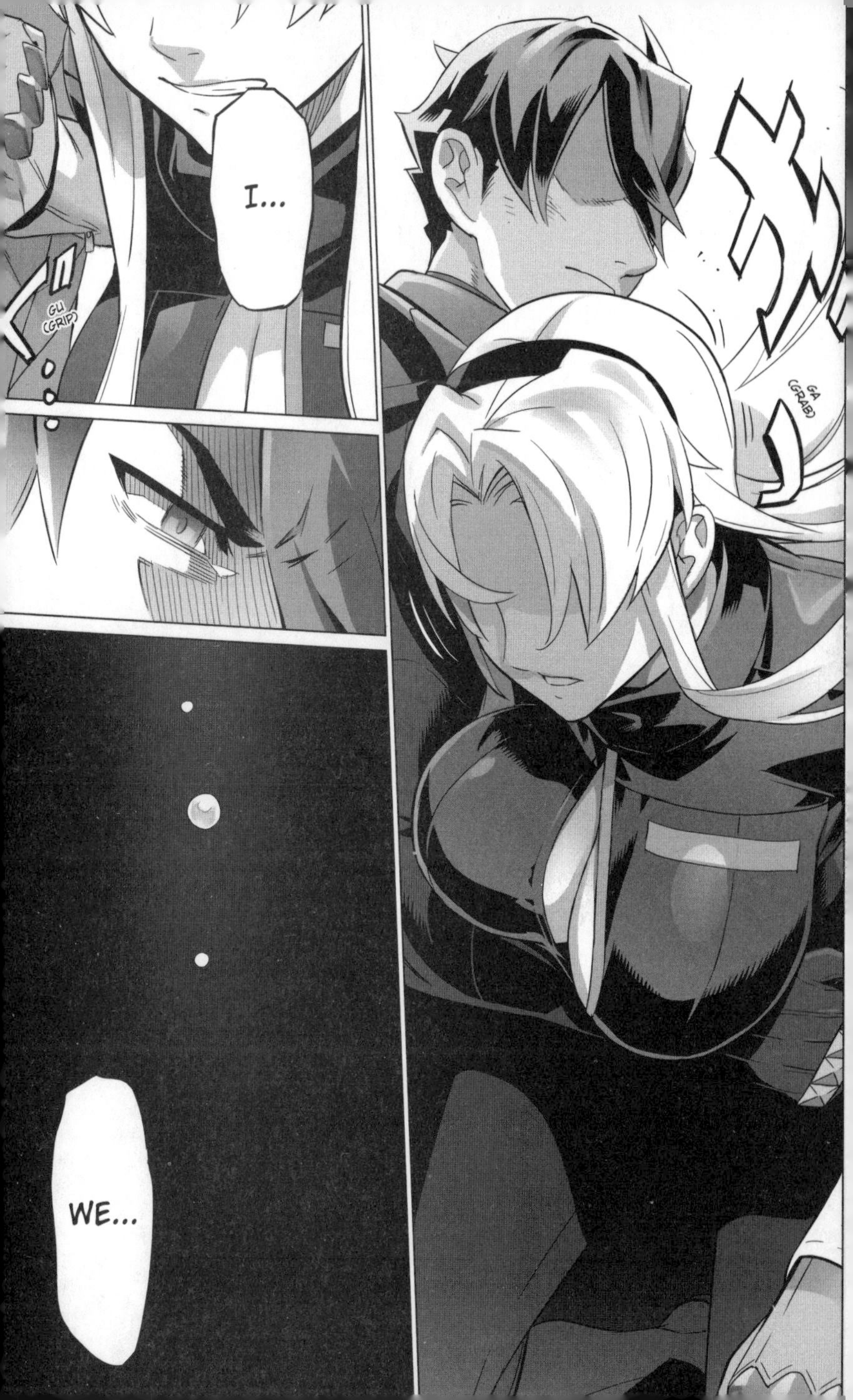
GA (GRAB)
I...
GU (GRIP)
WE...

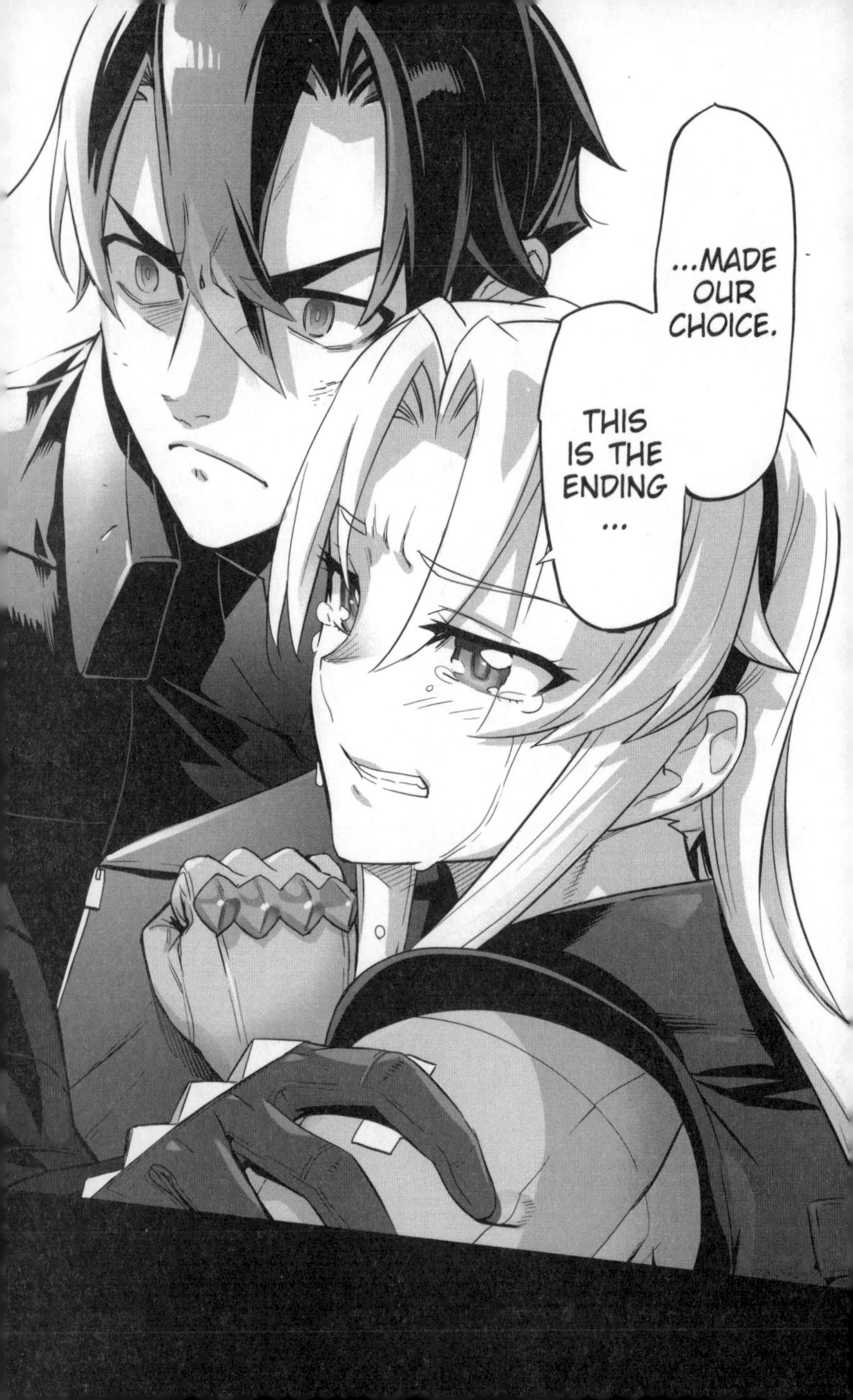
...MADE OUR CHOICE.
THIS IS THE ENDING ...

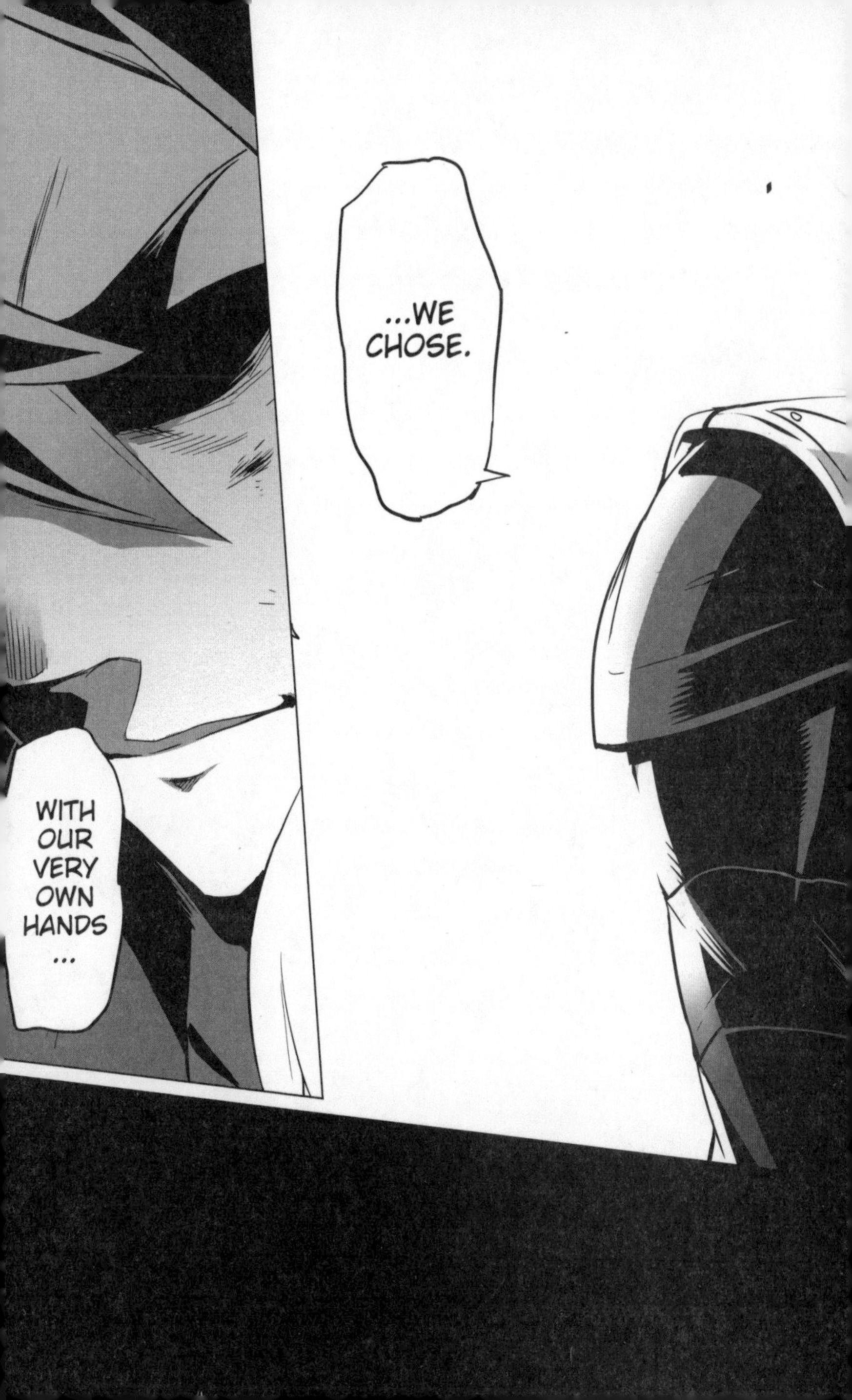
...WE CHOSE.
WITH OUR VERY OWN HANDS ...

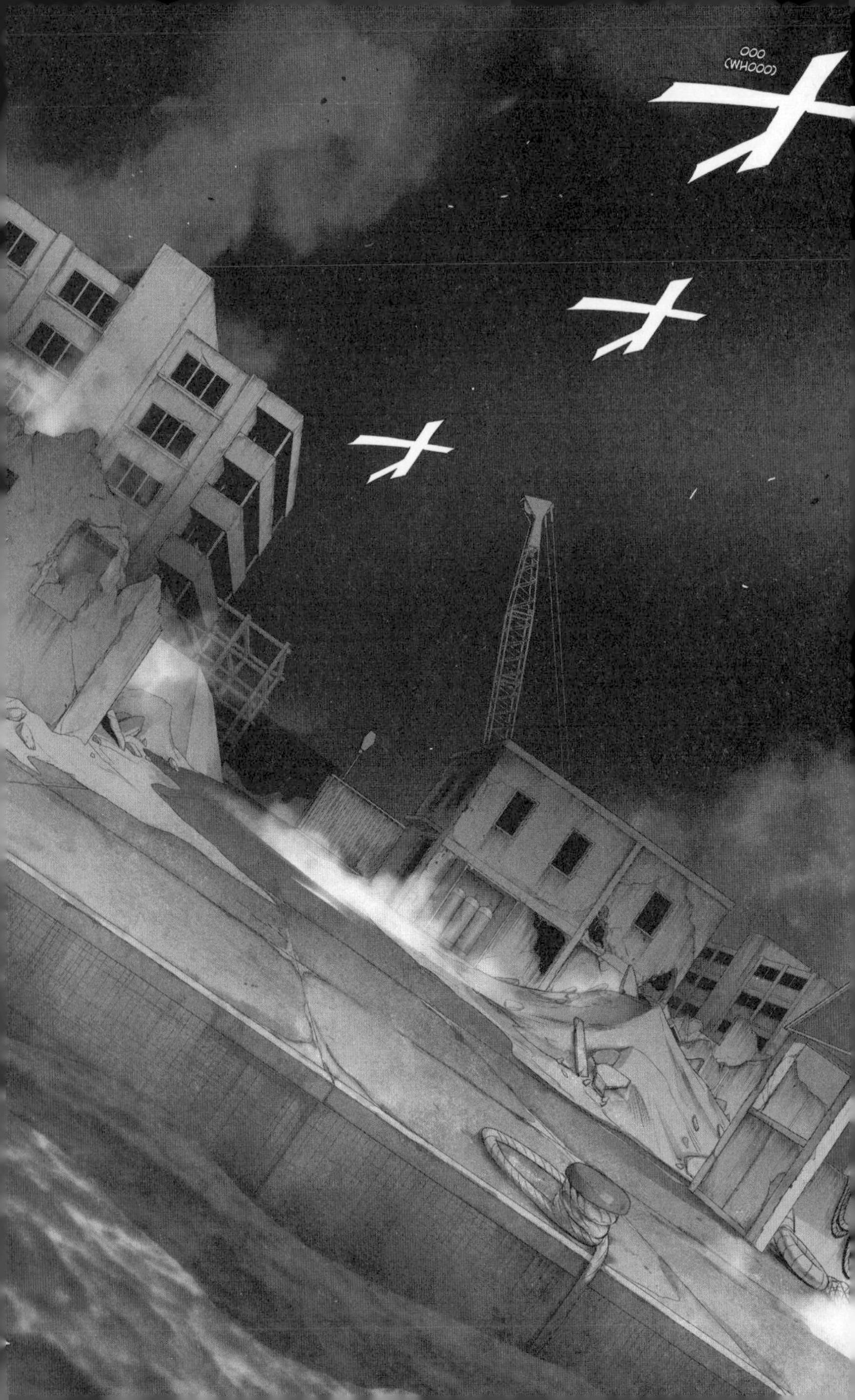
ナナナ
OOO
(WHOOOO)

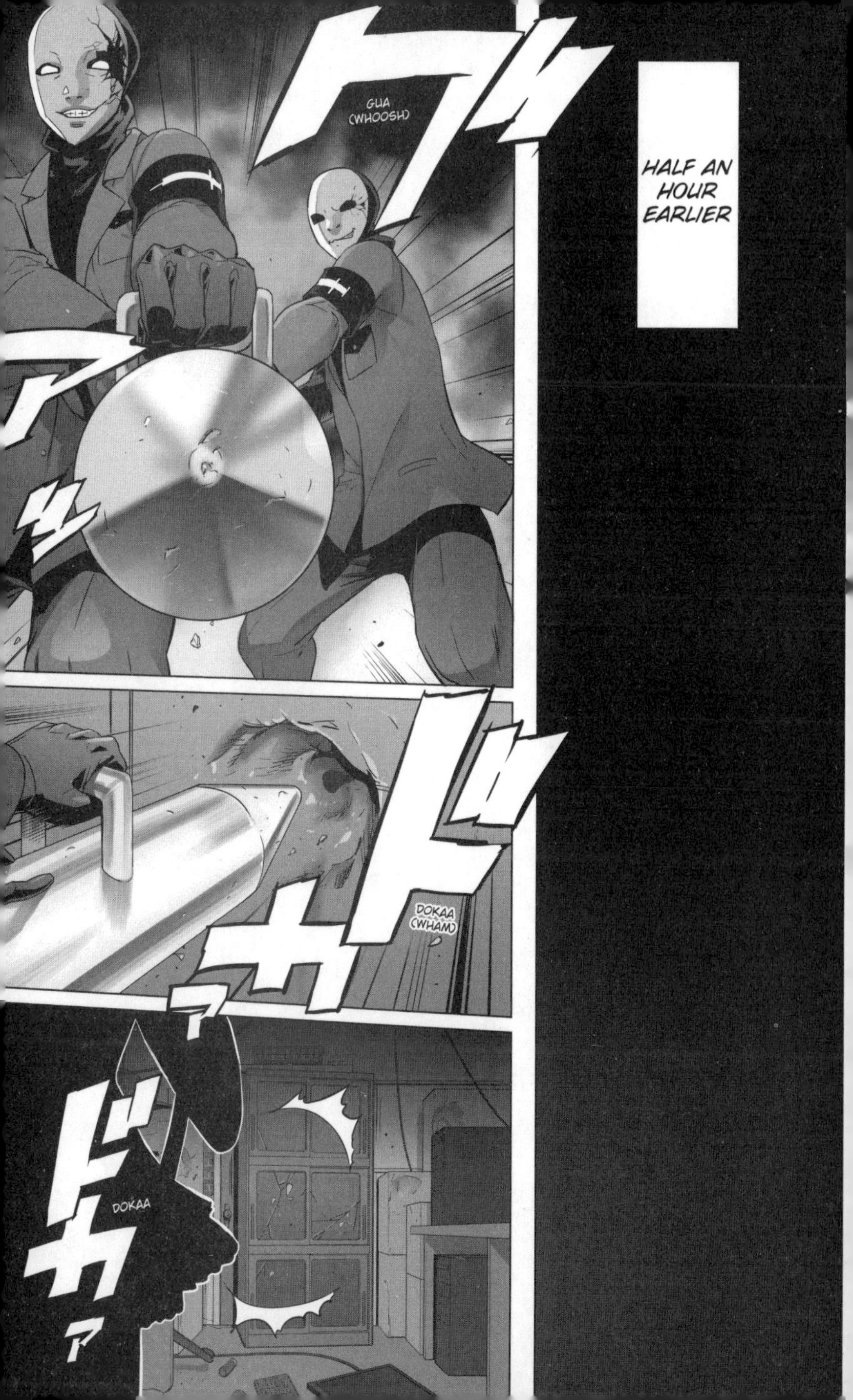
HALF AN HOUR EARLIER
GUA (WHOOSH)
DOKAA (WHAM)
DOKAA

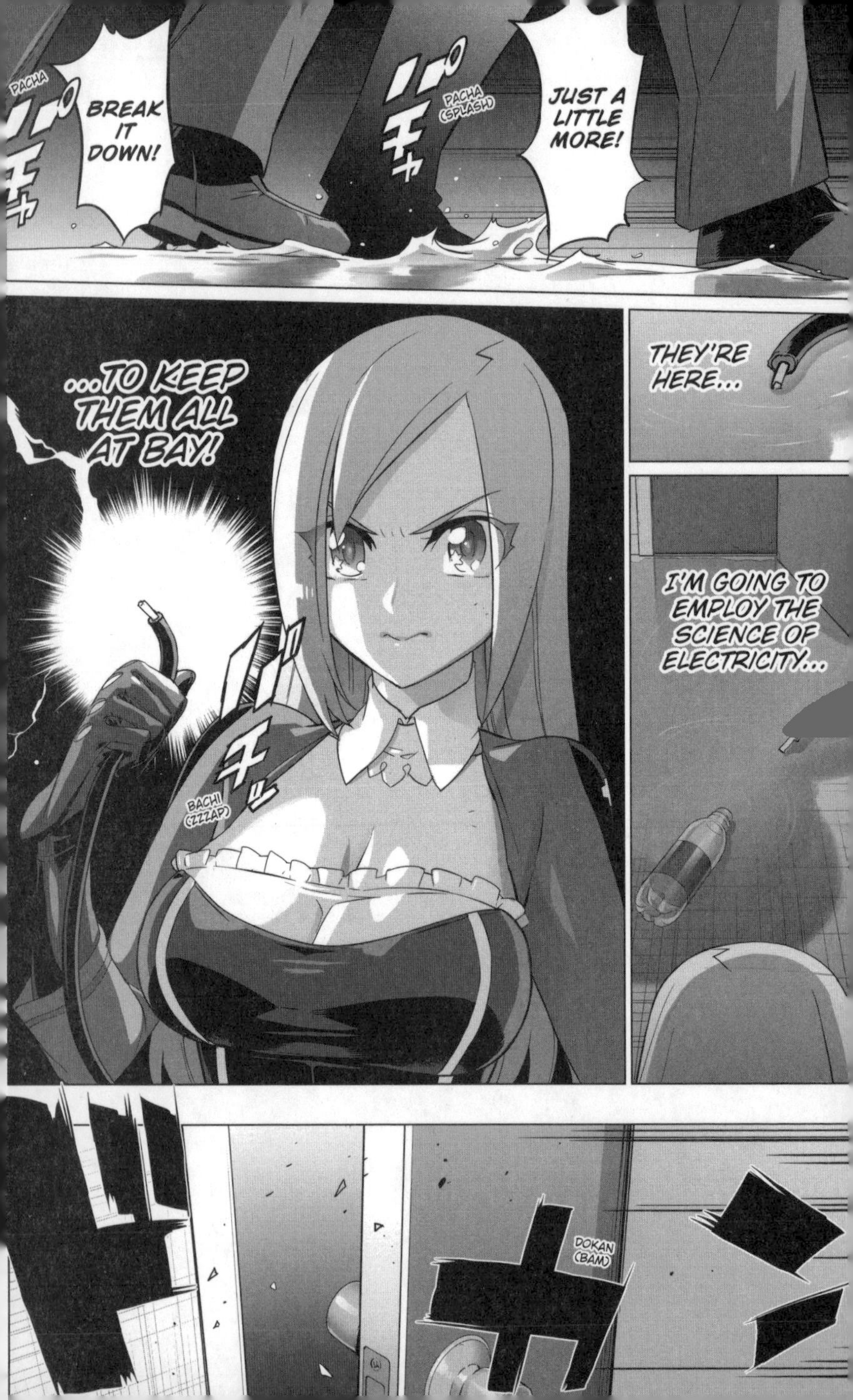
JUST A LITTLE MORE!
PACHA (SPLASH)
BREAK IT DOWN!
PACHA
THEY'RE HERE...
I'M GOING TO EMPLOY THE SCIENCE OF ELECTRICITY...
...TO KEEP THEM ALL AT BAY!
BACHI (ZZZAP)
DOKAN (BAM)

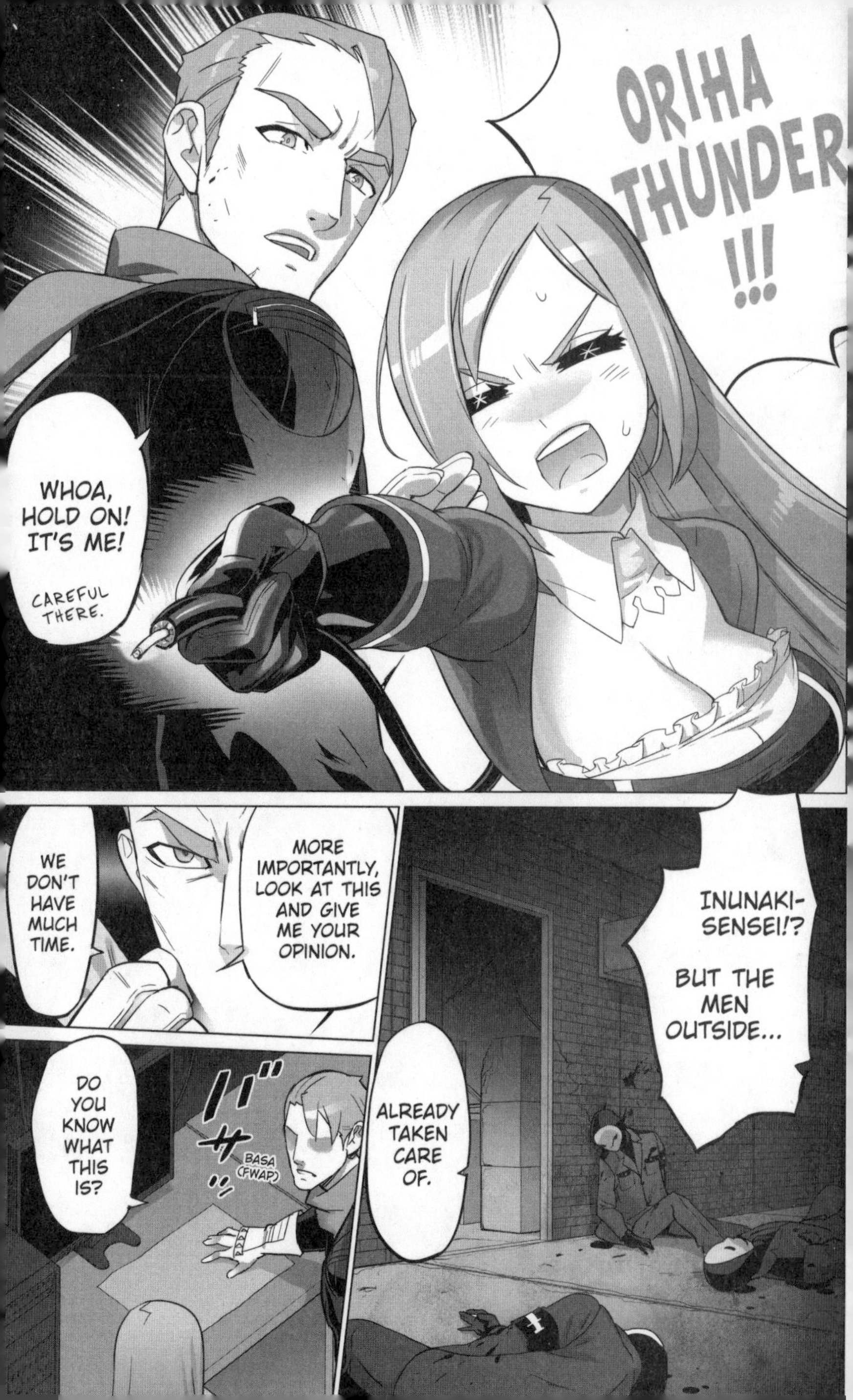
ORIHA THUNDER !!!
WHOA, HOLD ON! IT'S ME!
CAREFUL THERE.
INUNAKI-SENSEI!?
BUT THE MEN OUTSIDE...
ALREADY TAKEN CARE OF.
MORE IMPORTANTLY, LOOK AT THIS AND GIVE ME YOUR OPINION.
WE DON'T HAVE MUCH TIME.
BASA (FWAP)
DO YOU KNOW WHAT THIS IS?

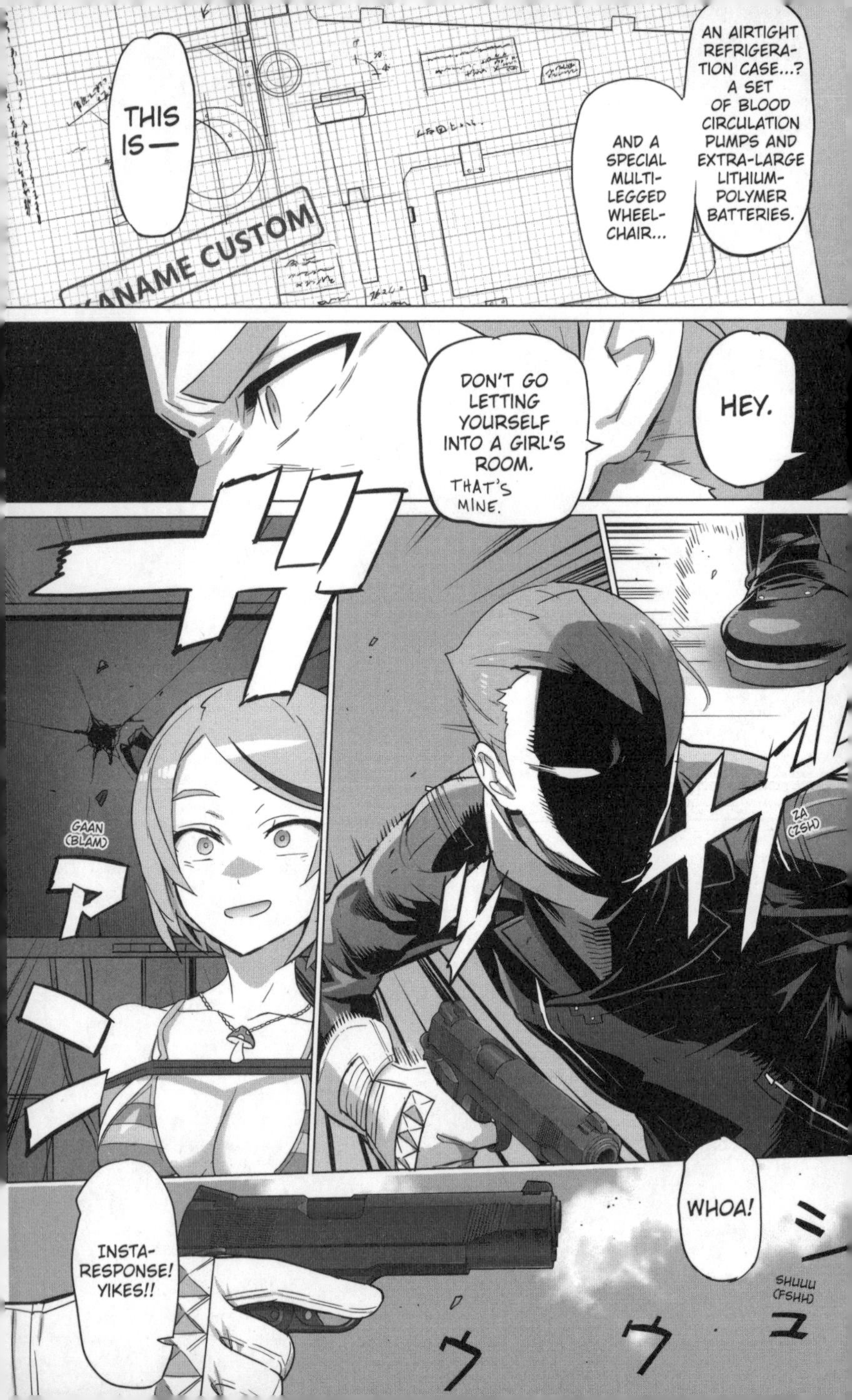
AN AIRTIGHT REFRIGERATION CASE...? A SET OF BLOOD CIRCULATION PUMPS AND EXTRA-LARGE LITHIUM-POLYMER BATTERIES.
AND A SPECIAL MULTI-LEGGED WHEELCHAIR...
THIS IS—
KANAME CUSTOM
HEY.
DON'T GO LETTING YOURSELF INTO A GIRL'S ROOM.
THAT'S MINE.
ZA (ZSH)
GAAN (BLAM)
WHOA!
SHUUU (FSHH)
INSTA-RESPONSE! YIKES!!

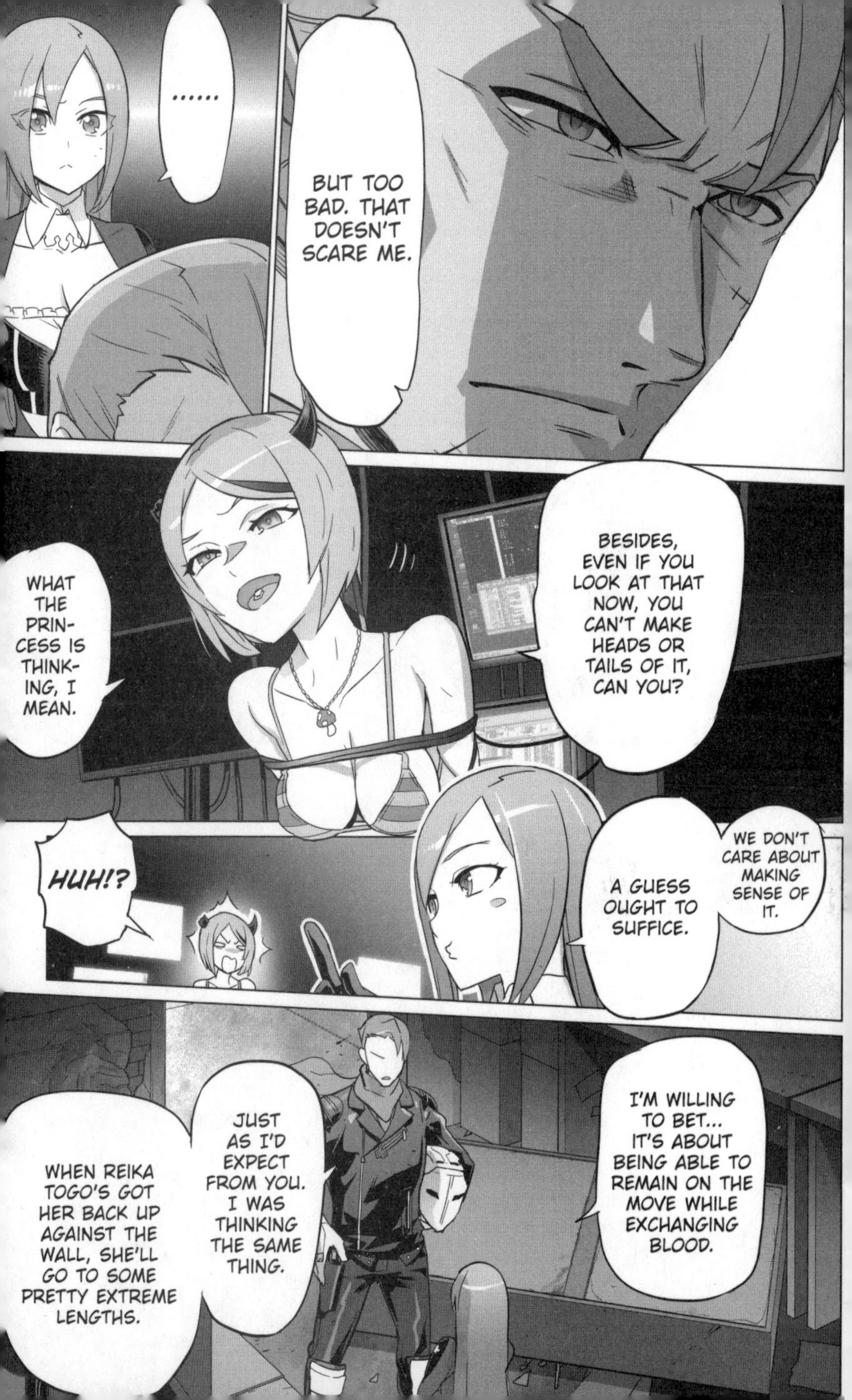

BUT TOO BAD. THAT DOESN'T SCARE ME.
......
BESIDES, EVEN IF YOU LOOK AT THAT NOW, YOU CAN'T MAKE HEADS OR TAILS OF IT, CAN YOU?
WHAT THE PRIN-CESS IS THINK-ING, I MEAN.
WE DON'T CARE ABOUT MAKING SENSE OF IT.
A GUESS OUGHT TO SUFFICE.
HUH!?
I'M WILLING TO BET... IT'S ABOUT BEING ABLE TO REMAIN ON THE MOVE WHILE EXCHANGING BLOOD.
JUST AS I'D EXPECT FROM YOU. I WAS THINKING THE SAME THING.
WHEN REIKA TOGO'S GOT HER BACK UP AGAINST THE WALL, SHE'LL GO TO SOME PRETTY EXTREME LENGTHS.

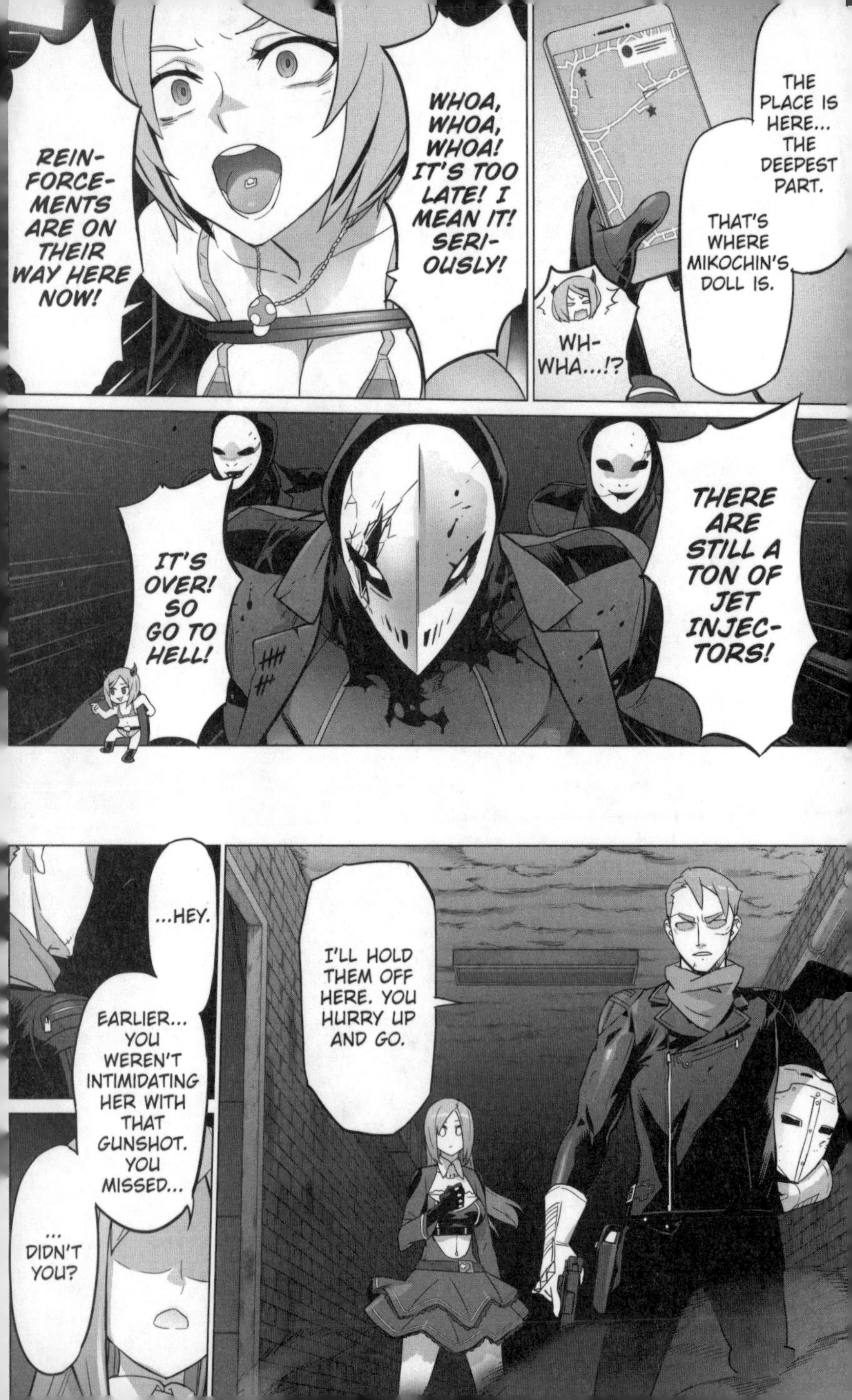

THE PLACE IS HERE... THE DEEPEST PART.
THAT'S WHERE MIKOCHIN'S DOLL IS.
WH-WHA...!?
WHOA, WHOA, WHOA! IT'S TOO LATE! I MEAN IT! SERIOUSLY!
REINFORCEMENTS ARE ON THEIR WAY HERE NOW!
THERE ARE STILL A TON OF JET INJECTORS!
IT'S OVER! SO GO TO HELL!
I'LL HOLD THEM OFF HERE. YOU HURRY UP AND GO.
...HEY.
EARLIER... YOU WEREN'T INTIMIDATING HER WITH THAT GUNSHOT. YOU MISSED...
...DIDN'T YOU?

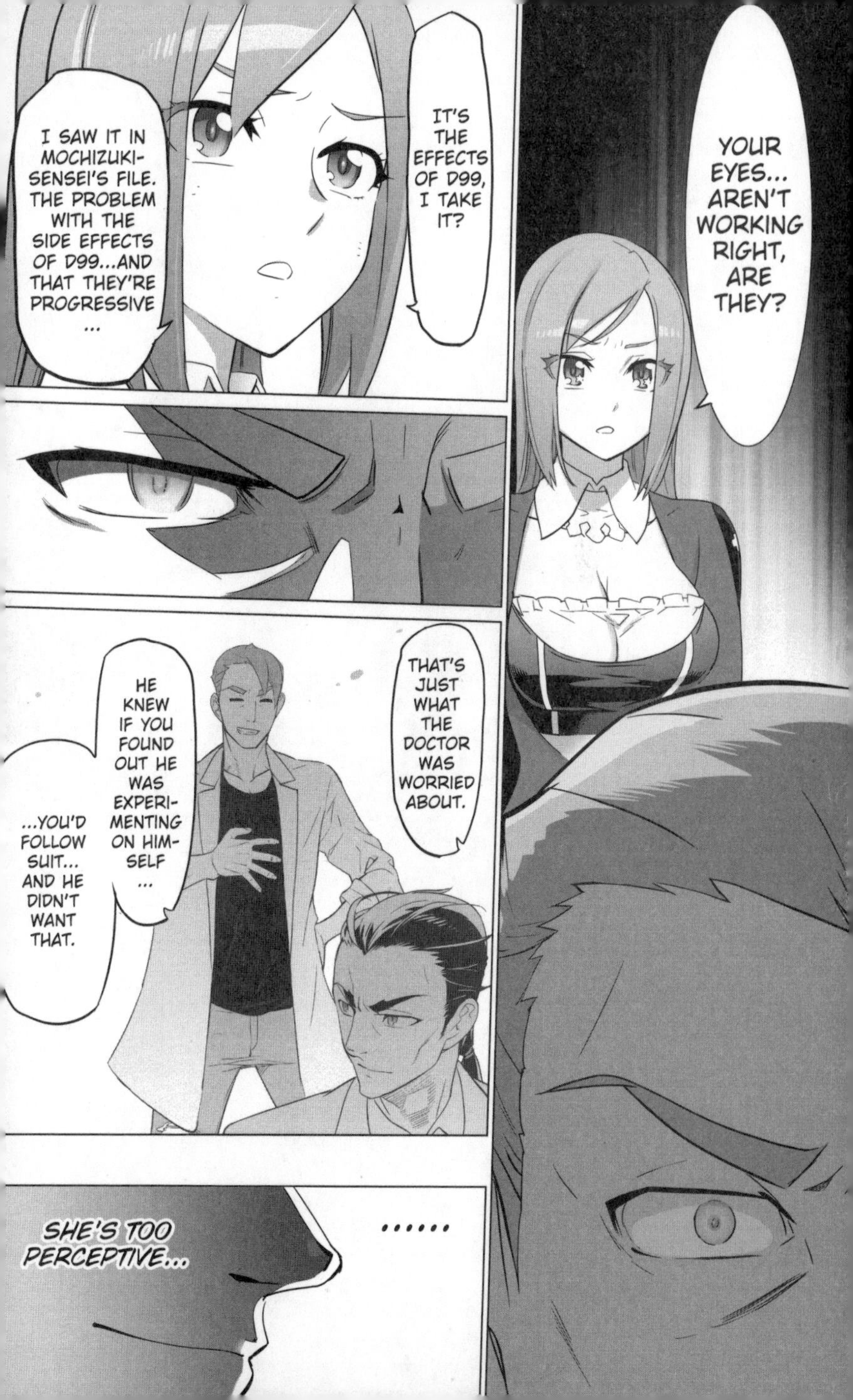
YOUR EYES... AREN'T WORKING RIGHT, ARE THEY?
IT'S THE EFFECTS OF D99, I TAKE IT?
I SAW IT IN MOCHIZUKI-SENSEI'S FILE. THE PROBLEM WITH THE SIDE EFFECTS OF D99...AND THAT THEY'RE PROGRESSIVE ...
THAT'S JUST WHAT THE DOCTOR WAS WORRIED ABOUT.
HE KNEW IF YOU FOUND OUT HE WAS EXPERIMENTING ON HIMSELF ...
...YOU'D FOLLOW SUIT... AND HE DIDN'T WANT THAT.
......
SHE'S TOO PERCEPTIVE...

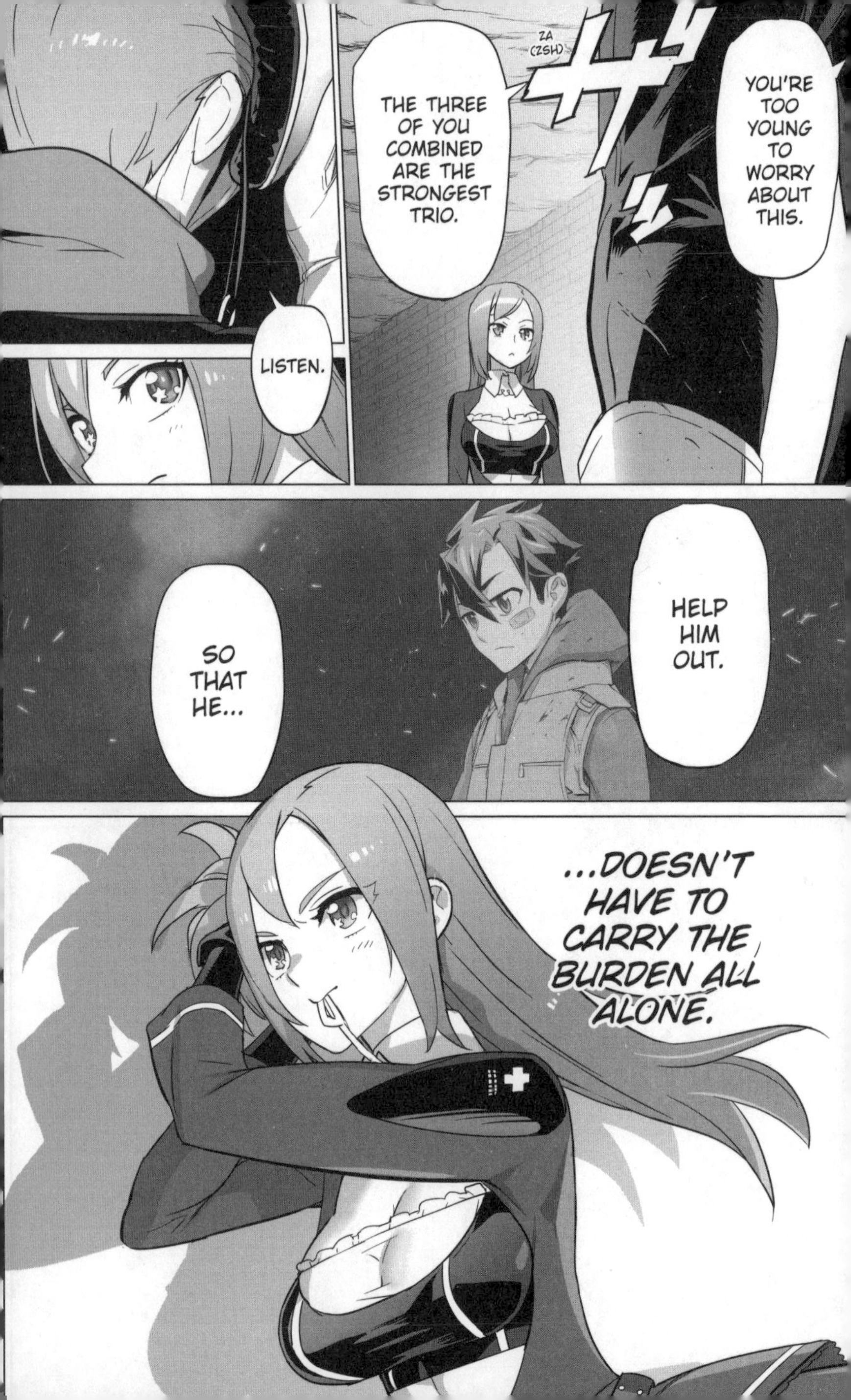
YOU'RE TOO YOUNG TO WORRY ABOUT THIS.
ZA (ZSH)
THE THREE OF YOU COMBINED ARE THE STRONGEST TRIO.
LISTEN.
HELP HIM OUT.
SO THAT HE...
...DOESN'T HAVE TO CARRY THE BURDEN ALL ALONE.

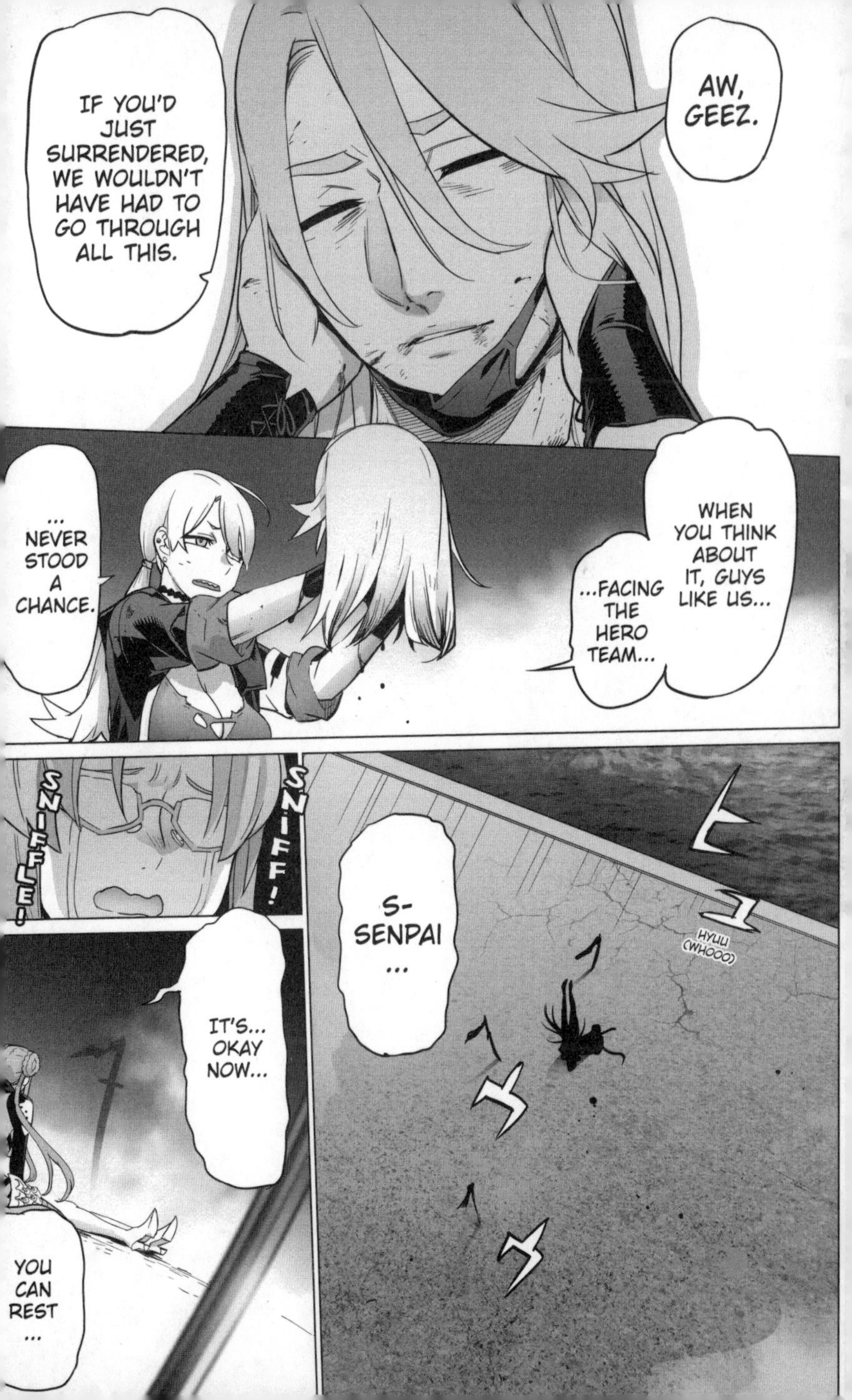
AW, GEEZ.
IF YOU'D JUST SURRENDERED, WE WOULDN'T HAVE HAD TO GO THROUGH ALL THIS.
WHEN YOU THINK ABOUT IT, GUYS LIKE US...
...FACING THE HERO TEAM...
...NEVER STOOD A CHANCE.
S-SENPAI...
HYUU (WHOOO)
SNIFF!
SNIFFLE!
IT'S... OKAY NOW...
YOU CAN REST...

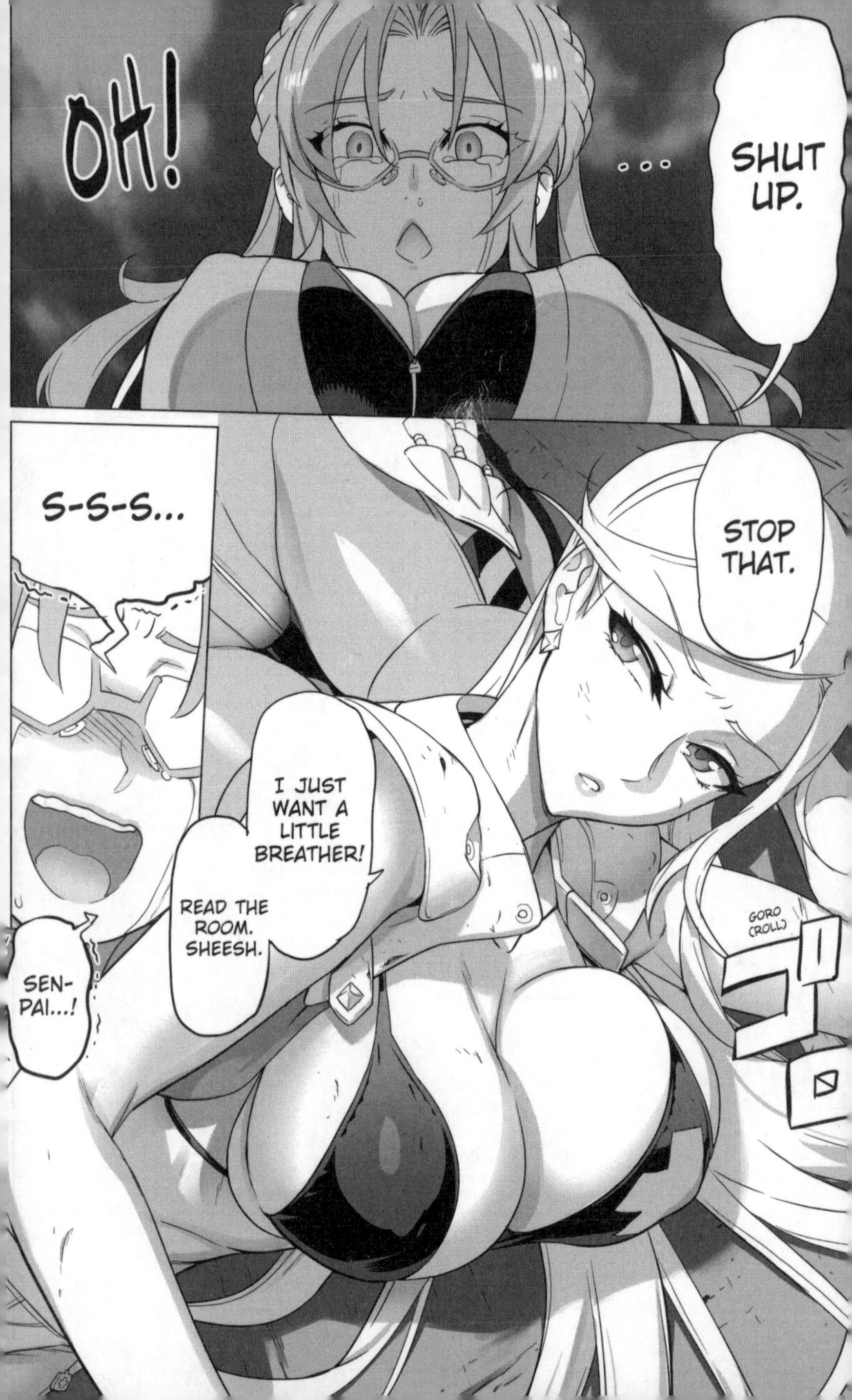
SHUT UP.
...
OH!
STOP THAT.
S-S-S...
GORO (ROLL)
I JUST WANT A LITTLE BREATHER!
READ THE ROOM. SHEESH.
SEN-PAI...!

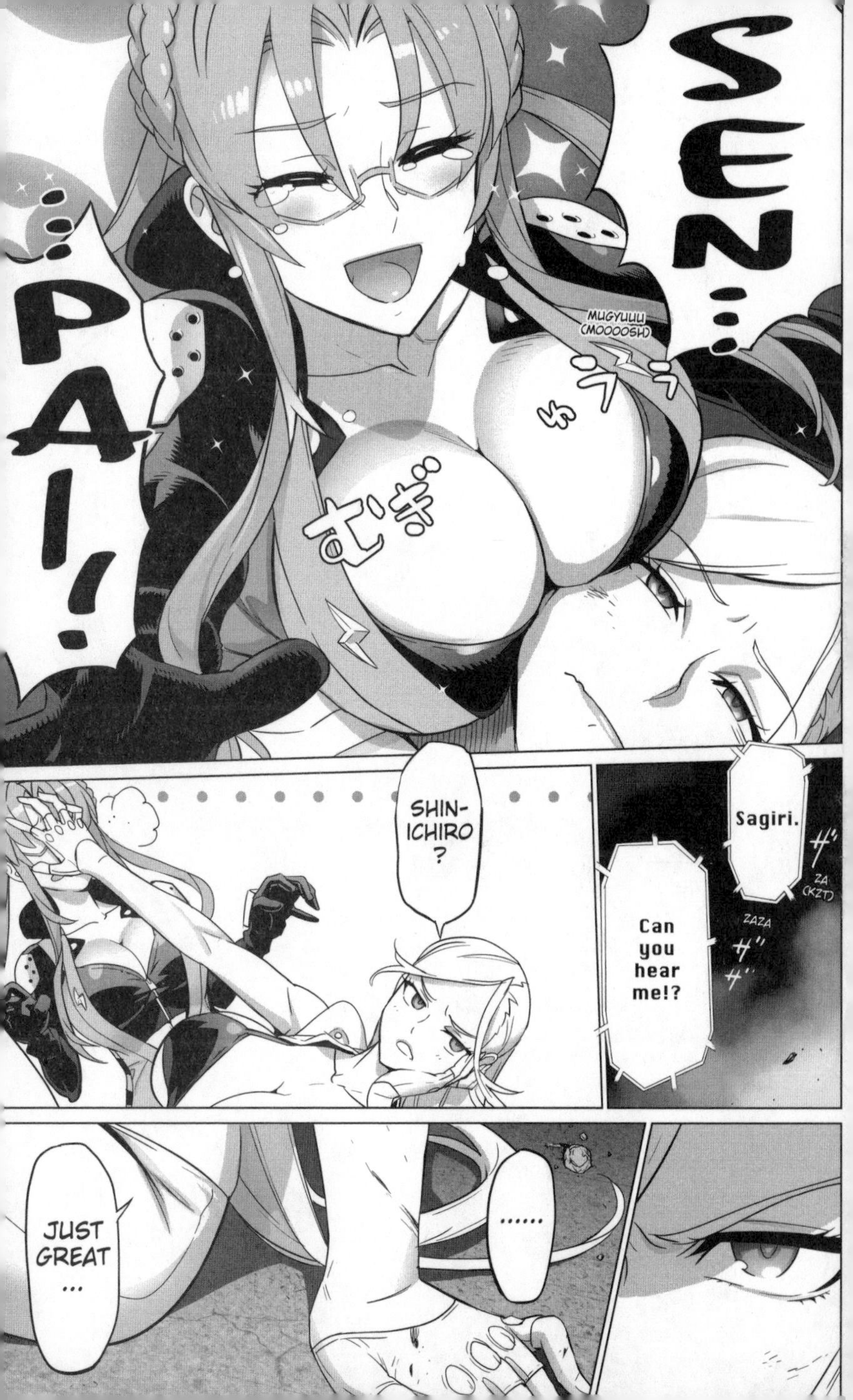
SEN...
......
MUGYUUU (MOOOOSH)
むぎゅうう
...
PAI!?
Sagiri.
ザ
ZA (KZT)
Can you hear me!?
ザザ
ZAZA
SHIN-ICHIRO?
......
JUST GREAT...

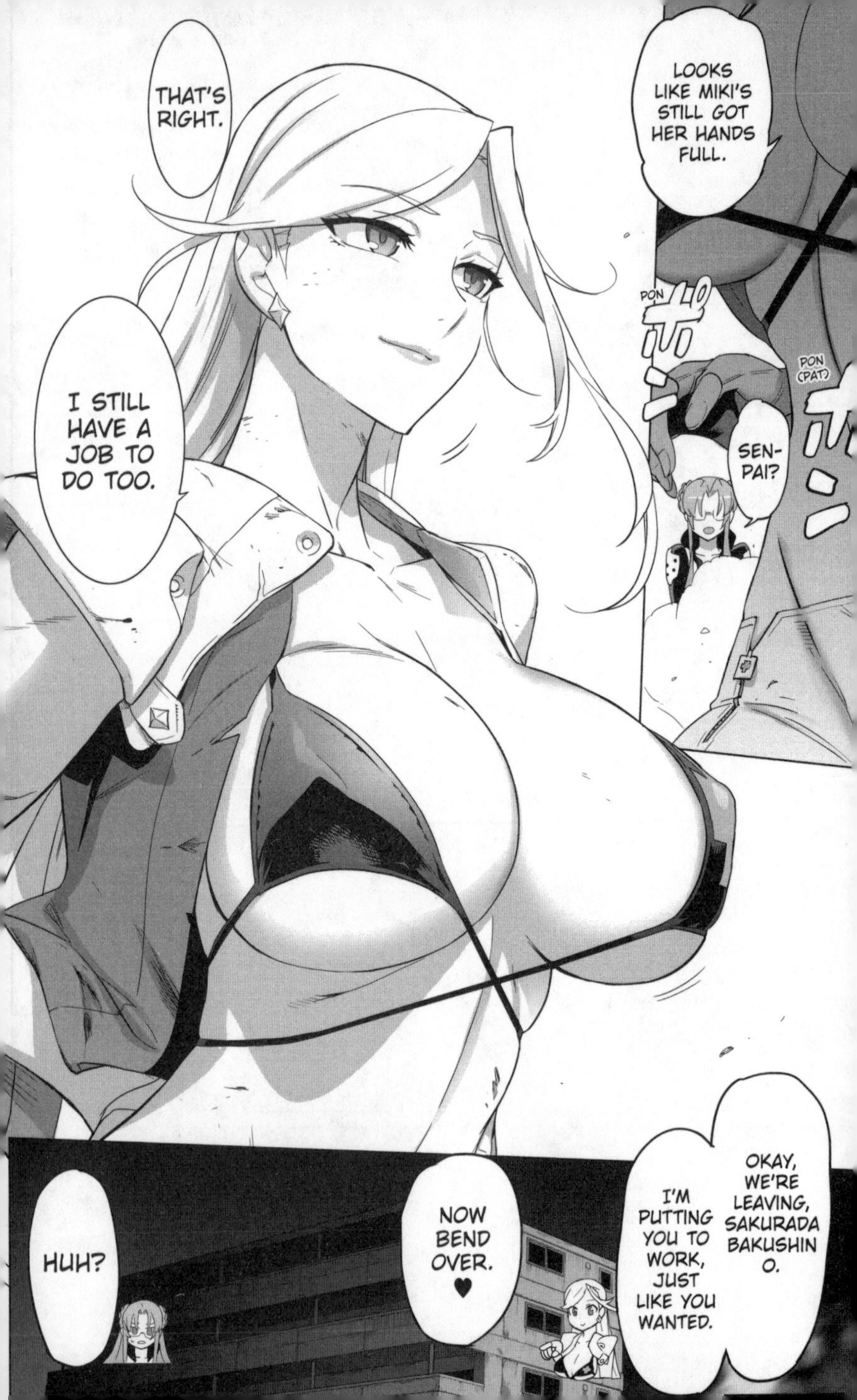

LOOKS LIKE MIKI'S STILL GOT HER HANDS FULL.
PON
PON (PAT)
SEN-PAI?
THAT'S RIGHT.
I STILL HAVE A JOB TO DO TOO.
OKAY, WE'RE LEAVING, SAKURADA BAKUSHIN O.
I'M PUTTING YOU TO WORK, JUST LIKE YOU WANTED.
NOW BEND OVER. ♥
HUH?

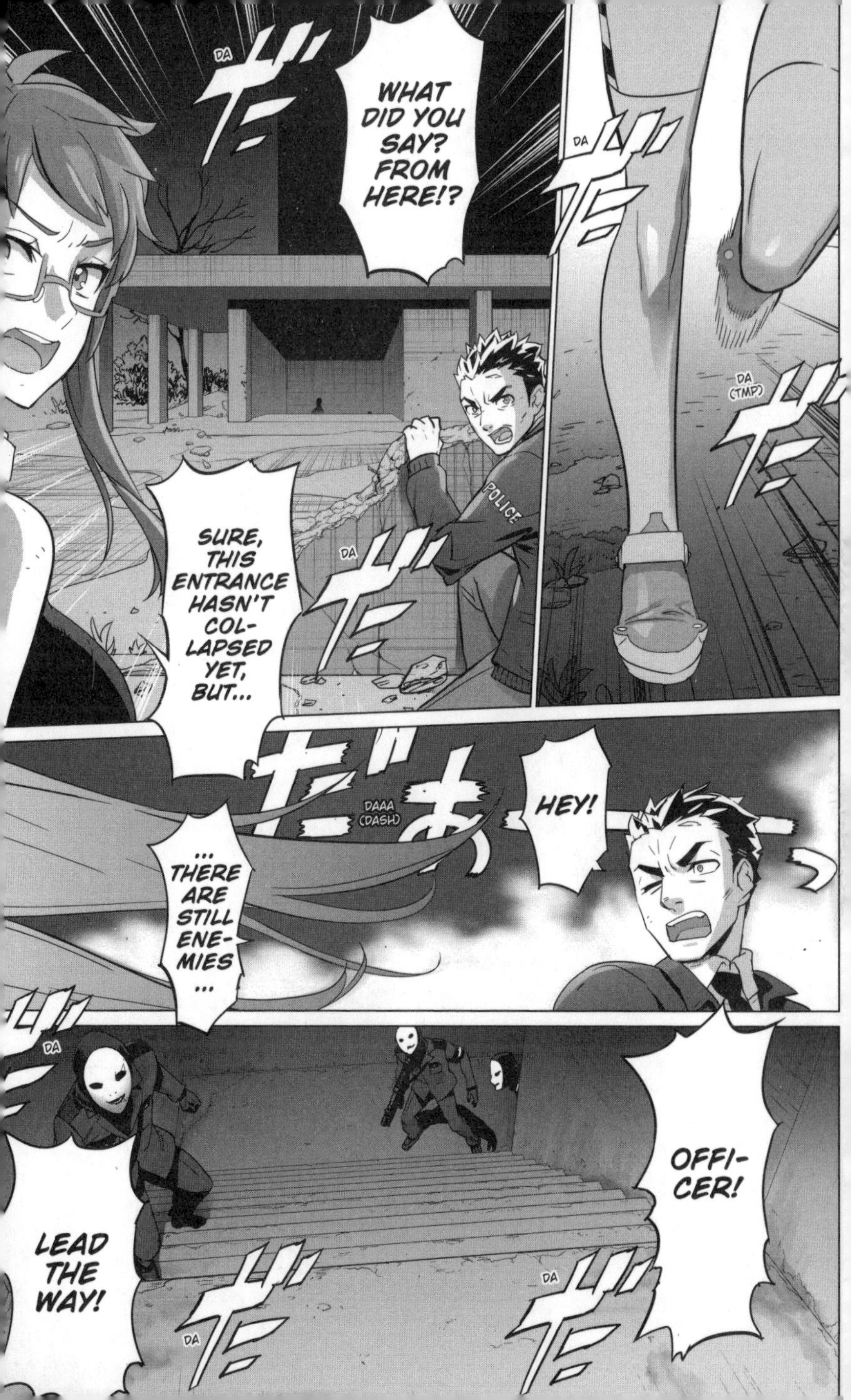
DA
DA (TMP)
WHAT DID YOU SAY? FROM HERE!?
DA
DA
SURE, THIS ENTRANCE HASN'T COL- LAPSED YET, BUT...
HEY!
DAAA (DASH)
... THERE ARE STILL ENE- MIES ...
OFFI- CER!
DA
DA
LEAD THE WAY!
DA

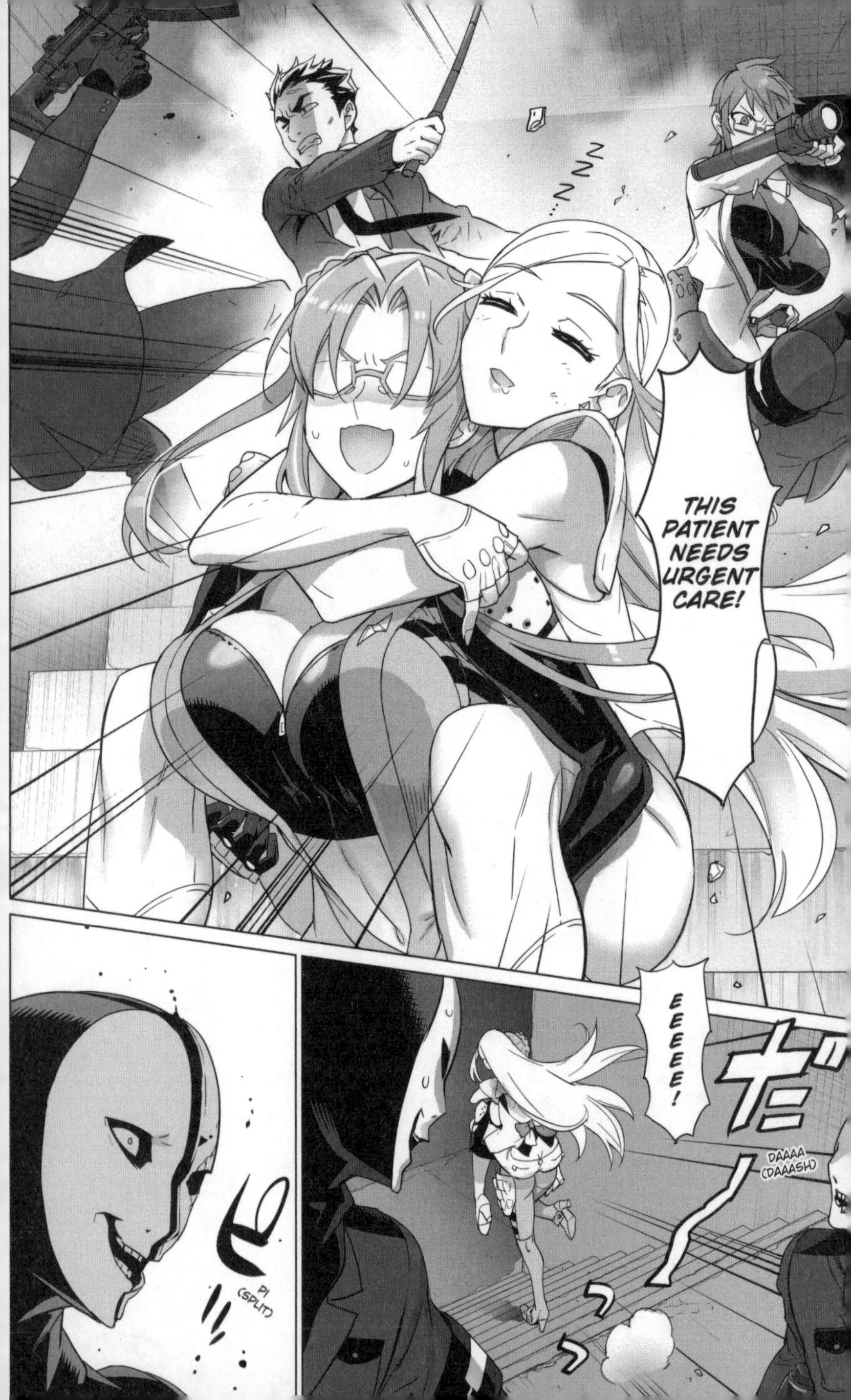
ZZZ...
THIS PATIENT NEEDS URGENT CARE!
EEEEEE!
DAAAA (DAAASH)
PI (SPLIT)

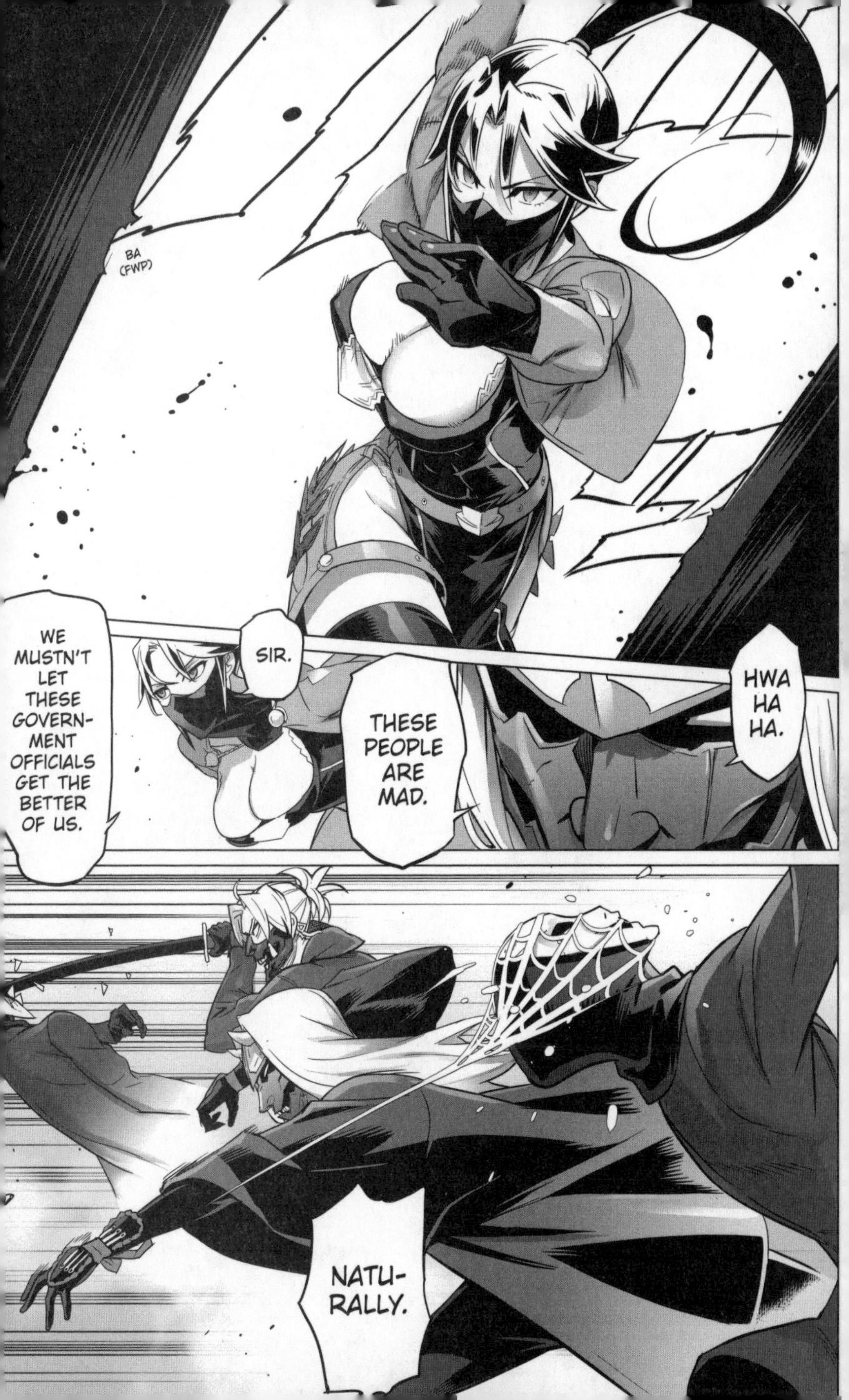
BA (FWP)
HWA HA HA.
THESE PEOPLE ARE MAD.
SIR.
WE MUSTN'T LET THESE GOVERN-MENT OFFICIALS GET THE BETTER OF US.
NATU-RALLY.

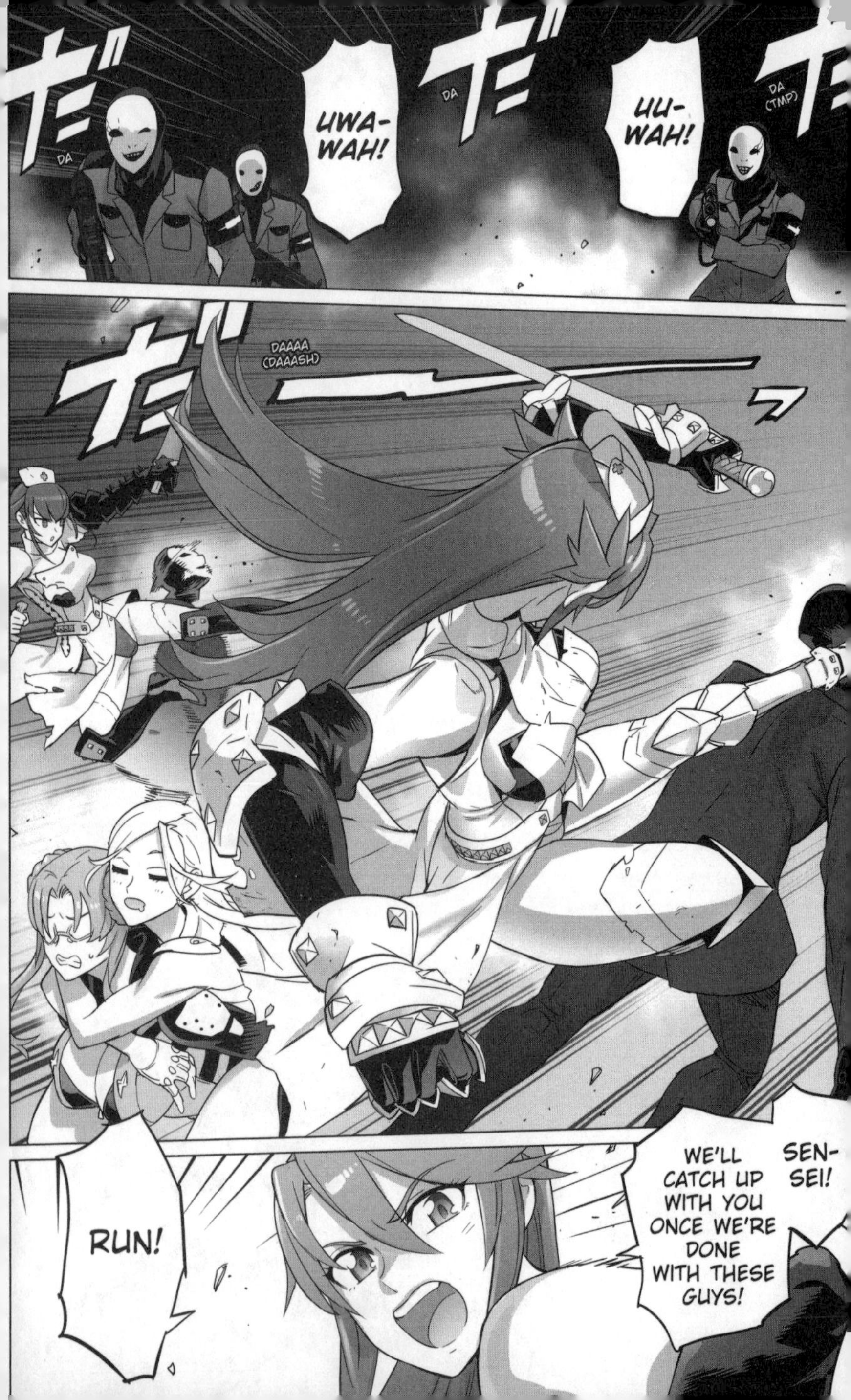
DA (TMP)
UU-WAH!
DA
UWA-WAH!
DA
DAAAA (DAAASH)
SEN-SEI!
WE'LL CATCH UP WITH YOU ONCE WE'RE DONE WITH THESE GUYS!
RUN!

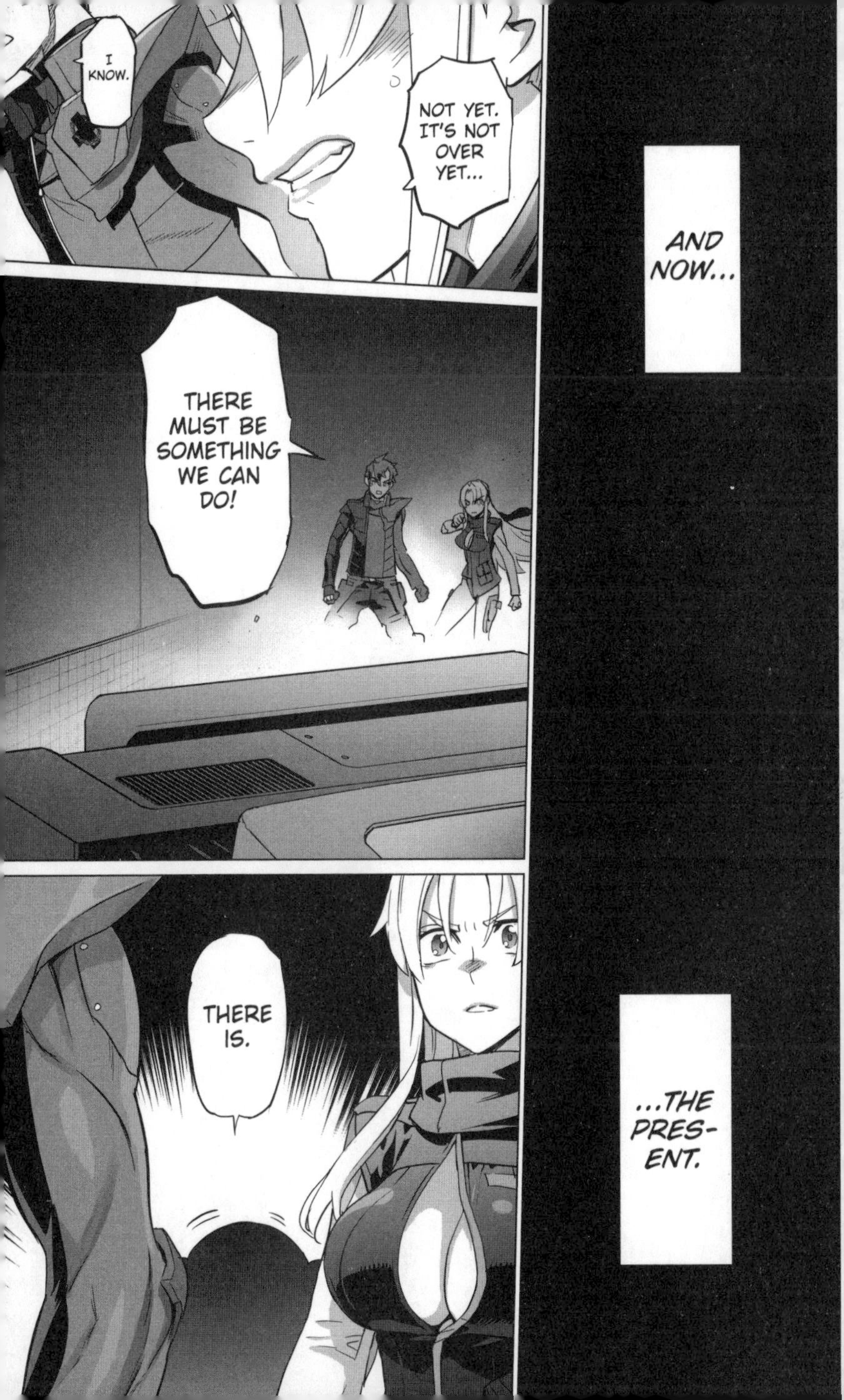
AND NOW...
...THE PRESENT.
NOT YET. IT'S NOT OVER YET...
I KNOW.
THERE MUST BE SOMETHING WE CAN DO!
THERE IS.

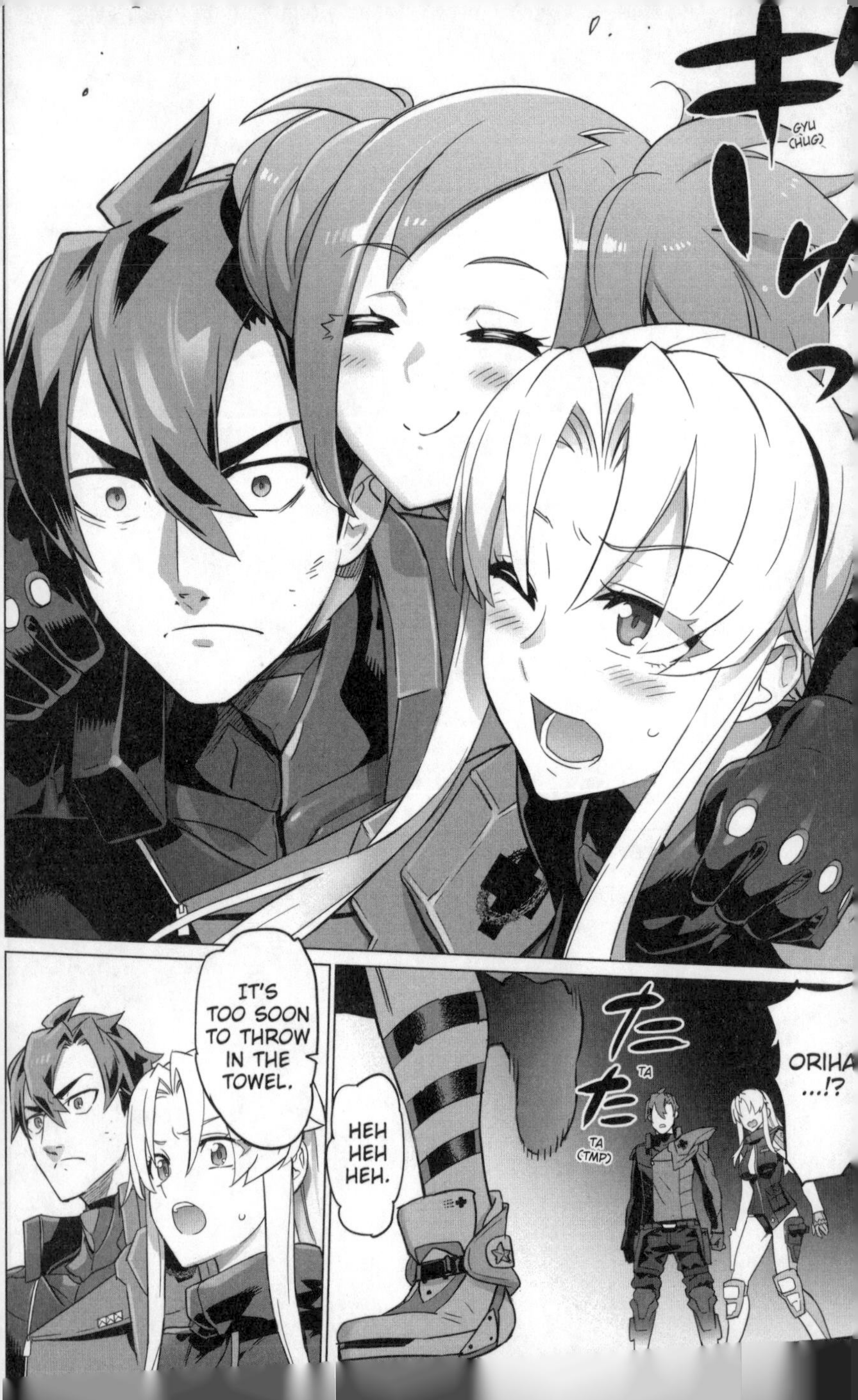
GYU
(HUG)
TA
TA
(TMP)
ORIHA ...!?
IT'S TOO SOON TO THROW IN THE TOWEL.
HEH HEH HEH.

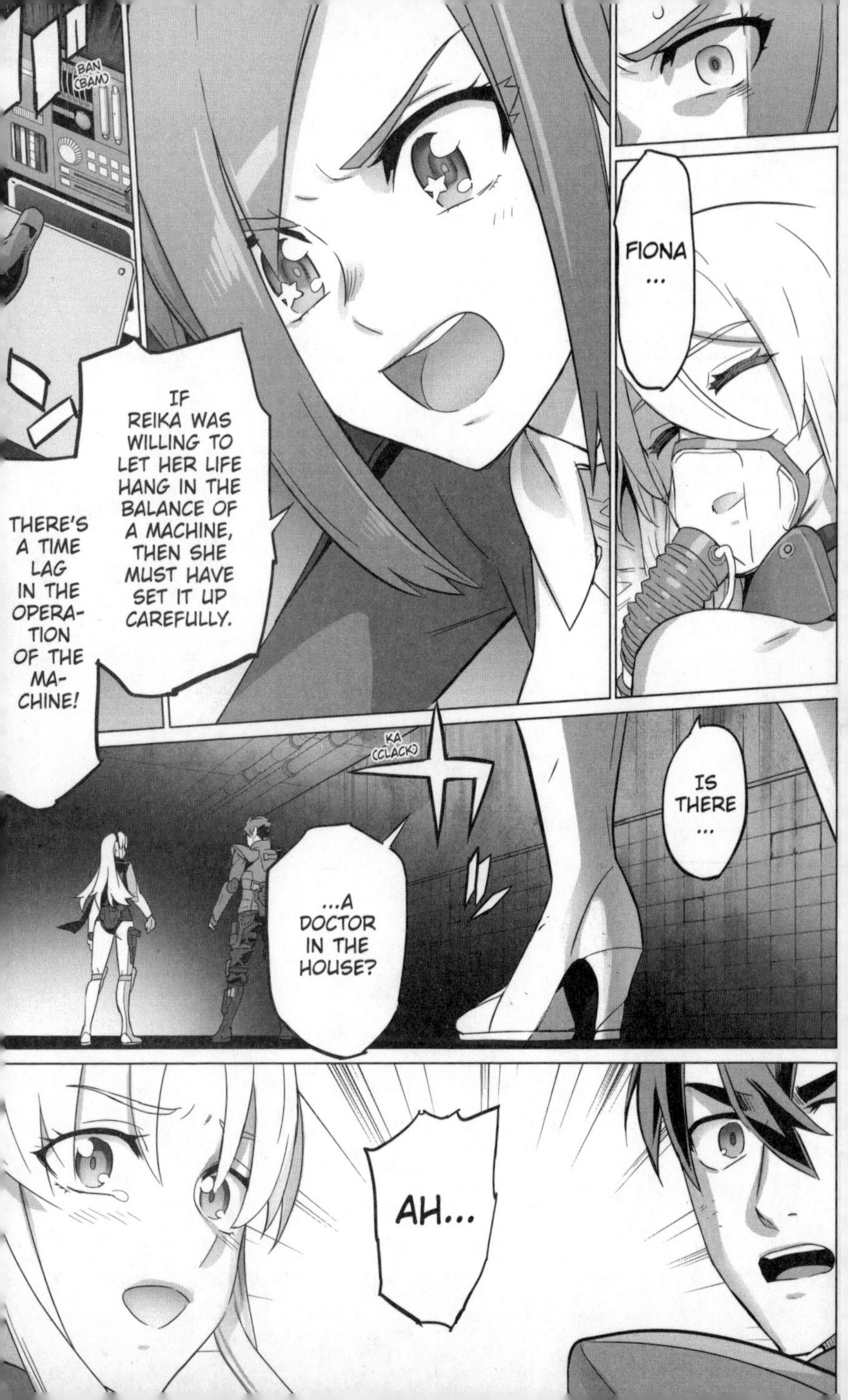
FIONA ...
BAN (BAM)
IF REIKA WAS WILLING TO LET HER LIFE HANG IN THE BALANCE OF A MACHINE, THEN SHE MUST HAVE SET IT UP CAREFULLY.
THERE'S A TIME LAG IN THE OPERATION OF THE MACHINE!
IS THERE ...
KA (CLACK)
...A DOCTOR IN THE HOUSE?
AH...

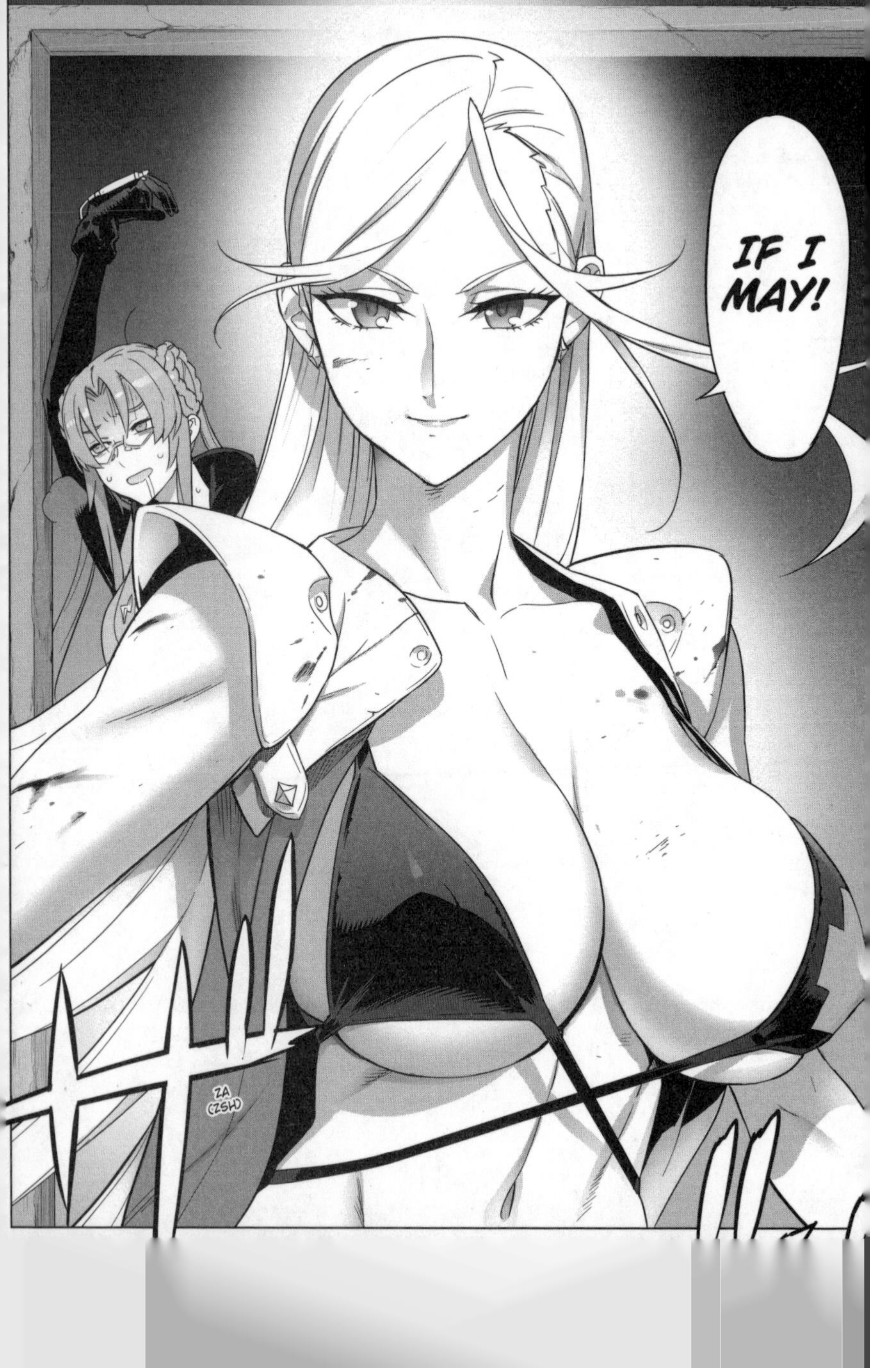
IF I MAY!
ZA
(ZSH)

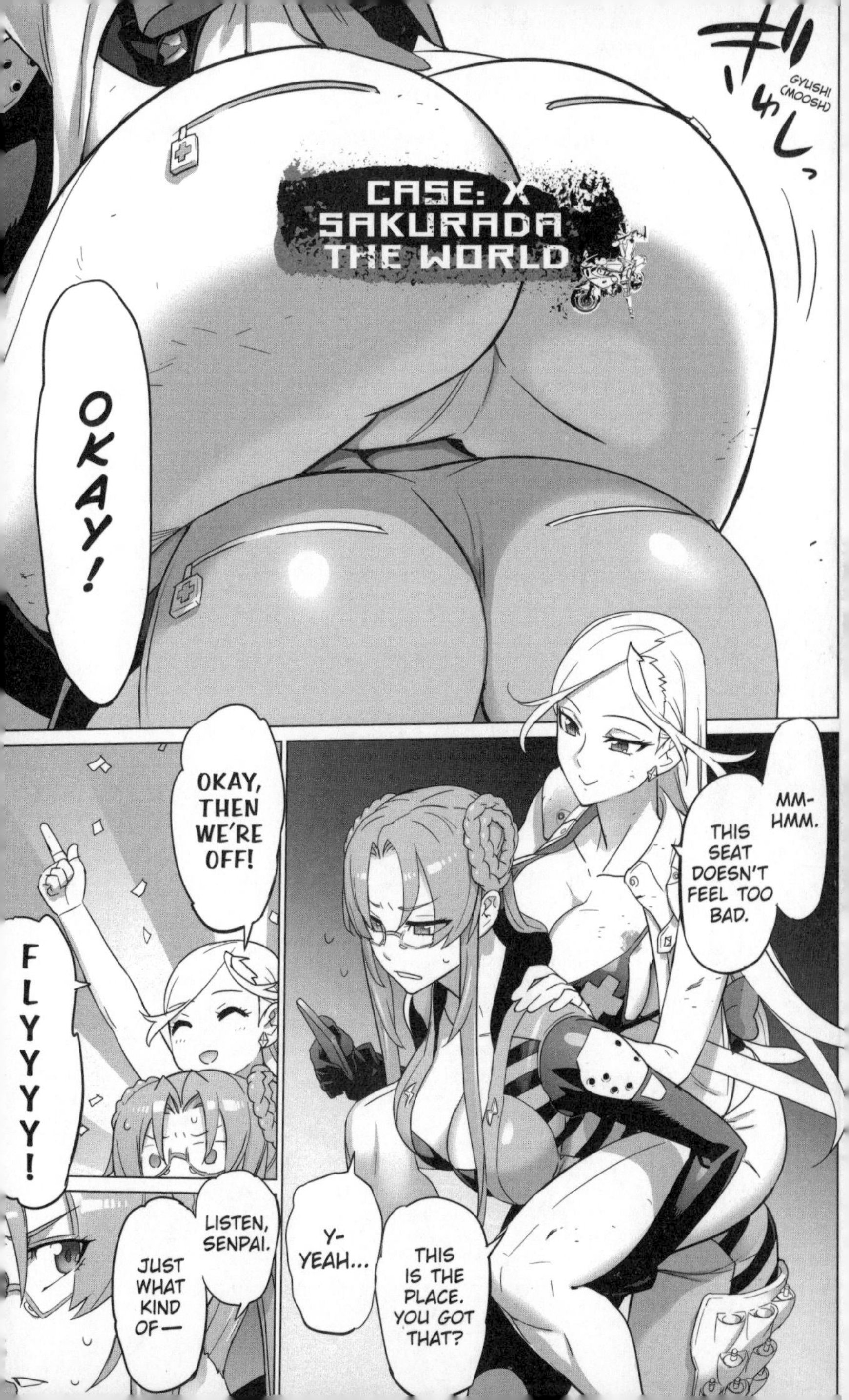

ぎゅしっ
GYUSHI (MOOSH)
CASE: X
SAKURADA THE WORLD
OKAY!
MM-HMM. THIS SEAT DOESN'T FEEL TOO BAD.
THIS IS THE PLACE. YOU GOT THAT?
Y-YEAH...
OKAY, THEN WE'RE OFF!
FLYYYY!
LISTEN, SENPAI.
JUST WHAT KIND OF—

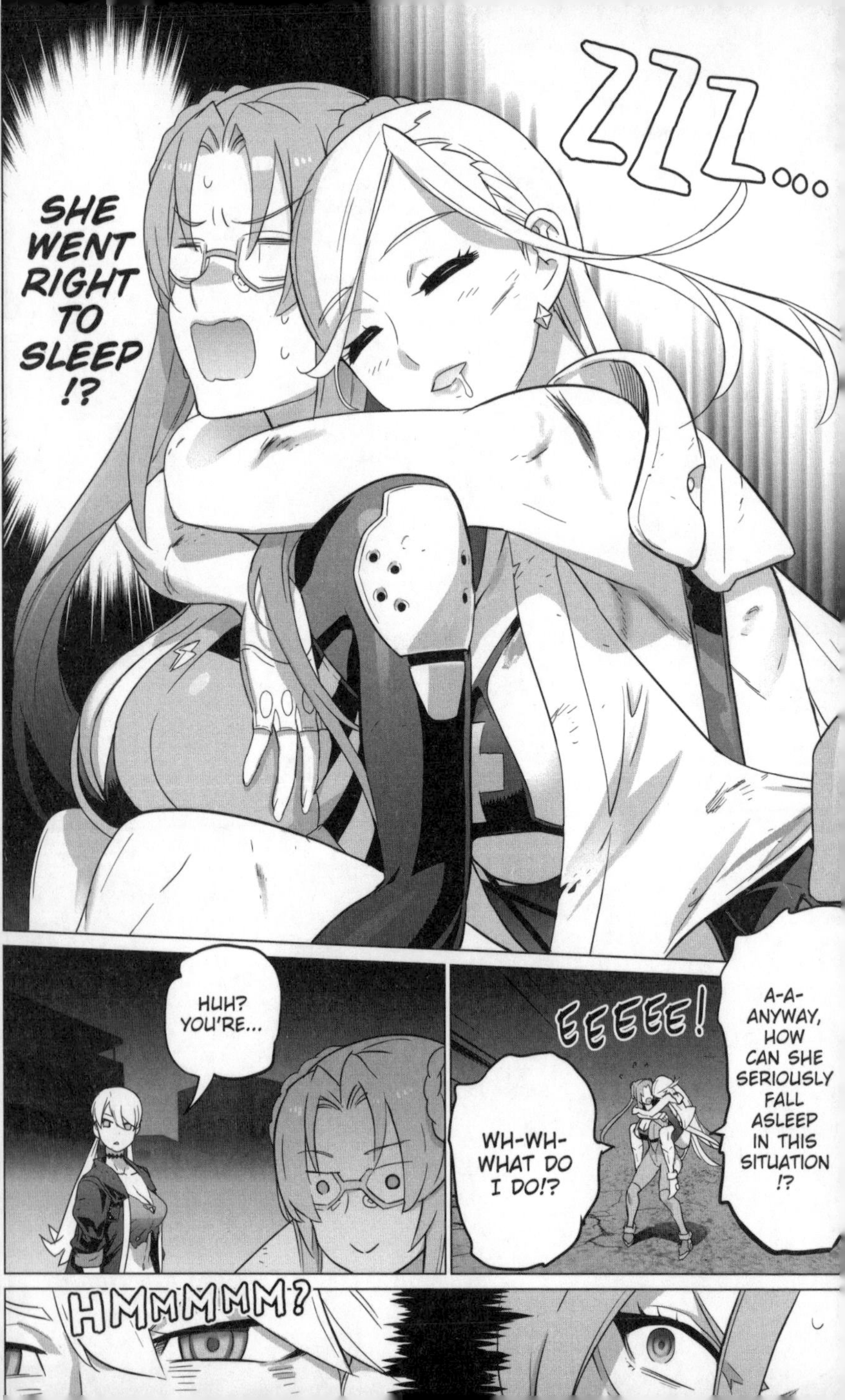
ZZZ...
SHE WENT RIGHT TO SLEEP!?
A-A-ANYWAY, HOW CAN SHE SERIOUSLY FALL ASLEEP IN THIS SITUATION!?
EEEEE!
WH-WH-WHAT DO I DO!?
HUH? YOU'RE...
HMMMMM?

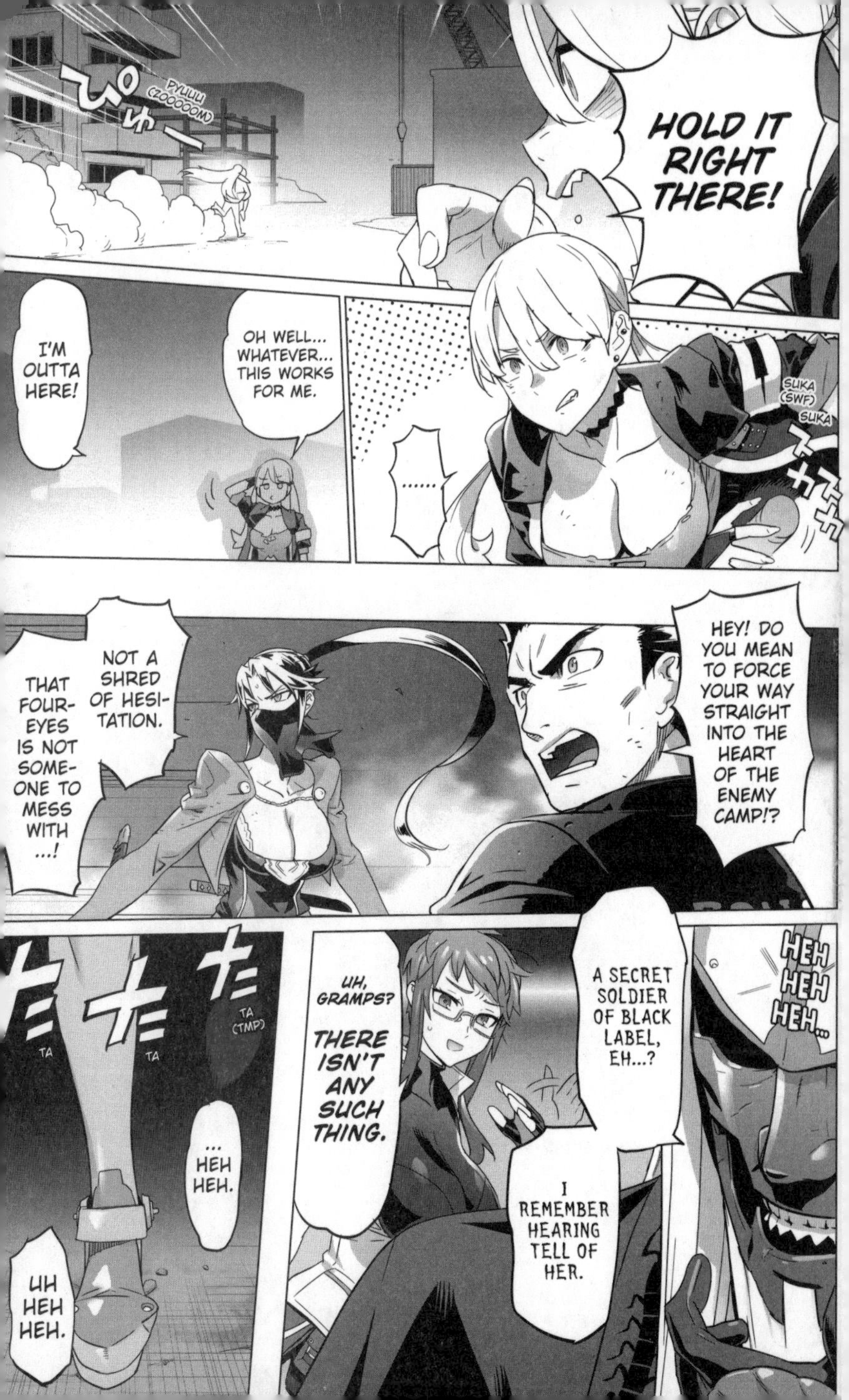
HOLD IT RIGHT THERE!
ぴゅー
PYUUU (ZOOOOOM)
SUKA (SWF) SUKA
......
OH WELL... WHATEVER... THIS WORKS FOR ME.
I'M OUTTA HERE!
HEY! DO YOU MEAN TO FORCE YOUR WAY STRAIGHT INTO THE HEART OF THE ENEMY CAMP!?
NOT A SHRED OF HESI-TATION.
THAT FOUR-EYES IS NOT SOME-ONE TO MESS WITH ...!
HEH HEH HEH...
A SECRET SOLDIER OF BLACK LABEL, EH...?
UH, GRAMPS? THERE ISN'T ANY SUCH THING.
I REMEMBER HEARING TELL OF HER.
TA (TMP)
TA
TA
... HEH HEH.
UH HEH HEH.

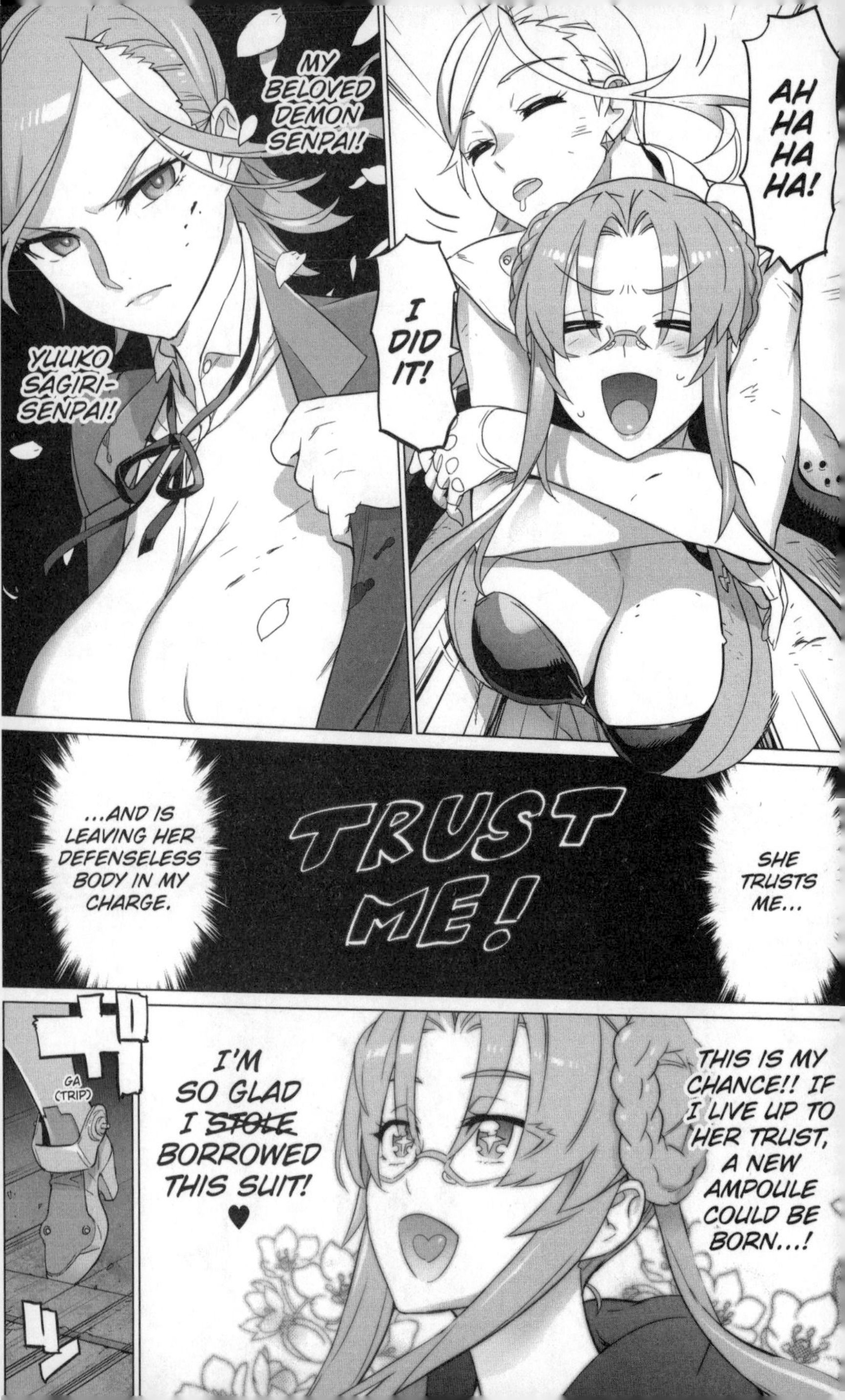
AH HA HA HA!
I DID IT!
MY BELOVED DEMON SENPAI!
YUUKO SAGIRI-SENPAI!
SHE TRUSTS ME...
TRUST ME!
...AND IS LEAVING HER DEFENSELESS BODY IN MY CHARGE.
THIS IS MY CHANCE!! IF I LIVE UP TO HER TRUST, A NEW AMPOULE COULD BE BORN...!
I'M SO GLAD I ~~STOLE~~ BORROWED THIS SUIT! ♥
GA (TRIP)

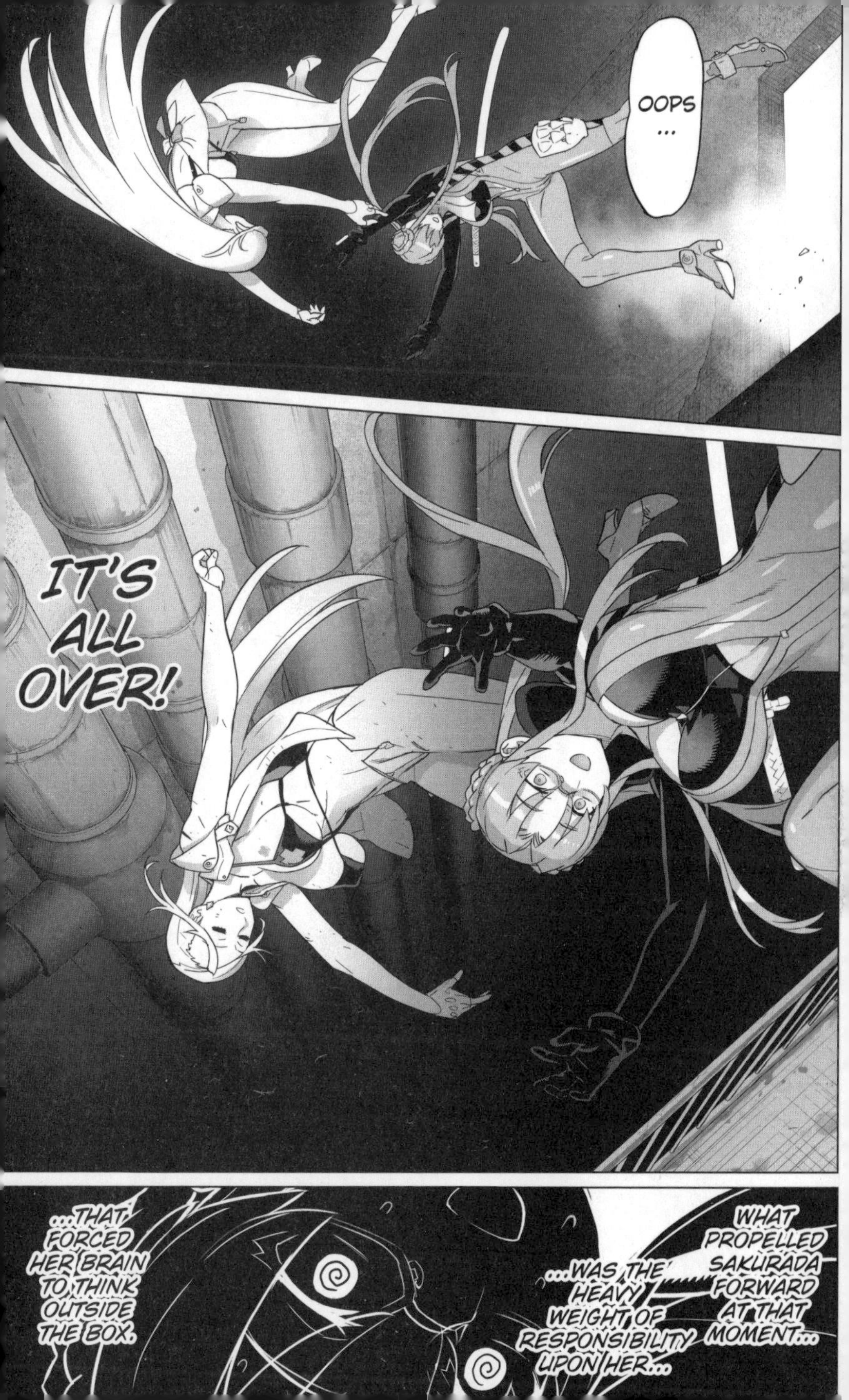
OOPS ...
IT'S ALL OVER!
WHAT PROPELLED SAKURADA FORWARD AT THAT MOMENT...
...WAS THE HEAVY WEIGHT OF RESPONSIBILITY UPON HER...
...THAT FORCED HER BRAIN TO THINK OUTSIDE THE BOX.

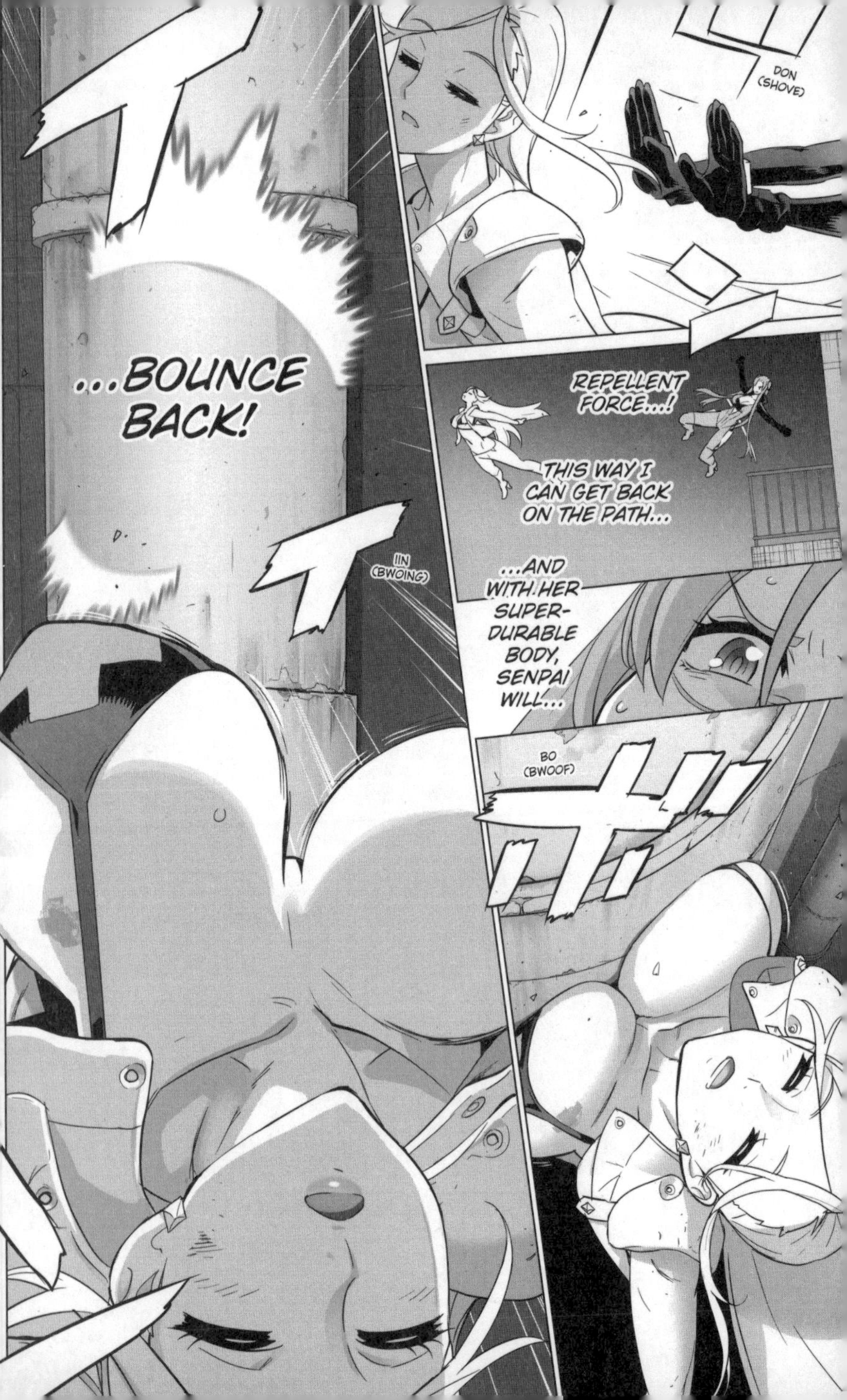
DON (SHOVE)
REPELLENT FORCE...!
THIS WAY I CAN GET BACK ON THE PATH...
...AND WITH HER SUPER-DURABLE BODY, SENPAI WILL...
BO (BWOOF)
...BOUNCE BACK!
IIN (BWOING)

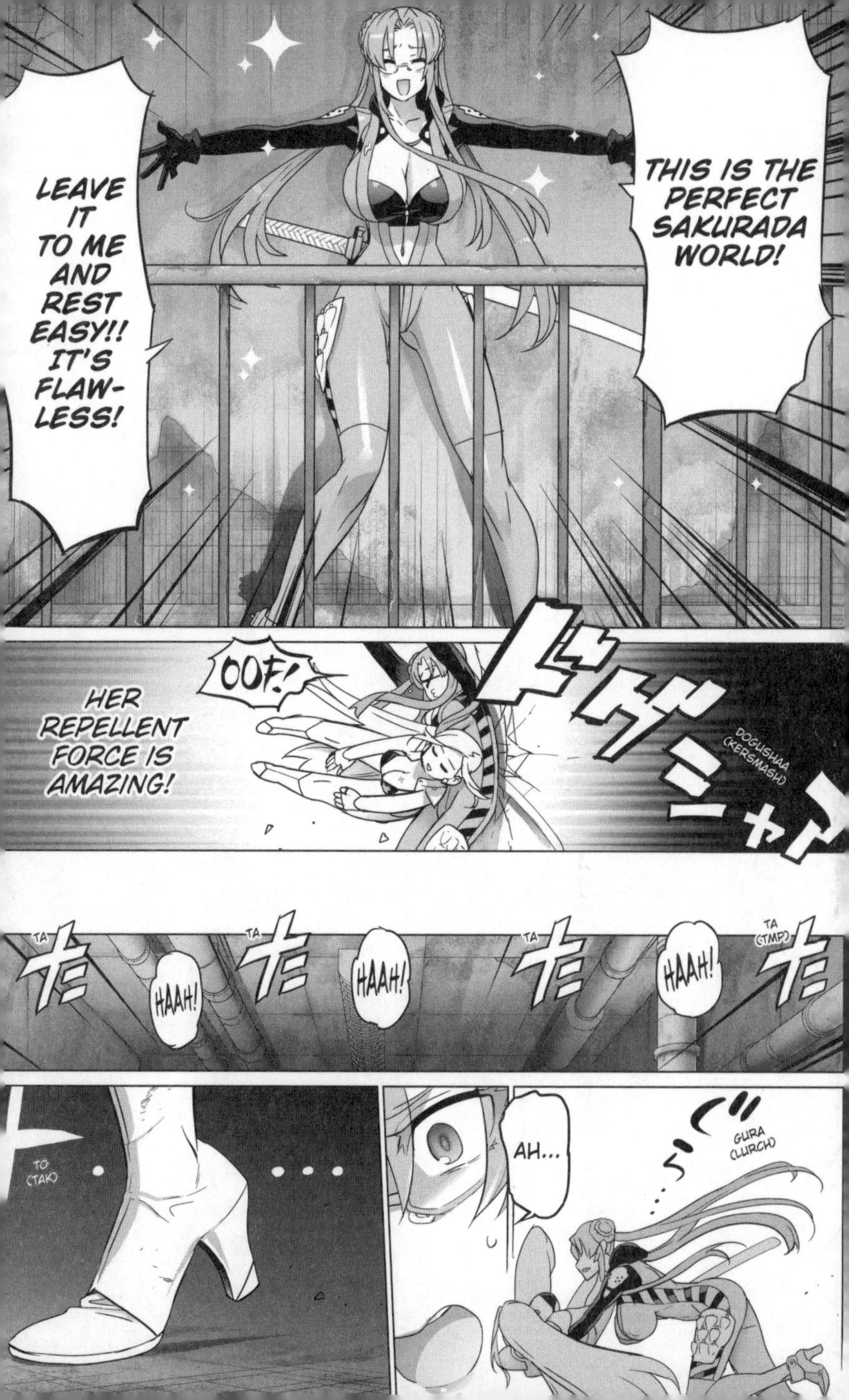
THIS IS THE PERFECT SAKURADA WORLD!
LEAVE IT TO ME AND REST EASY!! IT'S FLAWLESS!
DOGUSHAA (KERSMASH)
OOF!
HER REPELLENT FORCE IS AMAZING!
TA (TMP)
HAAH!
TA
HAAH!
TA
HAAH!
TA
GURA (LURCH)
AH...
TO (TAK)
. . . .

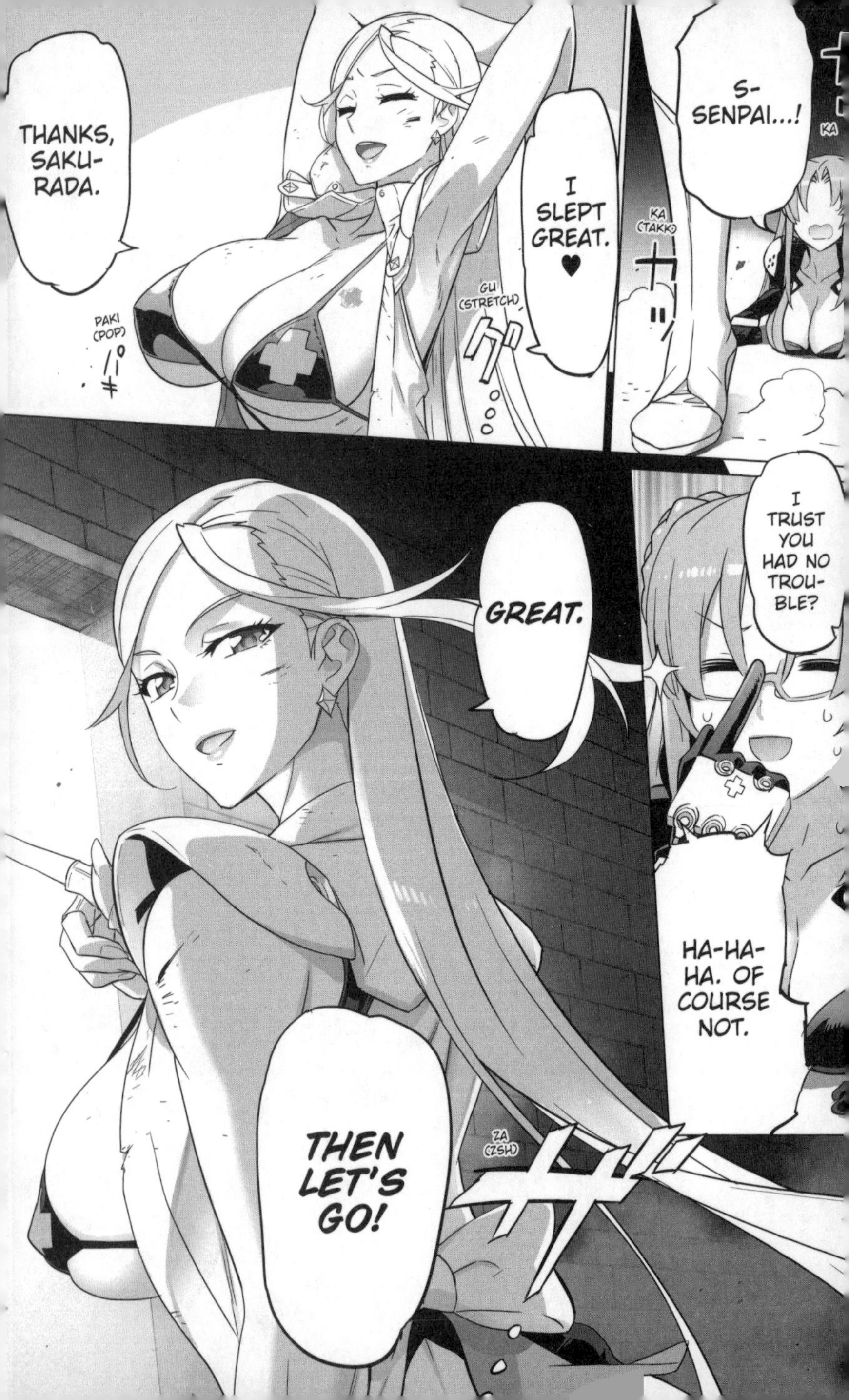
S-SENPAI...!
KA
KA (TAKK)
THANKS, SAKURADA.
I SLEPT GREAT. ♥
GU (STRETCH)
PAKI (POP)
I TRUST YOU HAD NO TROUBLE?
HA-HA-HA. OF COURSE NOT.
GREAT.
THEN LET'S GO!
ZA (ZSH)

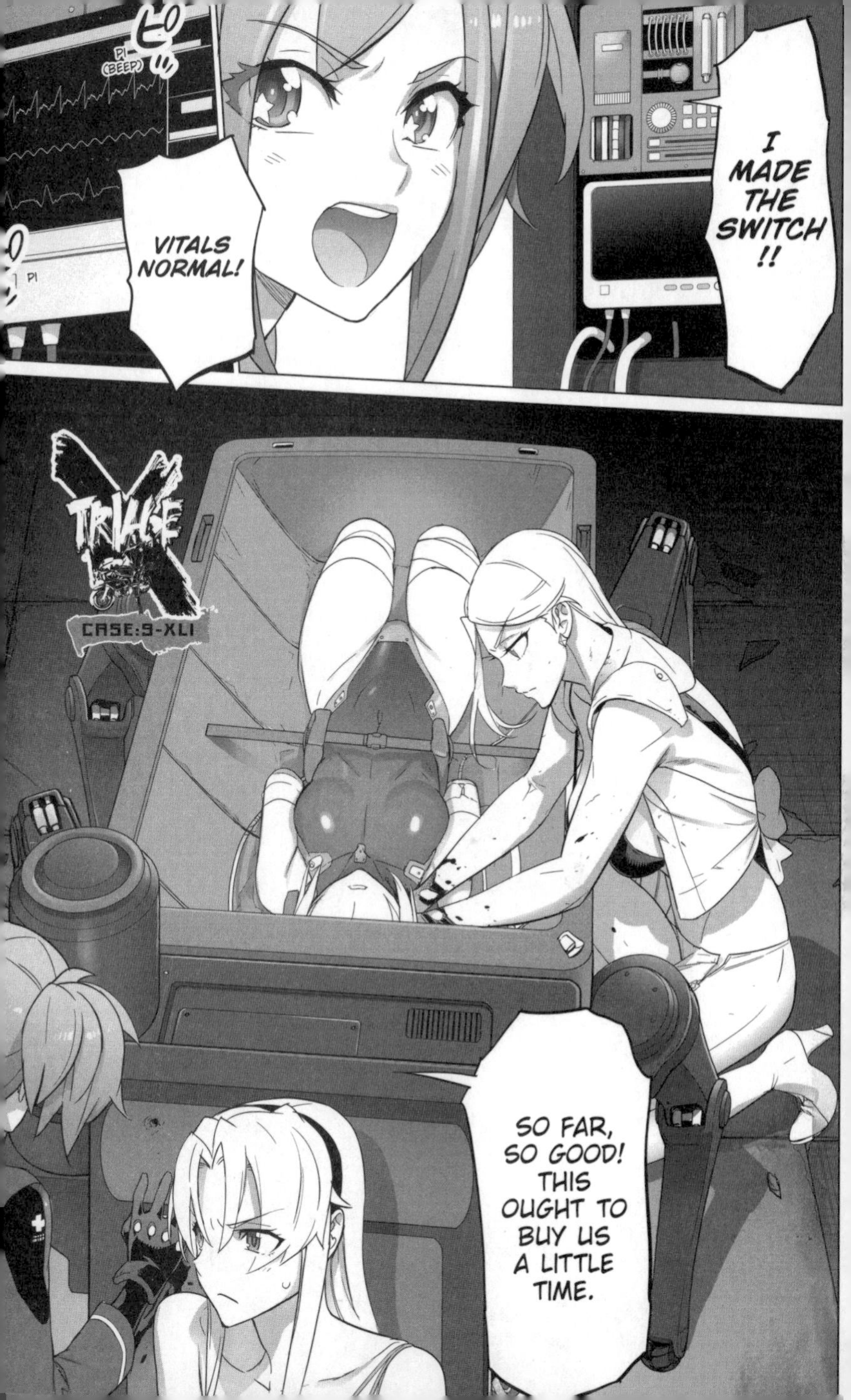
I MADE THE SWITCH!!
PI (BEEP)
VITALS NORMAL!
PI
TRIAGE X
CASE:9-XLI
SO FAR, SO GOOD! THIS OUGHT TO BUY US A LITTLE TIME.

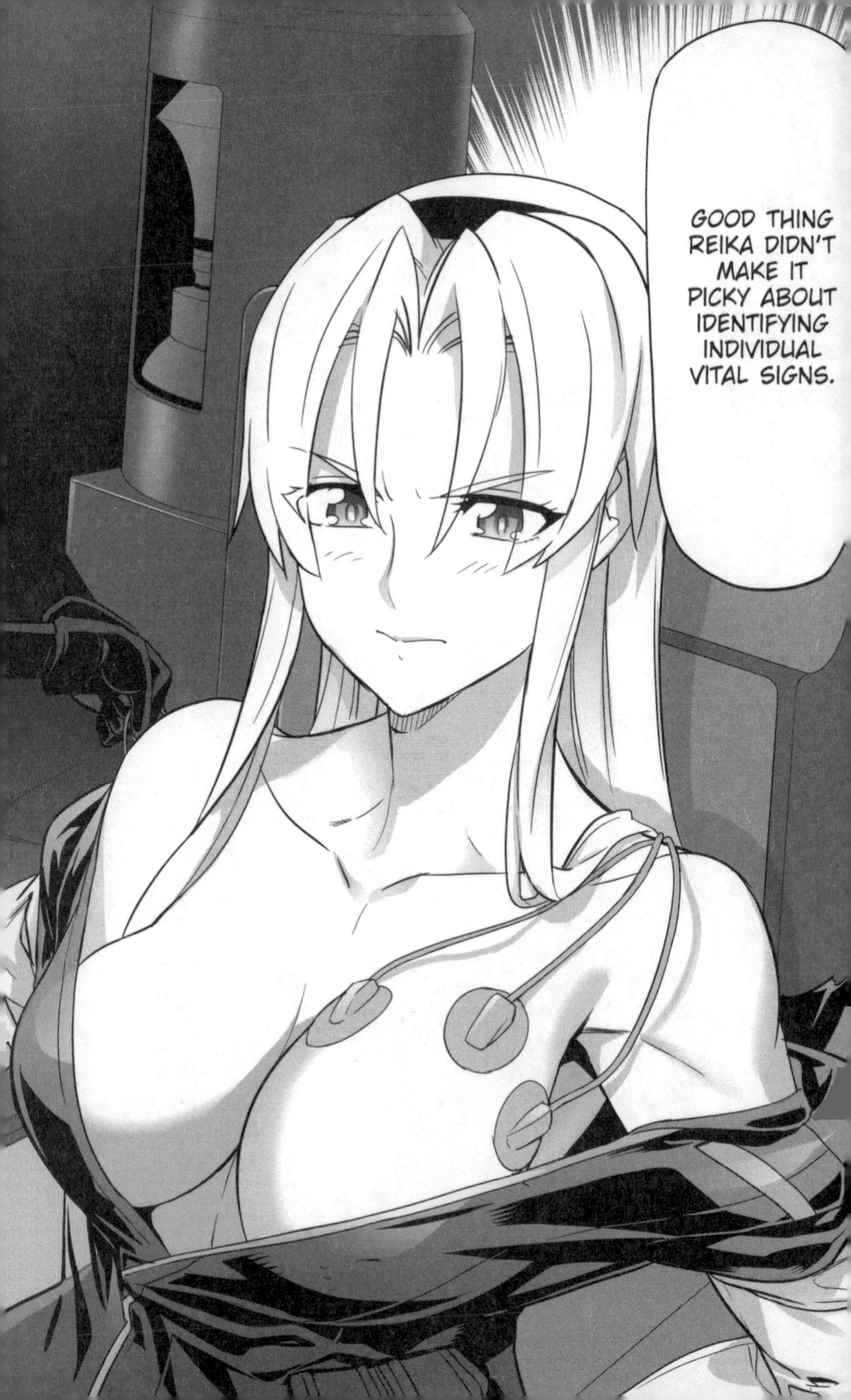
GOOD THING REIKA DIDN'T MAKE IT PICKY ABOUT IDENTIFYING INDIVIDUAL VITAL SIGNS.

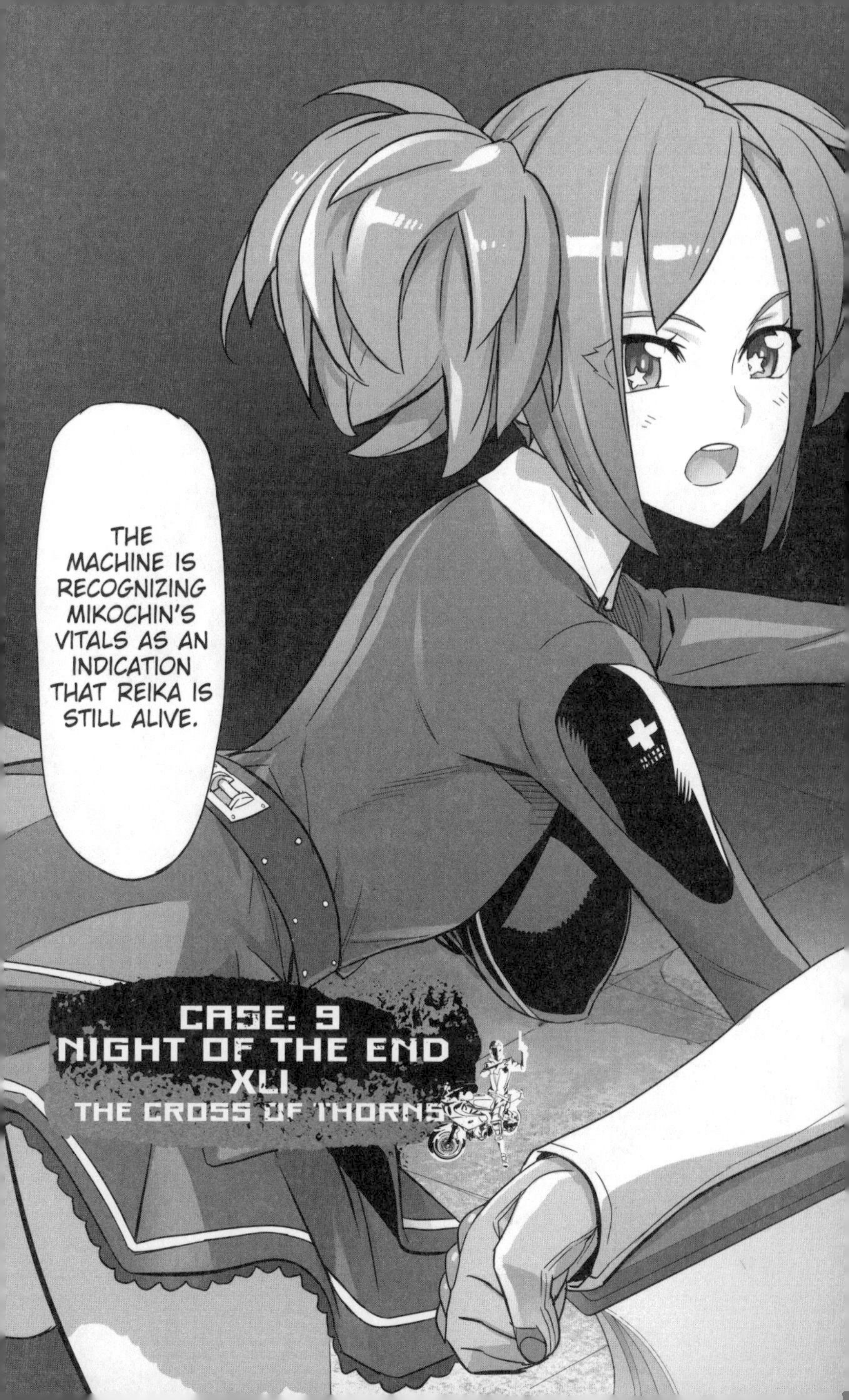
THE MACHINE IS RECOGNIZING MIKOCHIN'S VITALS AS AN INDICATION THAT REIKA IS STILL ALIVE.
CASE: 9
NIGHT OF THE END
XLI
THE CROSS OF THORNS

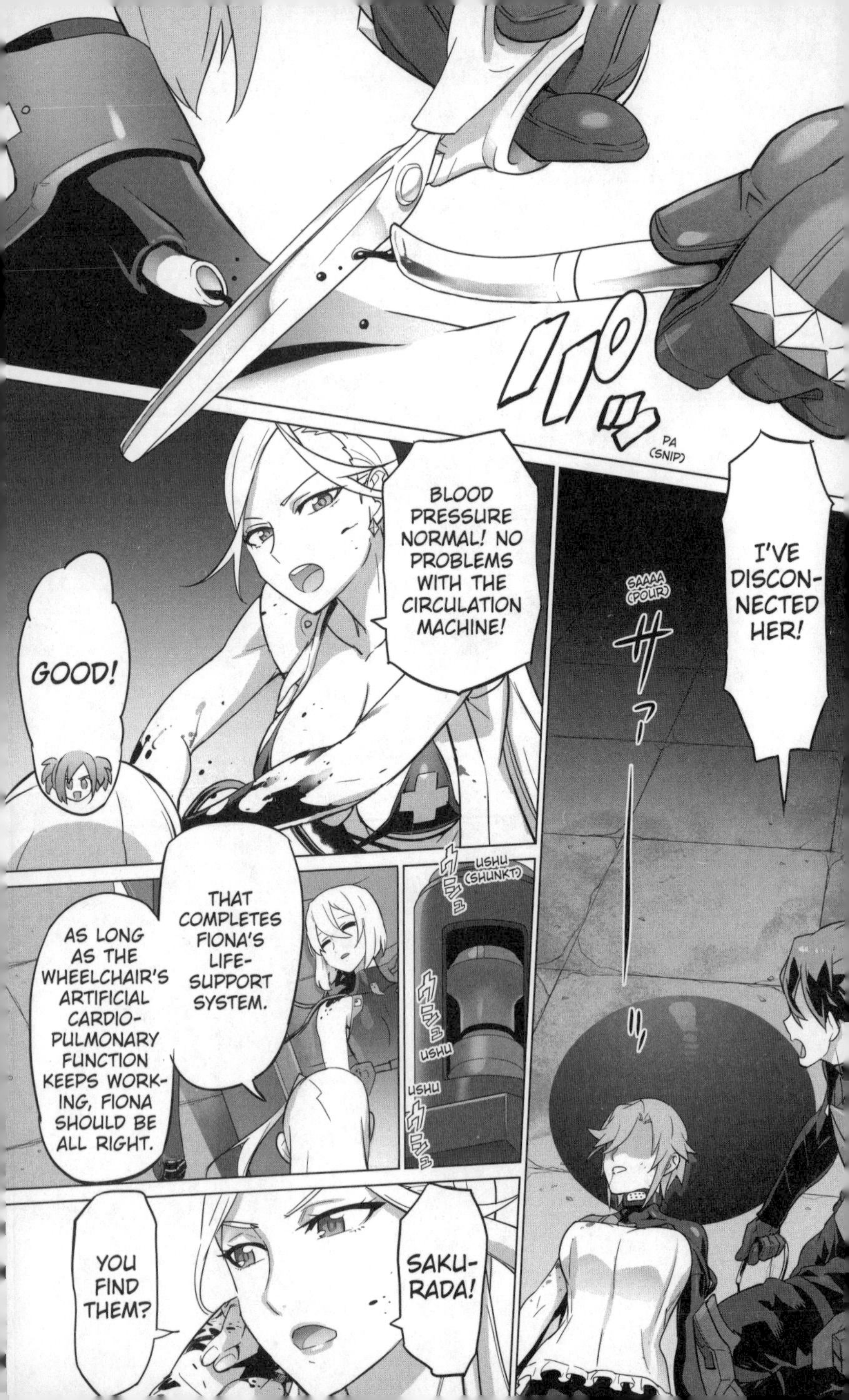
PA (SNIP)
I'VE DISCONNECTED HER!
SAAAA (POUR)
BLOOD PRESSURE NORMAL! NO PROBLEMS WITH THE CIRCULATION MACHINE!
GOOD!
USHU (SHUNKT)
USHU
USHU
THAT COMPLETES FIONA'S LIFE-SUPPORT SYSTEM.
AS LONG AS THE WHEELCHAIR'S ARTIFICIAL CARDIO-PULMONARY FUNCTION KEEPS WORKING, FIONA SHOULD BE ALL RIGHT.
SAKURADA!
YOU FIND THEM?

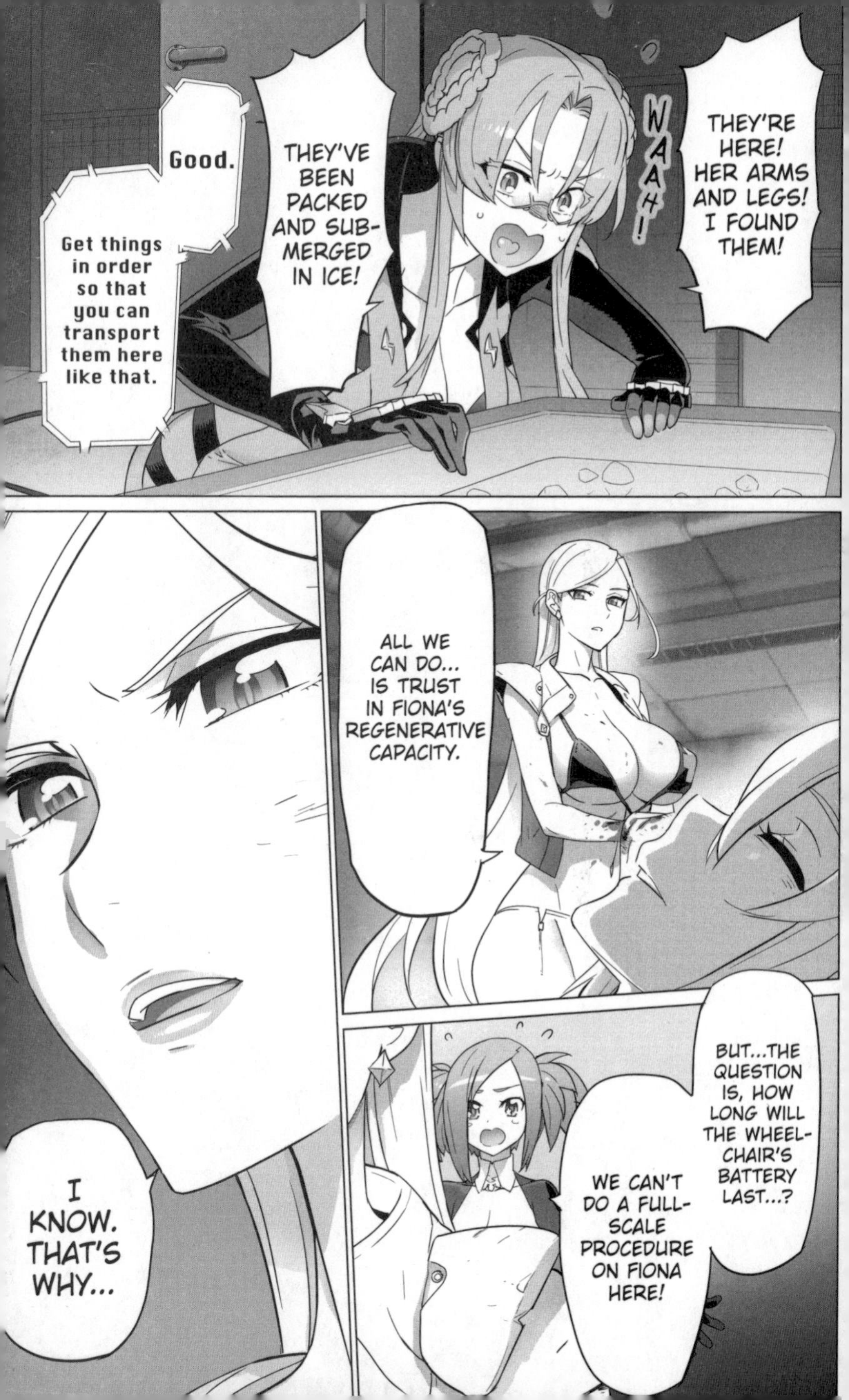
THEY'RE HERE! HER ARMS AND LEGS! I FOUND THEM!
WAAH!
THEY'VE BEEN PACKED AND SUBMERGED IN ICE!
Good.
Get things in order so that you can transport them here like that.
ALL WE CAN DO... IS TRUST IN FIONA'S REGENERATIVE CAPACITY.
BUT...THE QUESTION IS, HOW LONG WILL THE WHEELCHAIR'S BATTERY LAST...?
WE CAN'T DO A FULL-SCALE PROCEDURE ON FIONA HERE!
I KNOW. THAT'S WHY...

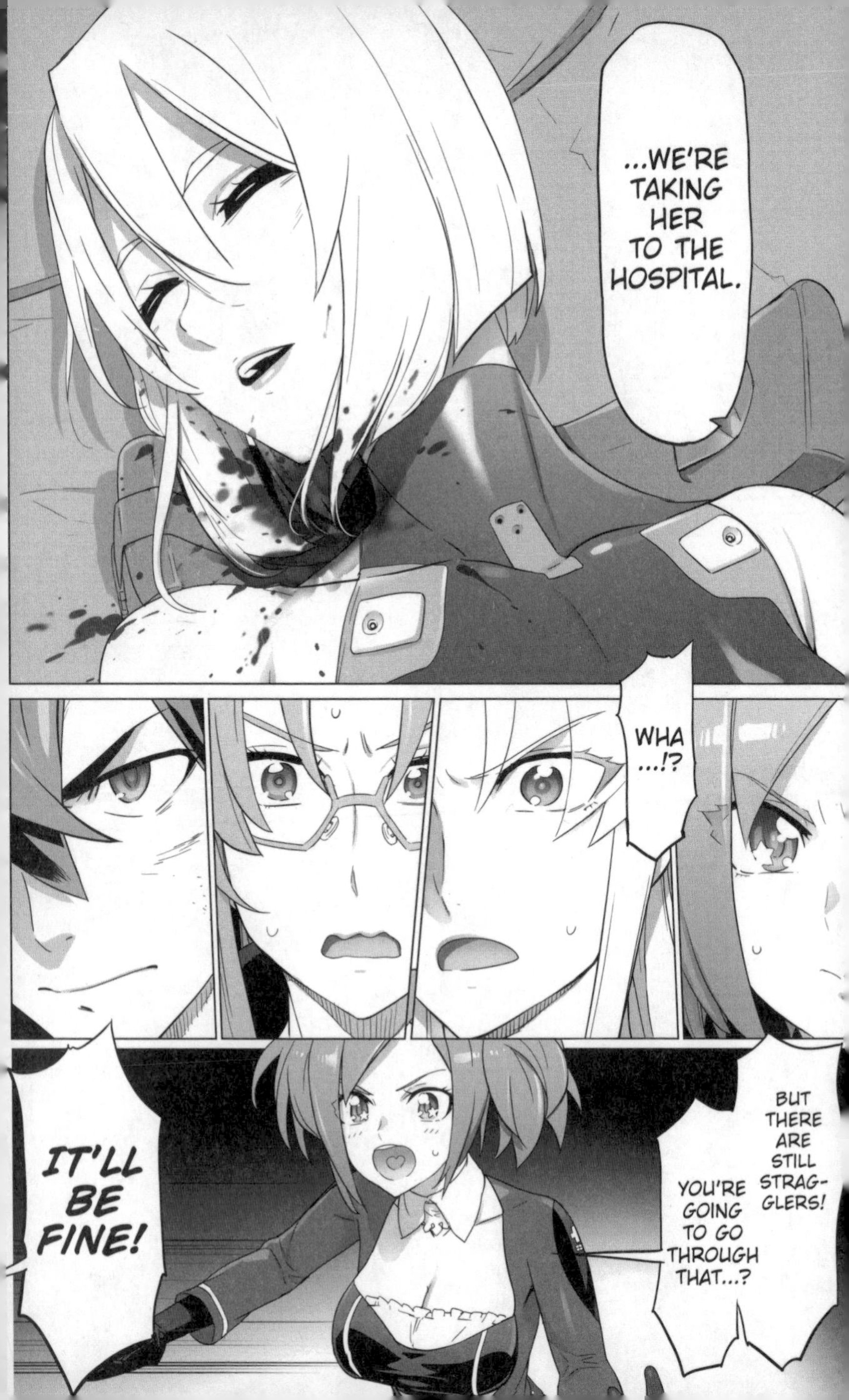
...WE'RE TAKING HER TO THE HOSPITAL.
WHA ...!?
BUT THERE ARE STILL STRAG-GLERS!
YOU'RE GOING TO GO THROUGH THAT...?
IT'LL BE FINE!

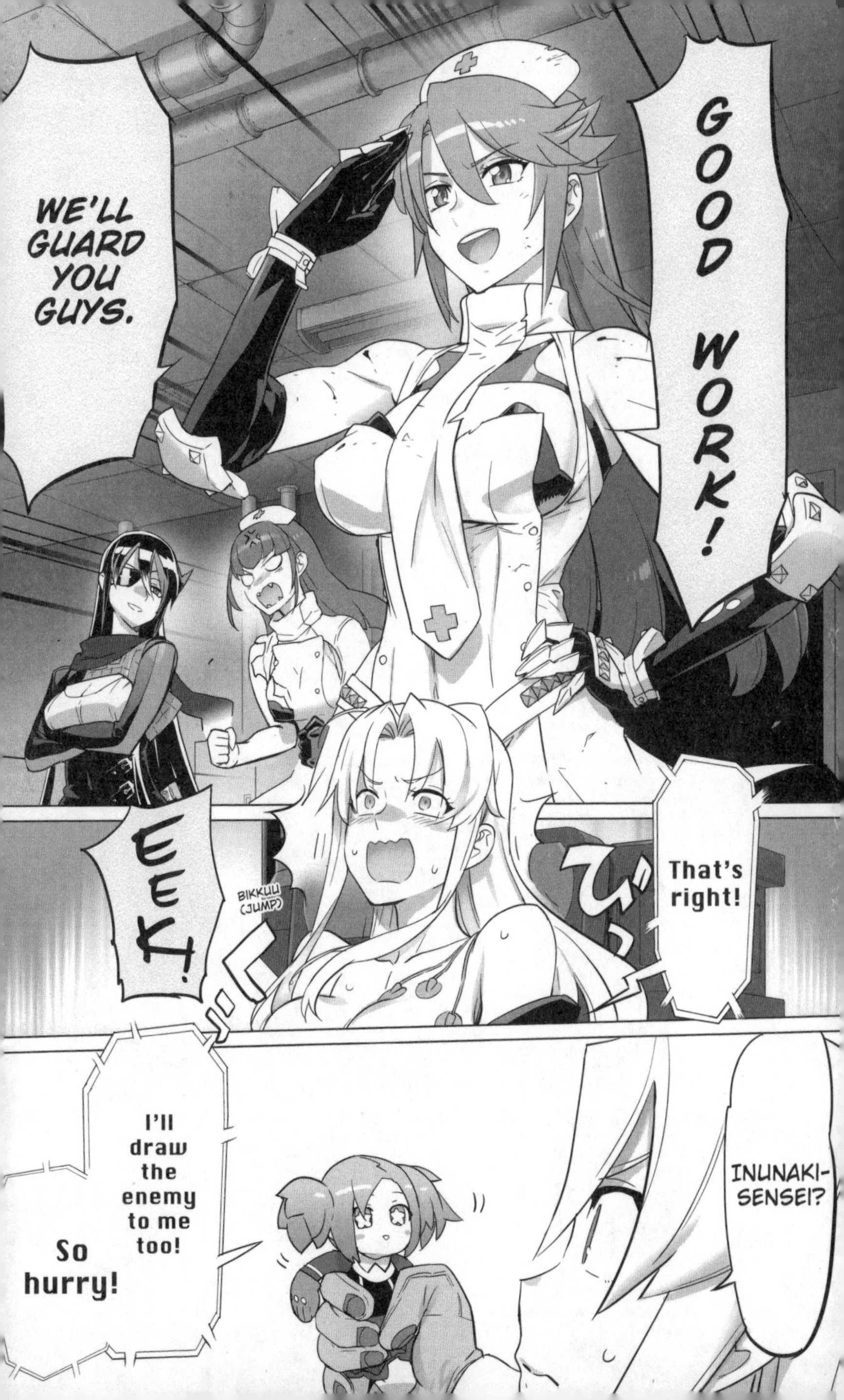
GOOD WORK!
WE'LL GUARD YOU GUYS.
That's right!
BIKKUU (JUMP)
EEK!
INUNAKI-SENSEI?
I'll draw the enemy to me too!
So hurry!

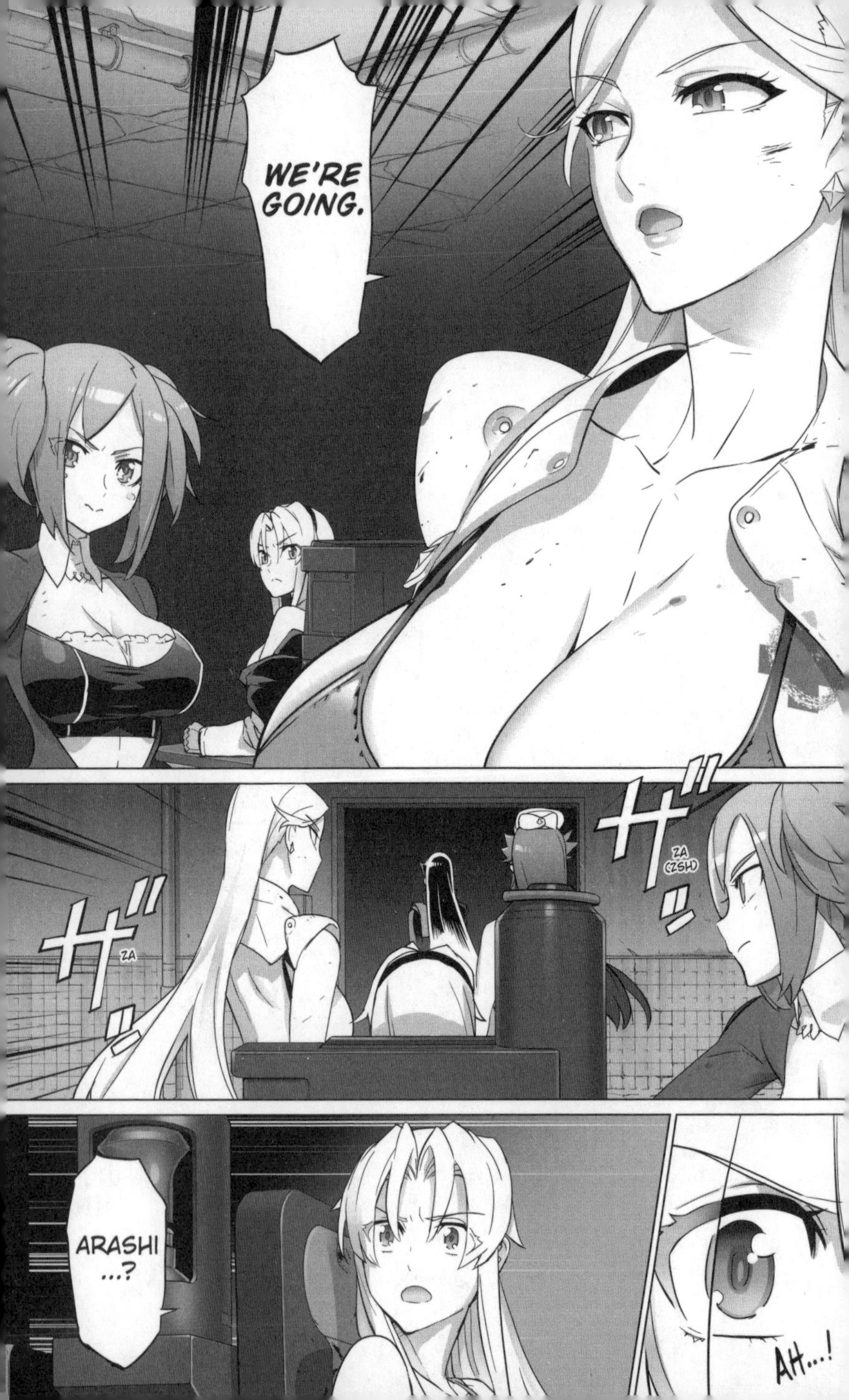
WE'RE GOING.
ZA (ZSH)
ZA
AH...!
ARASHI ...?

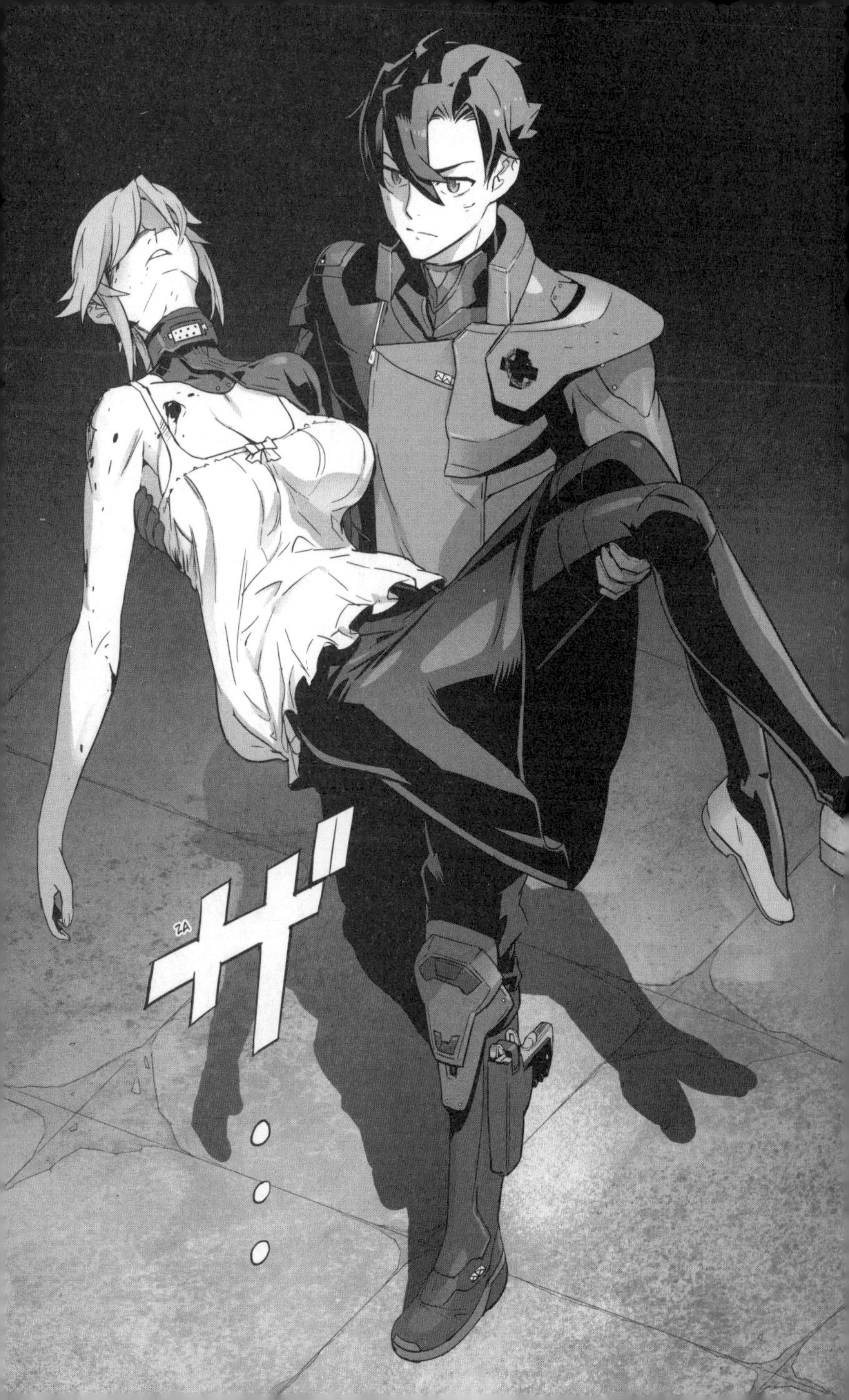
ザ
ZA

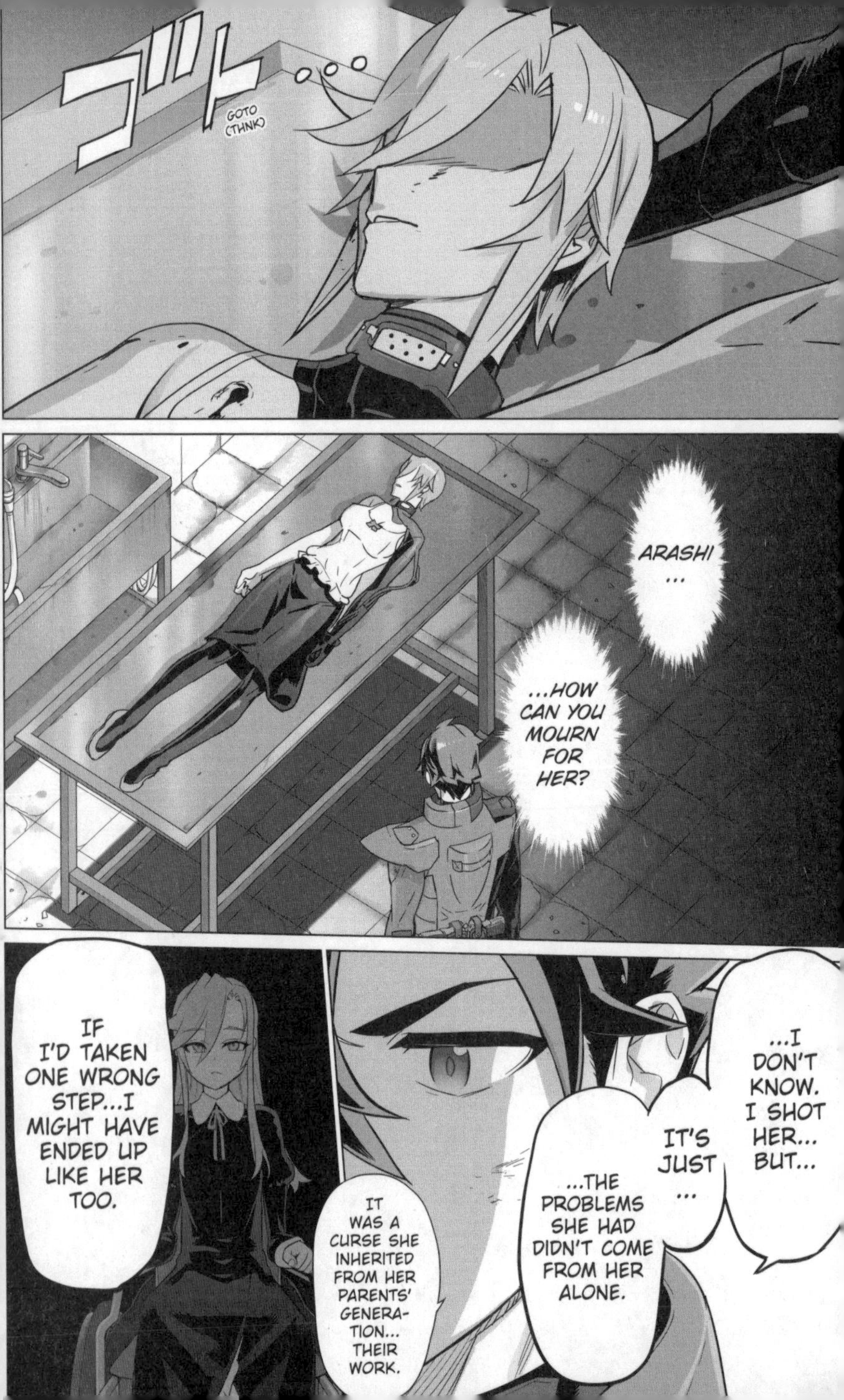
GOTO (THNK)
ARASHI ...
...HOW CAN YOU MOURN FOR HER?
...I DON'T KNOW. I SHOT HER... BUT...
IT'S JUST ...
...THE PROBLEMS SHE HAD DIDN'T COME FROM HER ALONE.
IT WAS A CURSE SHE INHERITED FROM HER PARENTS' GENERATION... THEIR WORK.
IF I'D TAKEN ONE WRONG STEP...I MIGHT HAVE ENDED UP LIKE HER TOO.

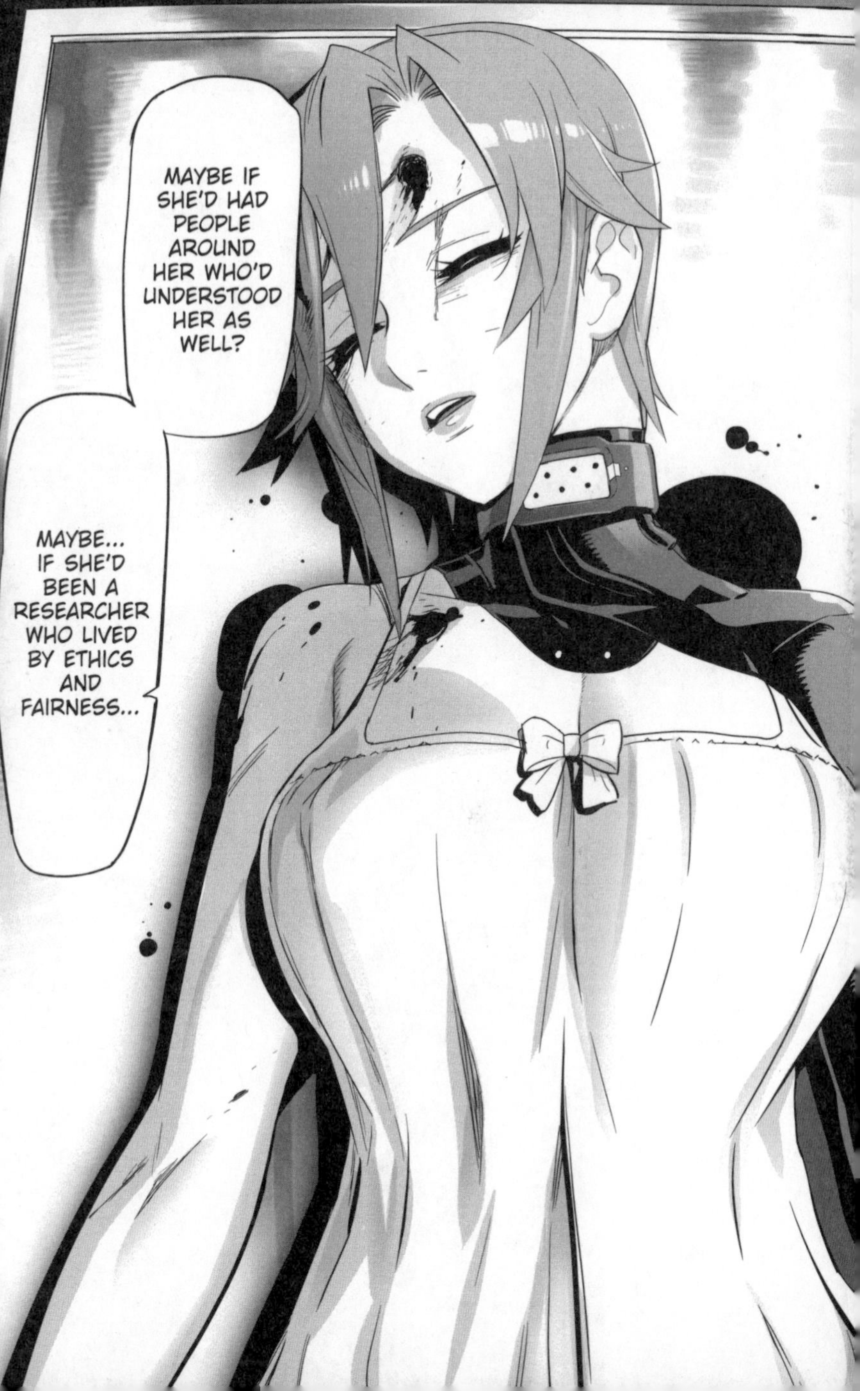
MAYBE IF SHE'D HAD PEOPLE AROUND HER WHO'D UNDERSTOOD HER AS WELL?
MAYBE... IF SHE'D BEEN A RESEARCHER WHO LIVED BY ETHICS AND FAIRNESS...

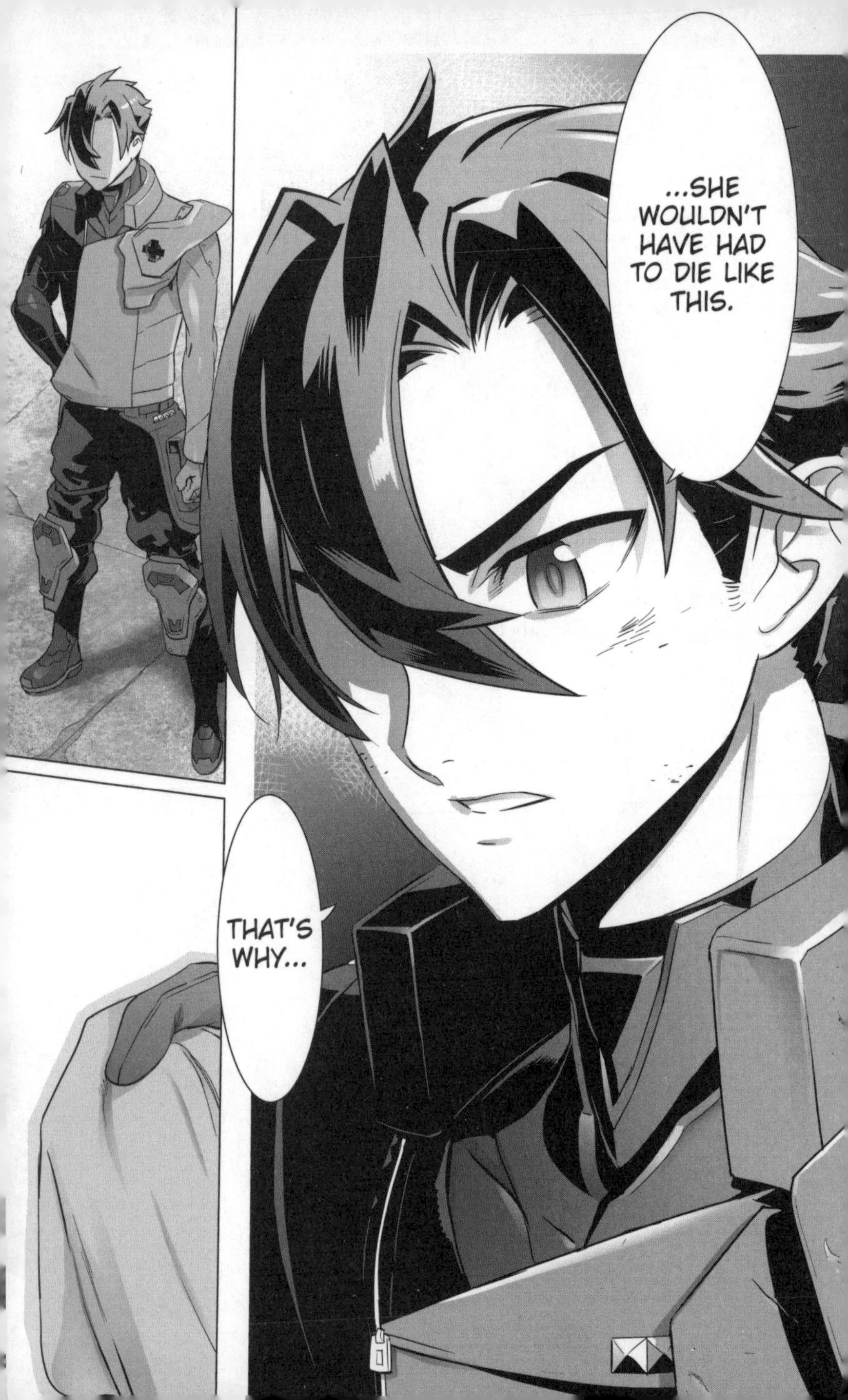
...SHE WOULDN'T HAVE HAD TO DIE LIKE THIS.
THAT'S WHY...

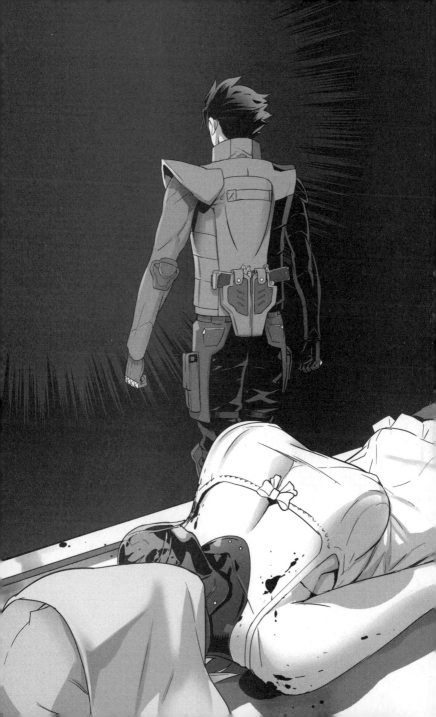

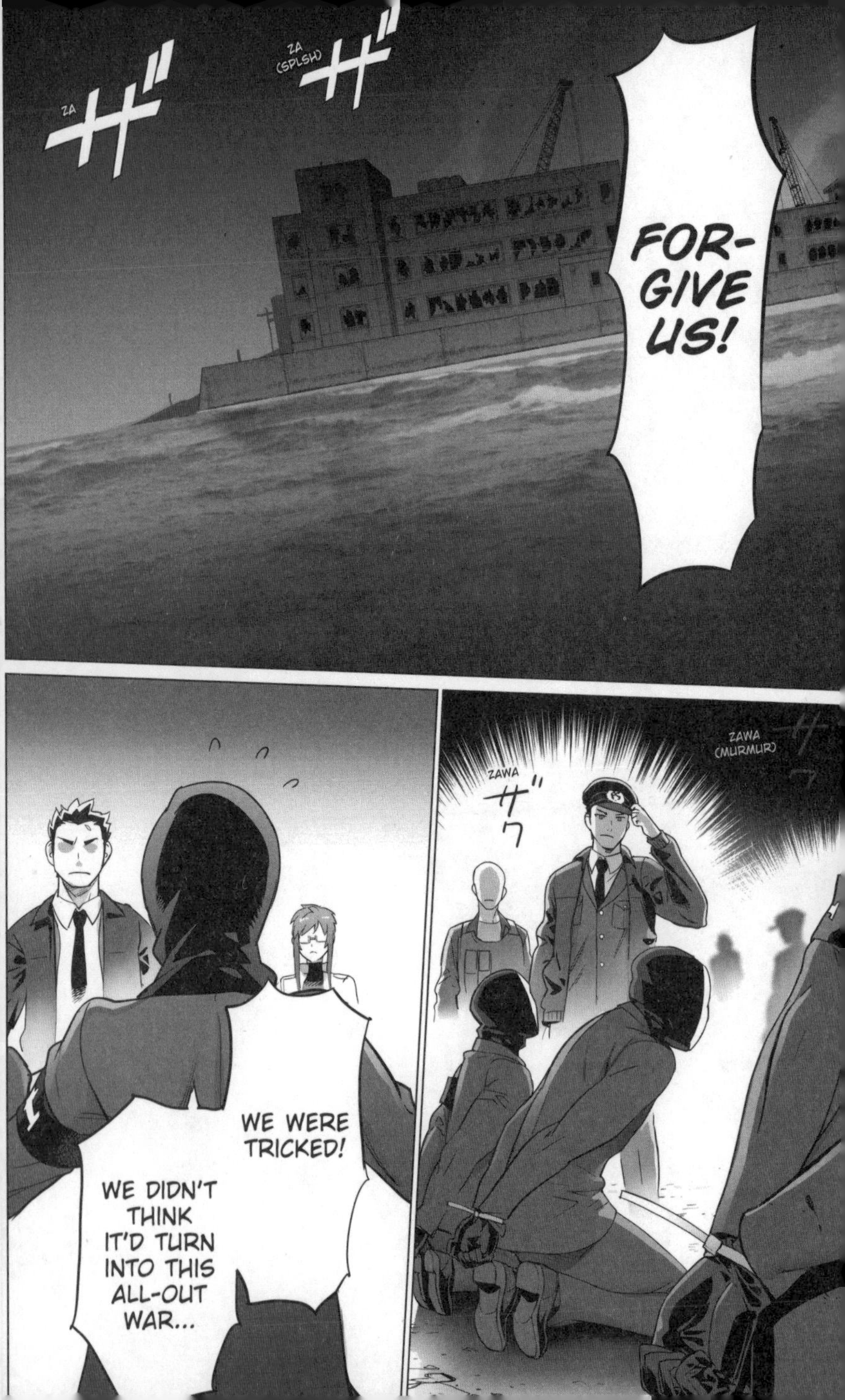
FOR-GIVE US!
ZA (SPLSH)
ZA
ZAWA (MURMUR)
ZAWA
WE WERE TRICKED!
WE DIDN'T THINK IT'D TURN INTO THIS ALL-OUT WAR...

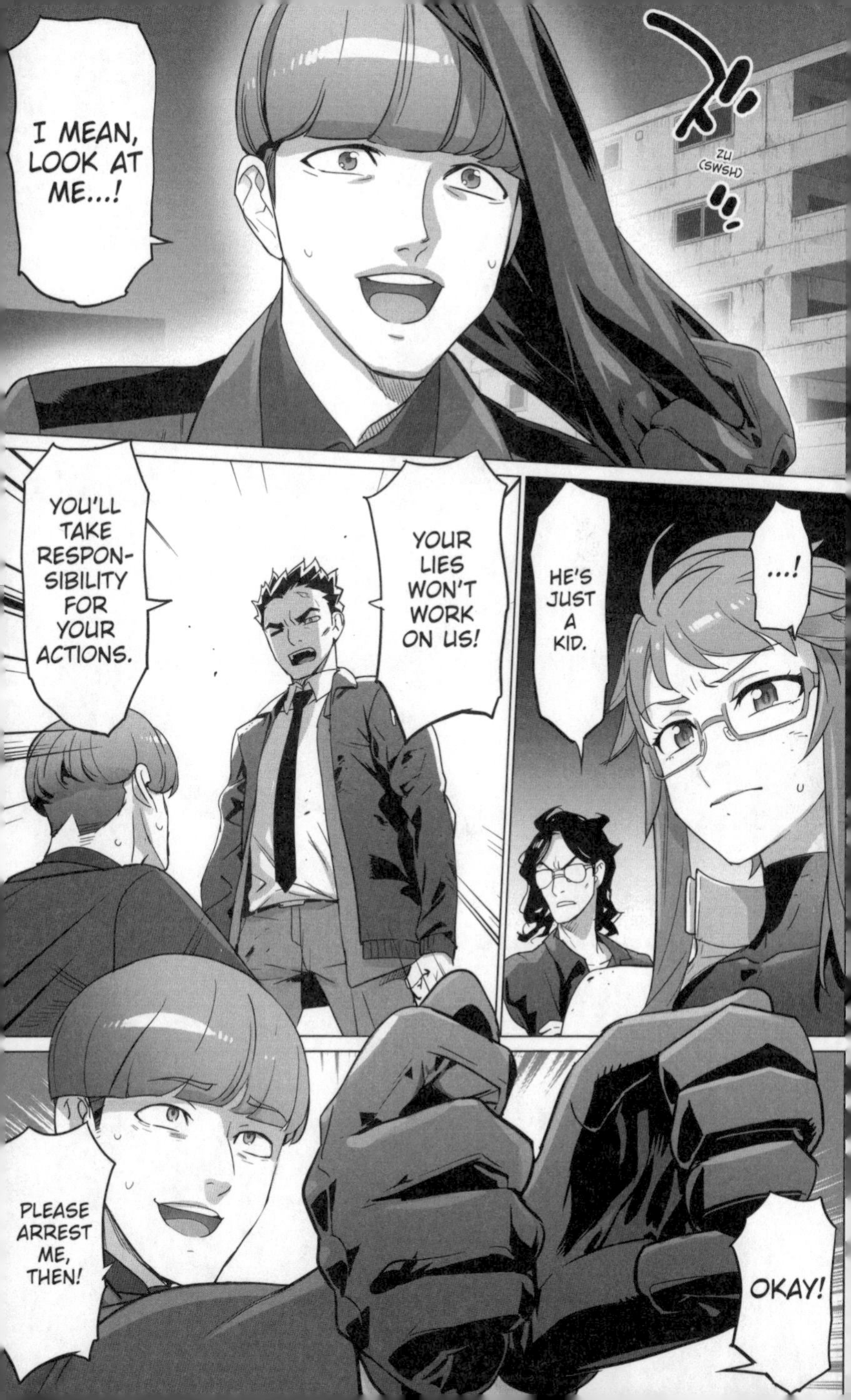
ZU
(SWSH)
I MEAN, LOOK AT ME...!
...!
HE'S JUST A KID.
YOUR LIES WON'T WORK ON US!
YOU'LL TAKE RESPON-SIBILITY FOR YOUR ACTIONS.
PLEASE ARREST ME, THEN!
OKAY!

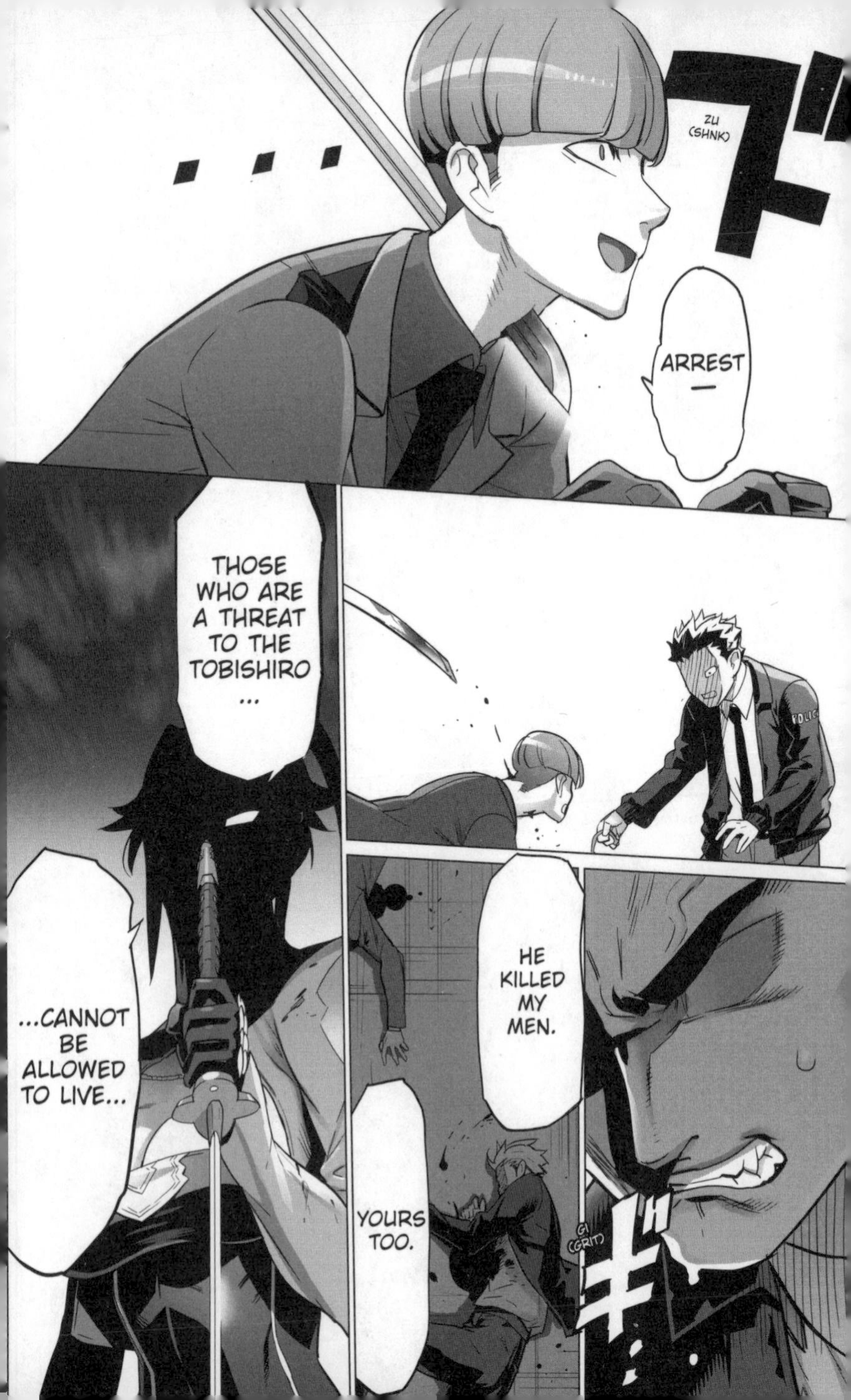
ZU (SHNK)
ARREST —
...
GI (GRIT)
HE KILLED MY MEN.
YOURS TOO.
THOSE WHO ARE A THREAT TO THE TOBISHIRO ...
...CANNOT BE ALLOWED TO LIVE...

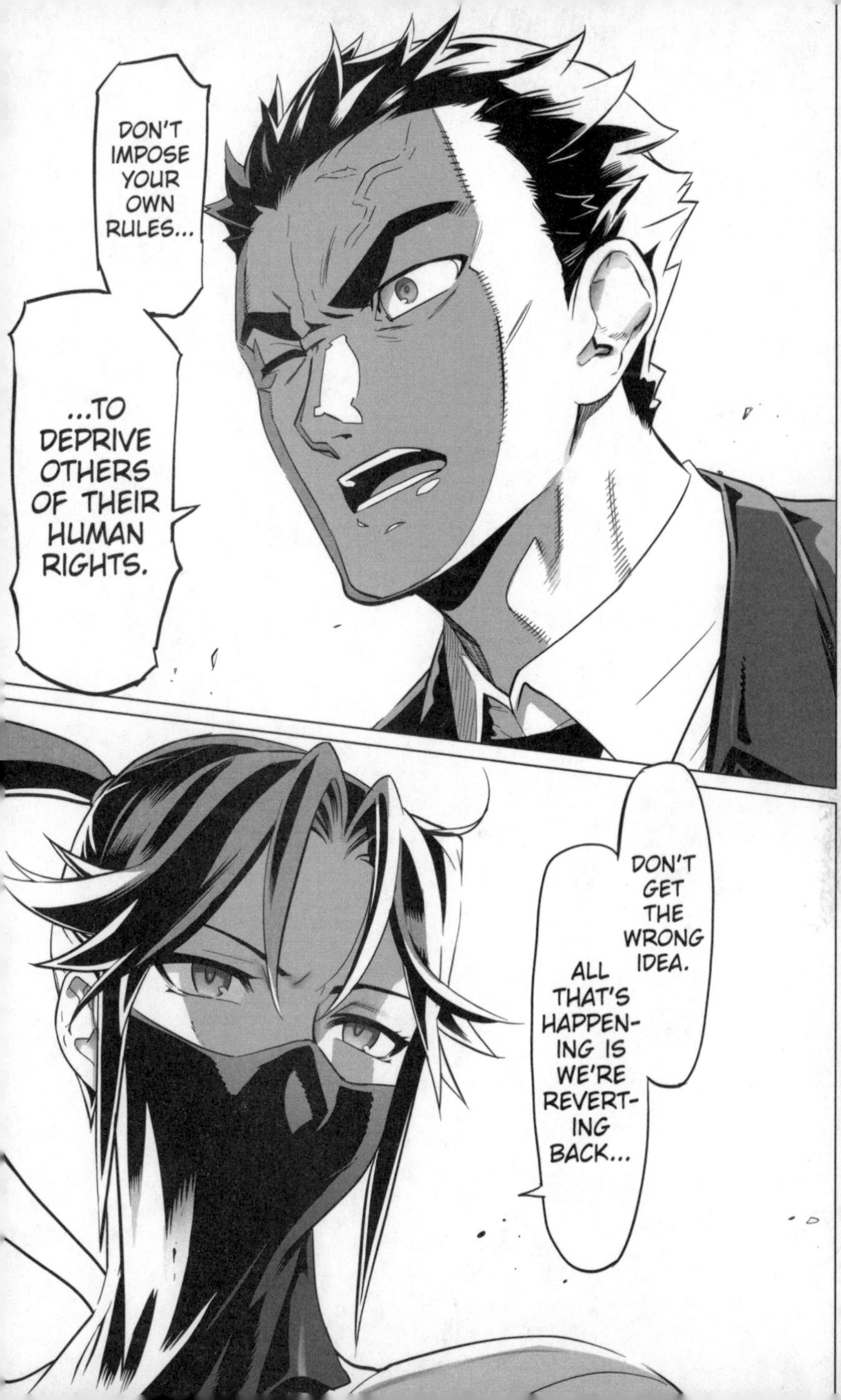
DON'T IMPOSE YOUR OWN RULES...
...TO DEPRIVE OTHERS OF THEIR HUMAN RIGHTS.
DON'T GET THE WRONG IDEA.
ALL THAT'S HAPPENING IS WE'RE REVERTING BACK...

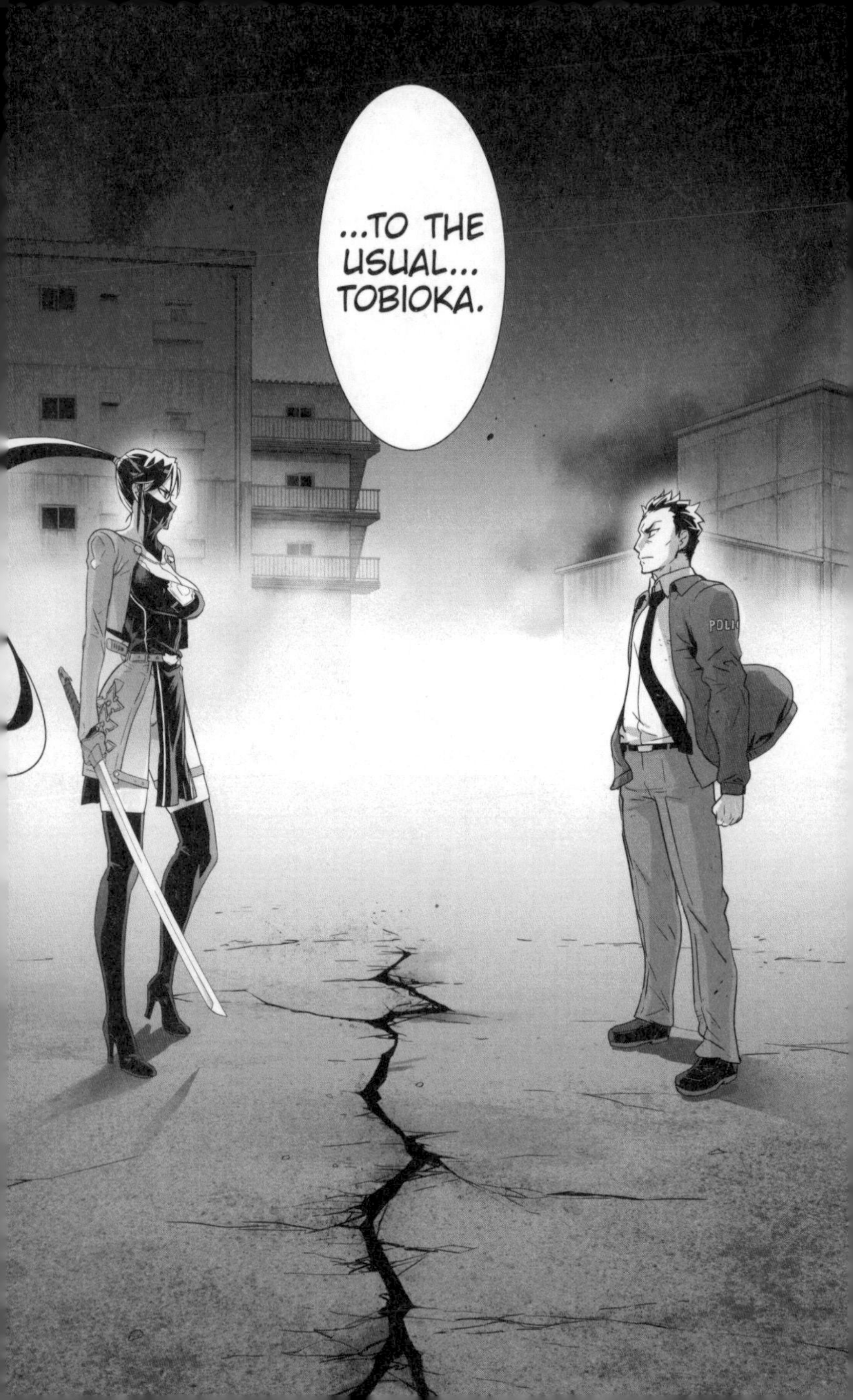
...TO THE USUAL... TOBIOKA.
POLIC

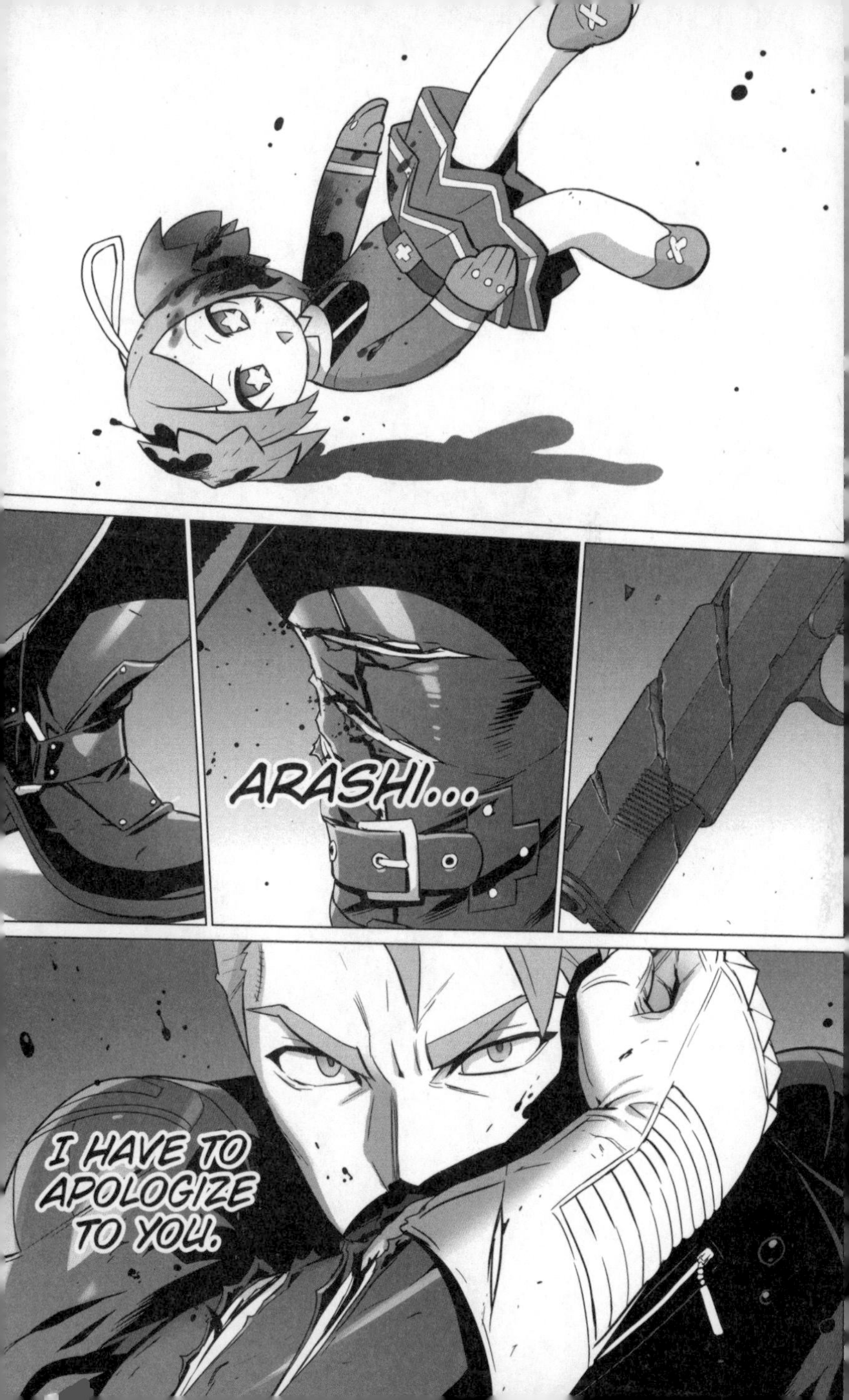
ARASHI...
I HAVE TO APOLOGIZE TO YOU.

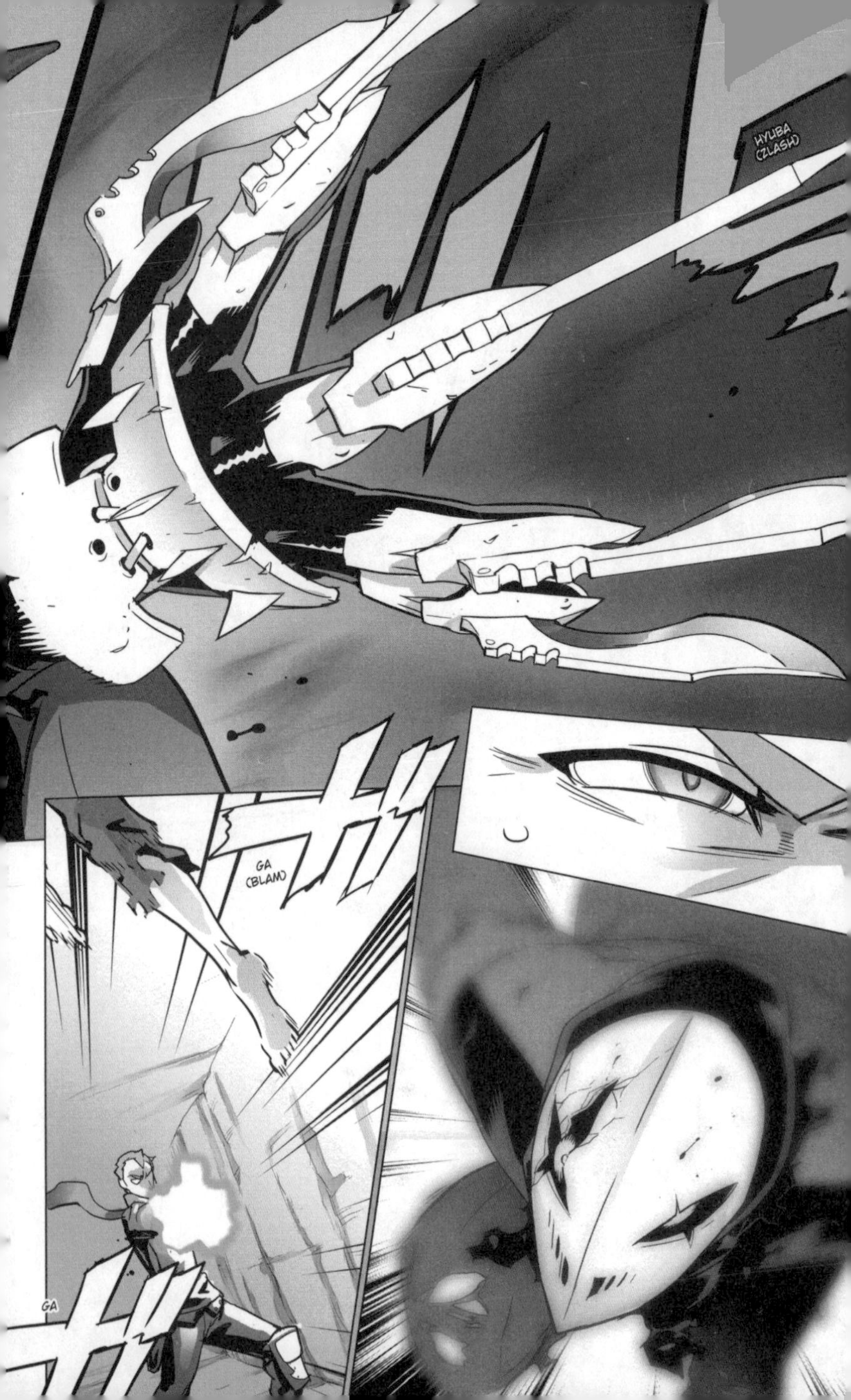
HYUBA
(ZLASH)
GA
(BLAM)
GA

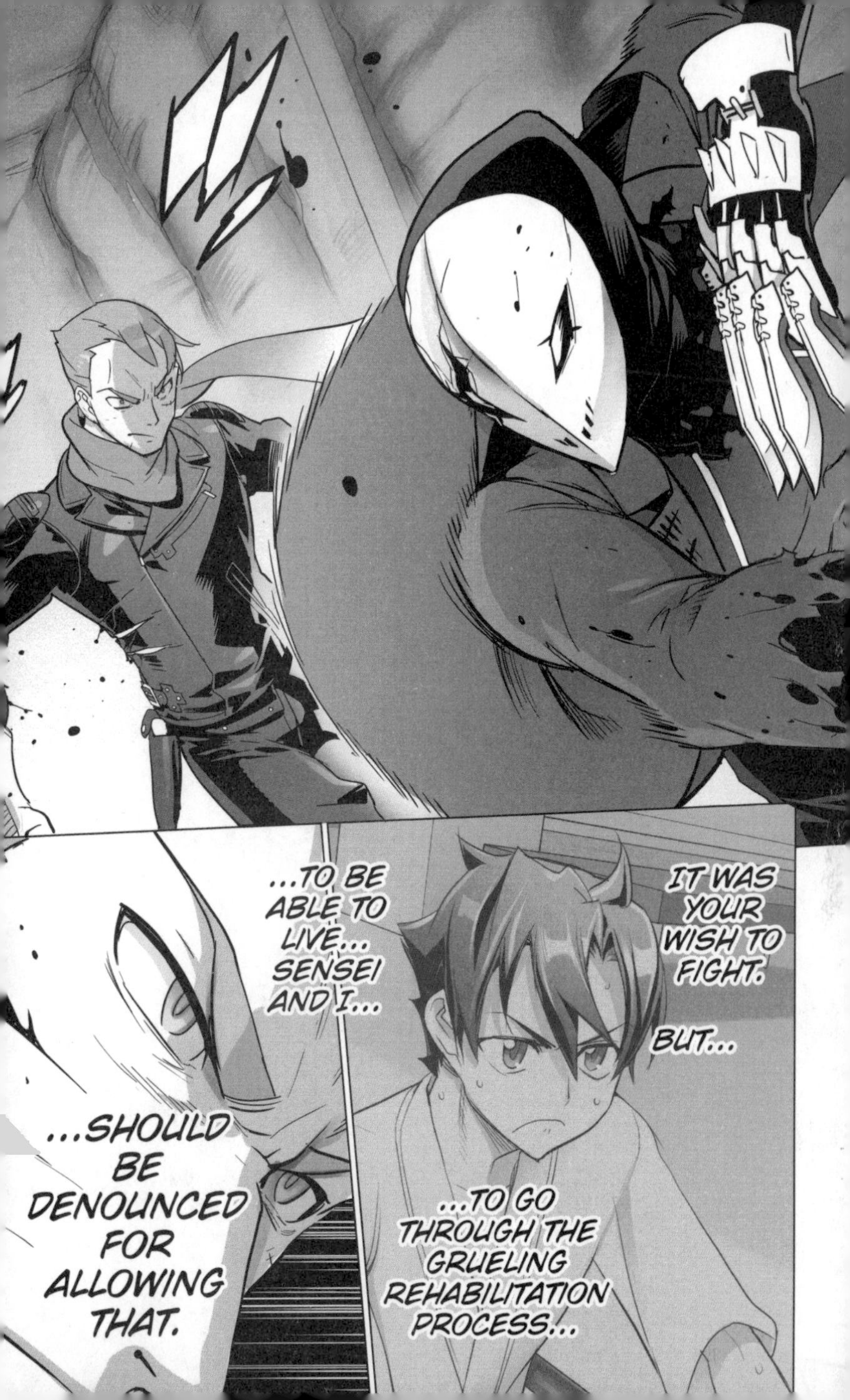
IT WAS YOUR WISH TO FIGHT.
...TO BE ABLE TO LIVE... SENSEI AND I...
BUT...
...TO GO THROUGH THE GRUELING REHABILITATION PROCESS...
...SHOULD BE DENOUNCED FOR ALLOWING THAT.

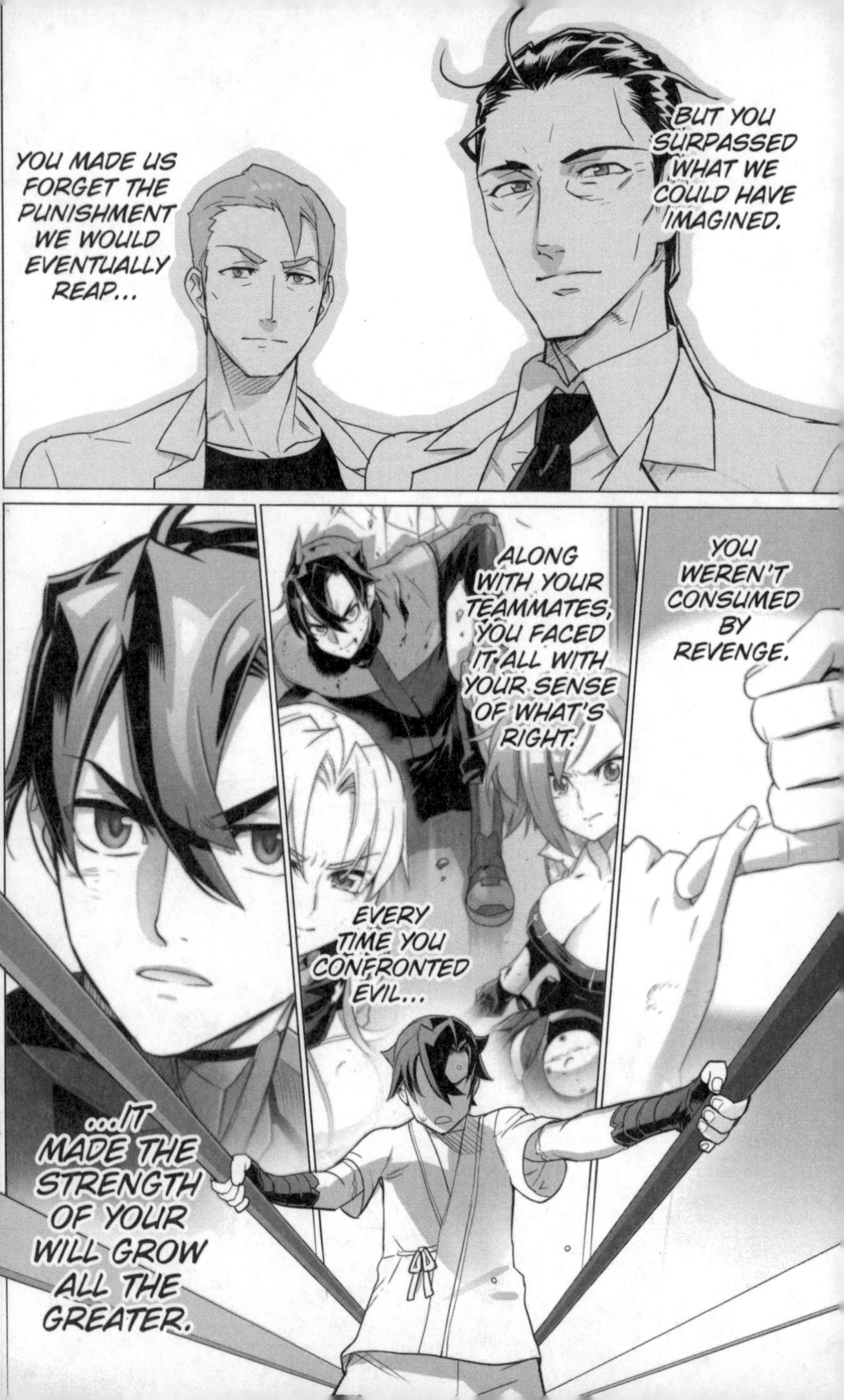
BUT YOU SURPASSED WHAT WE COULD HAVE IMAGINED.
YOU MADE US FORGET THE PUNISHMENT WE WOULD EVENTUALLY REAP...
YOU WEREN'T CONSUMED BY REVENGE.
ALONG WITH YOUR TEAMMATES, YOU FACED IT ALL WITH YOUR SENSE OF WHAT'S RIGHT.
EVERY TIME YOU CONFRONTED EVIL...
...IT MADE THE STRENGTH OF YOUR WILL GROW ALL THE GREATER.

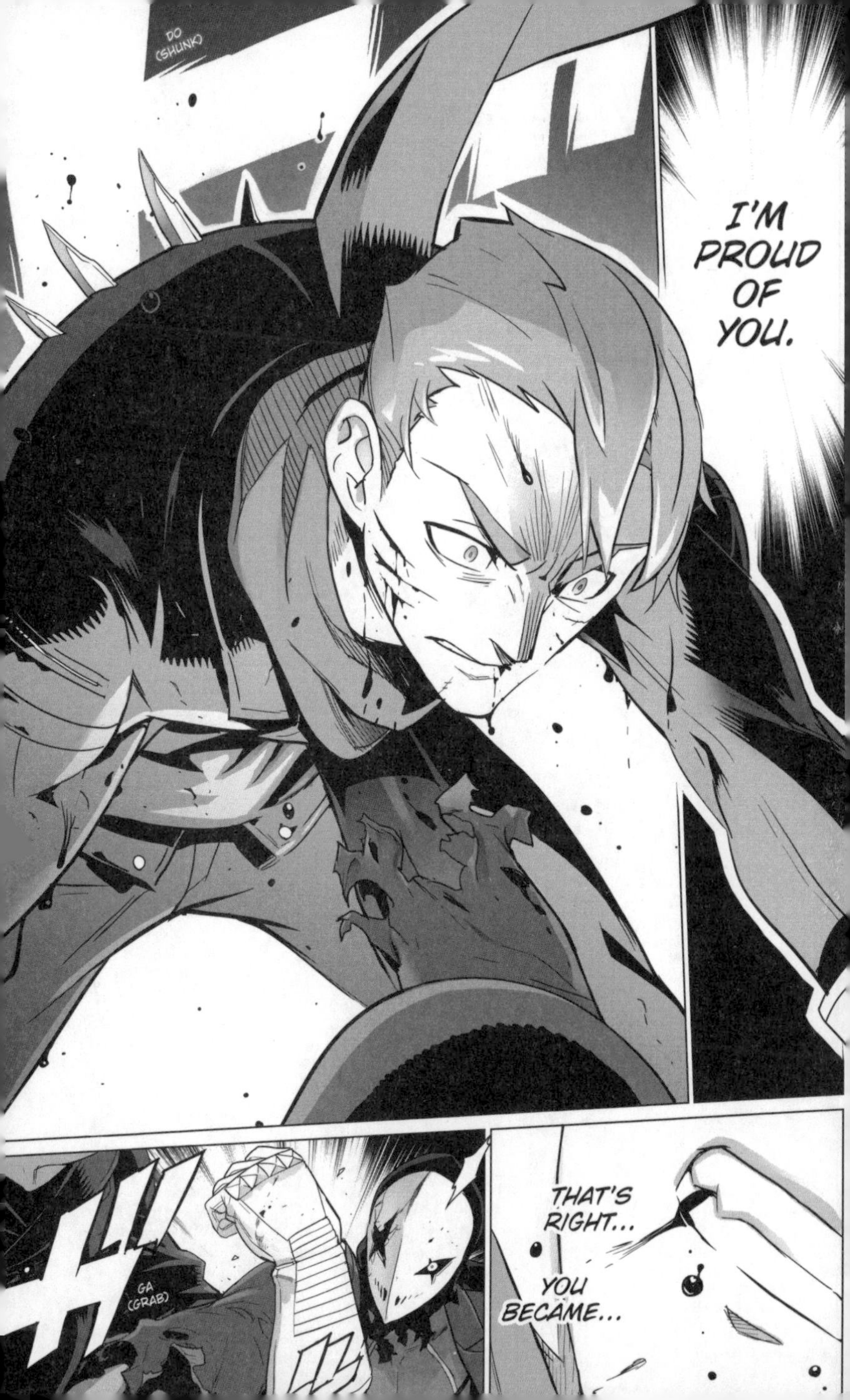
DO (SHUNK)
I'M PROUD OF YOU.
THAT'S RIGHT...
YOU BECAME...
GA (GRAB)

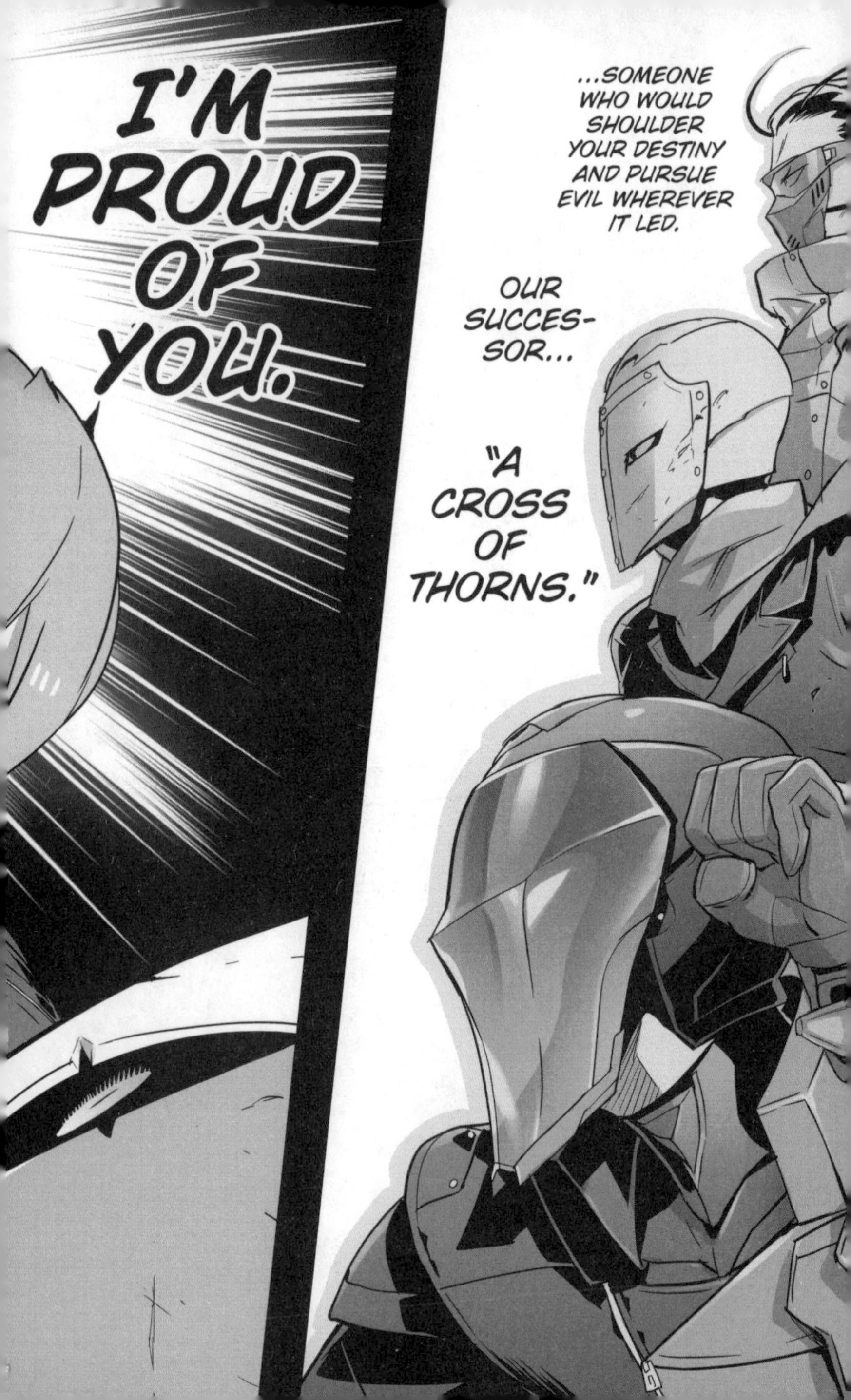
...SOMEONE WHO WOULD SHOULDER YOUR DESTINY AND PURSUE EVIL WHEREVER IT LED.
OUR SUCCES-SOR...
"A CROSS OF THORNS."
I'M PROUD OF YOU.

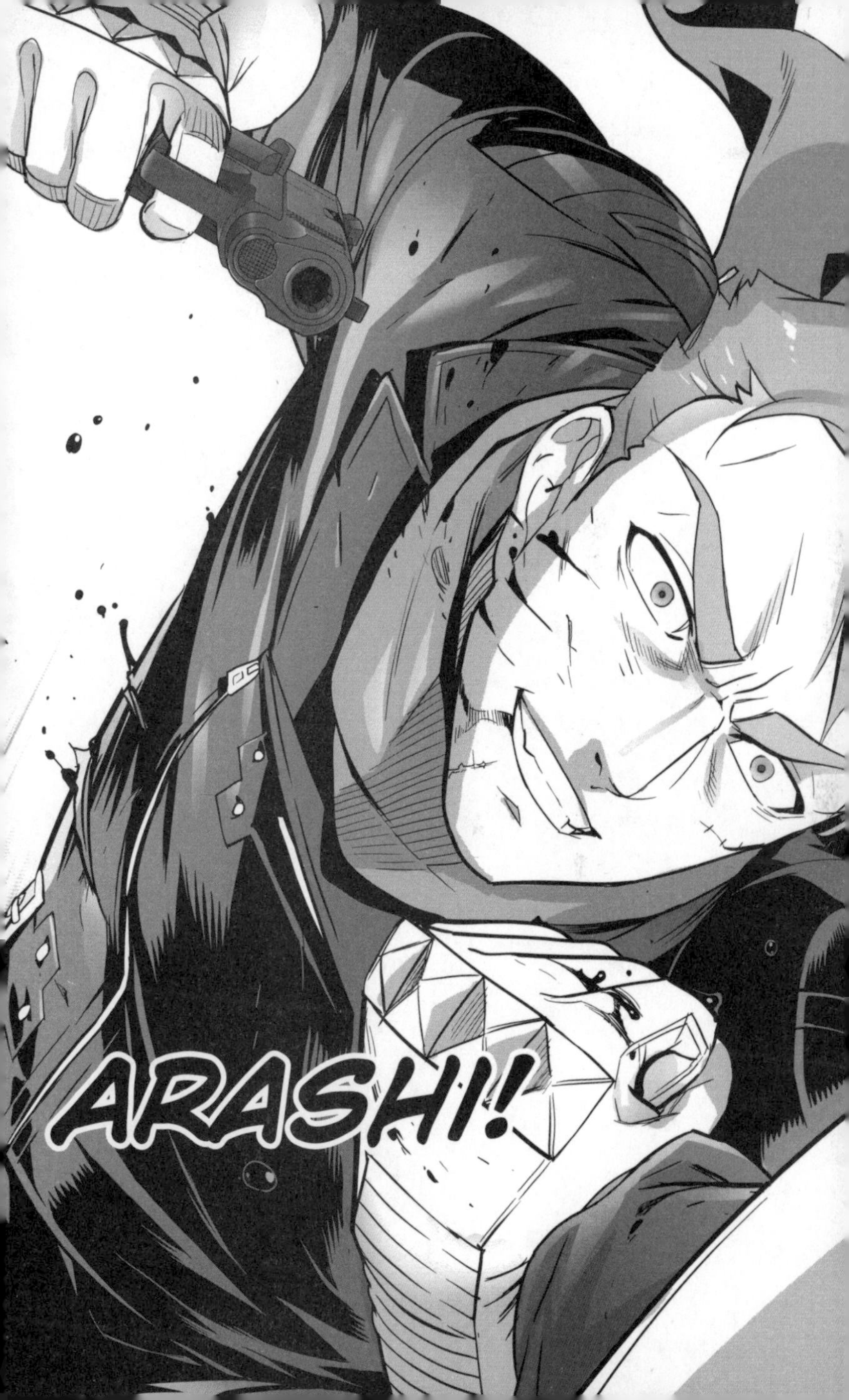
ARASHI!

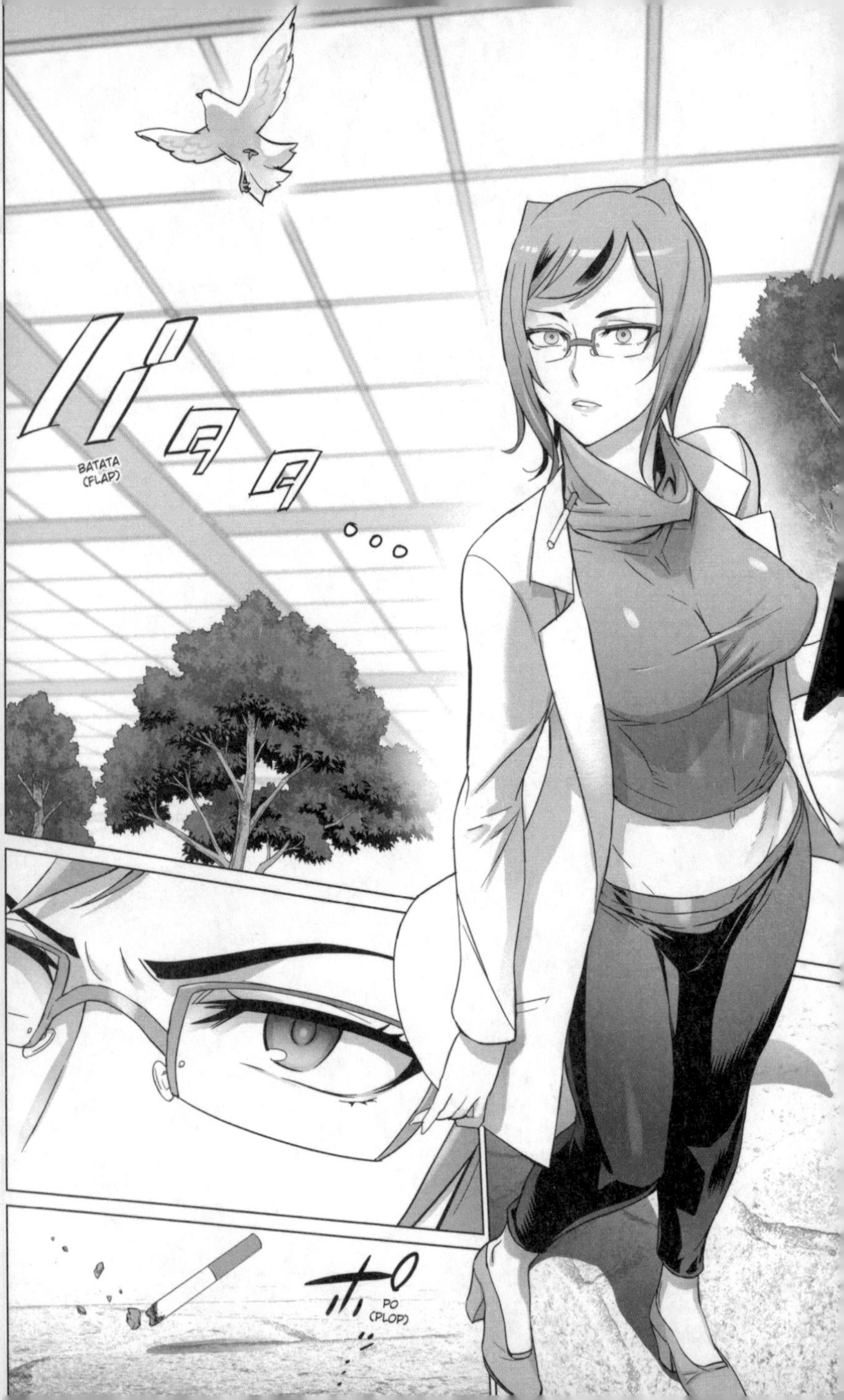
BATATA
(FLAP)
PO
(PLOP)

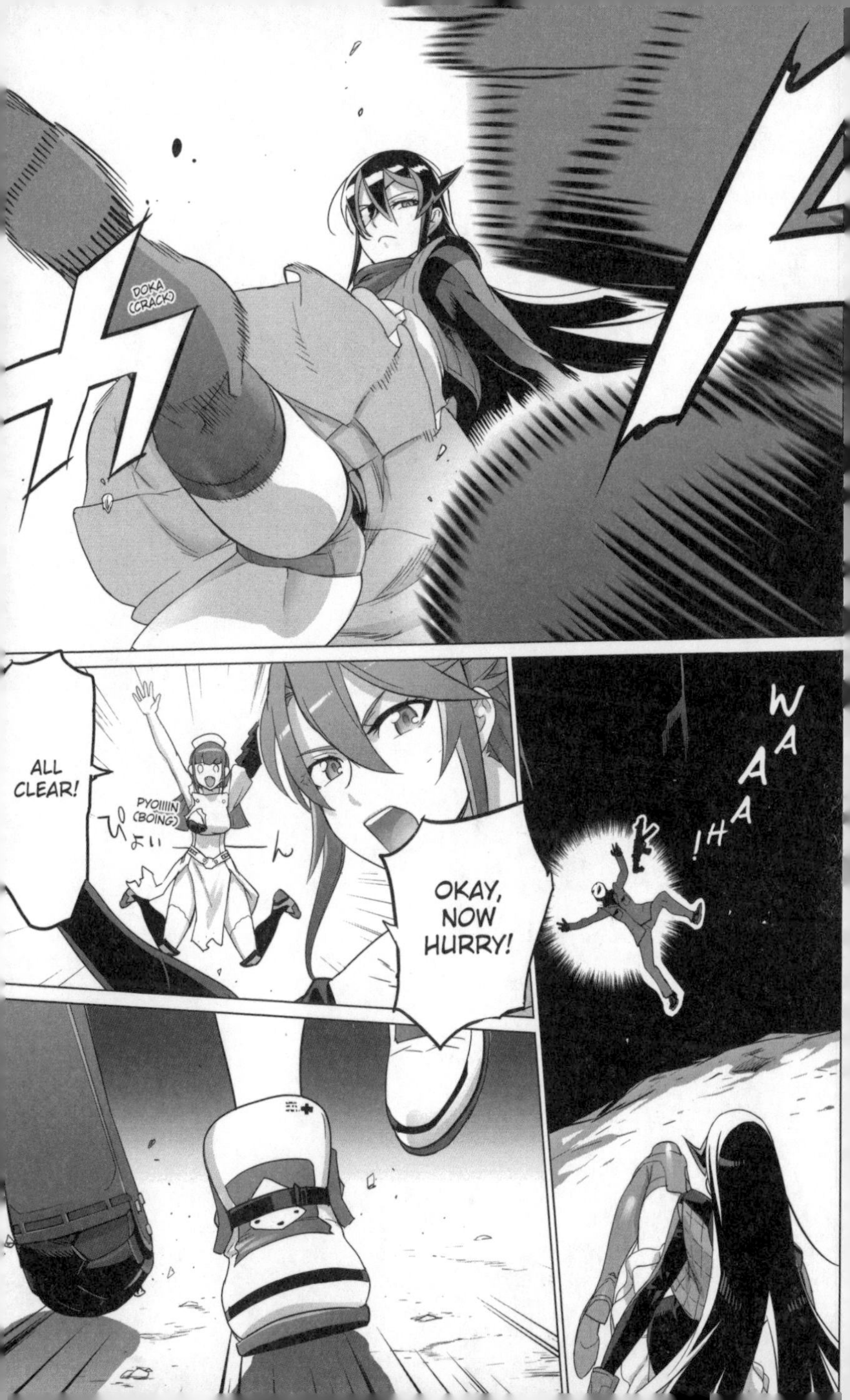
DOKA (CRACK)
WAAAAH!
ALL CLEAR!
PYOIIIIN (BOING)
ぴょい——ん
OKAY, NOW HURRY!

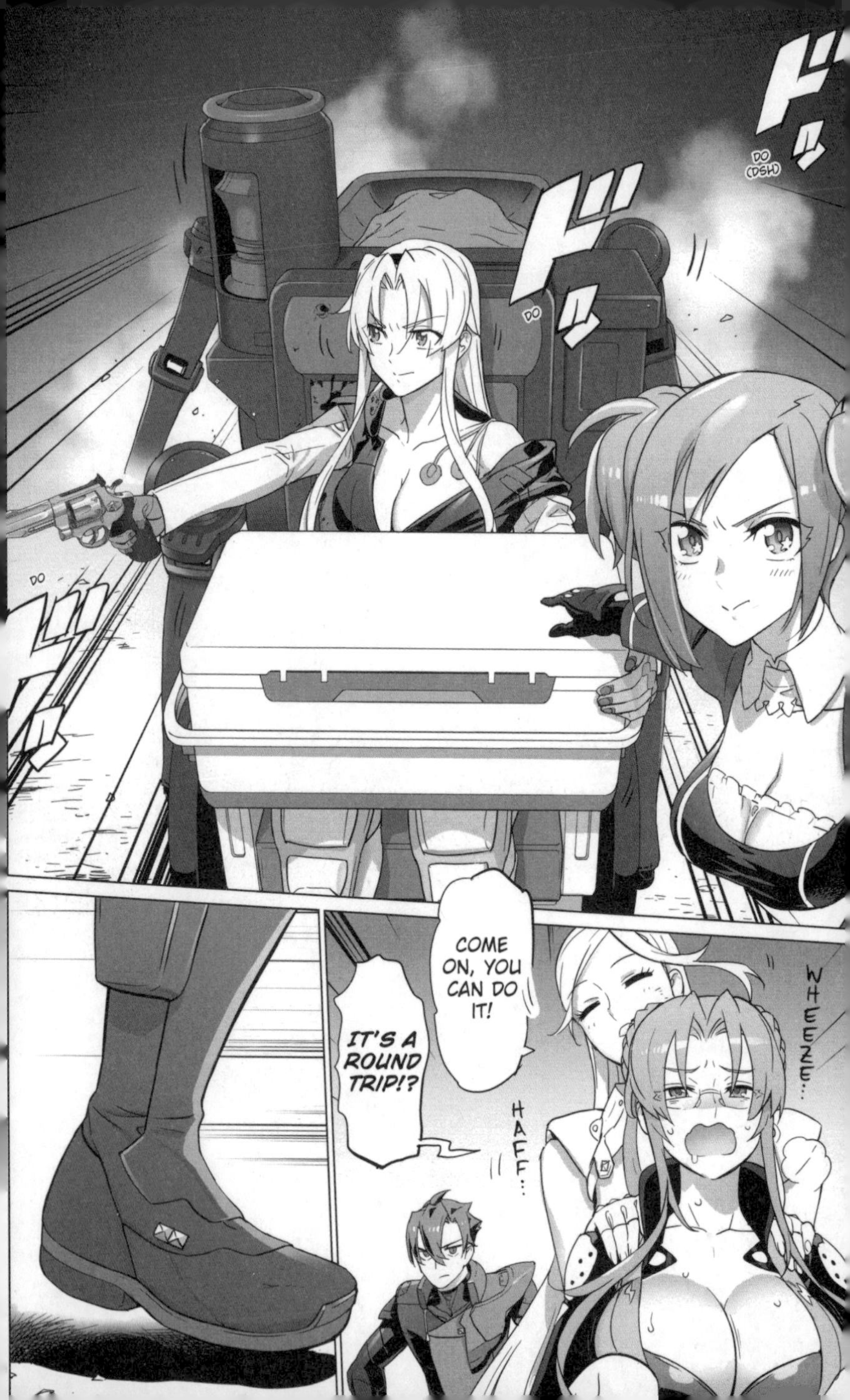
DO (DSH)
DO
DO
WHEEZE...
COME ON, YOU CAN DO IT!
HAFF...
IT'S A ROUND TRIP!?

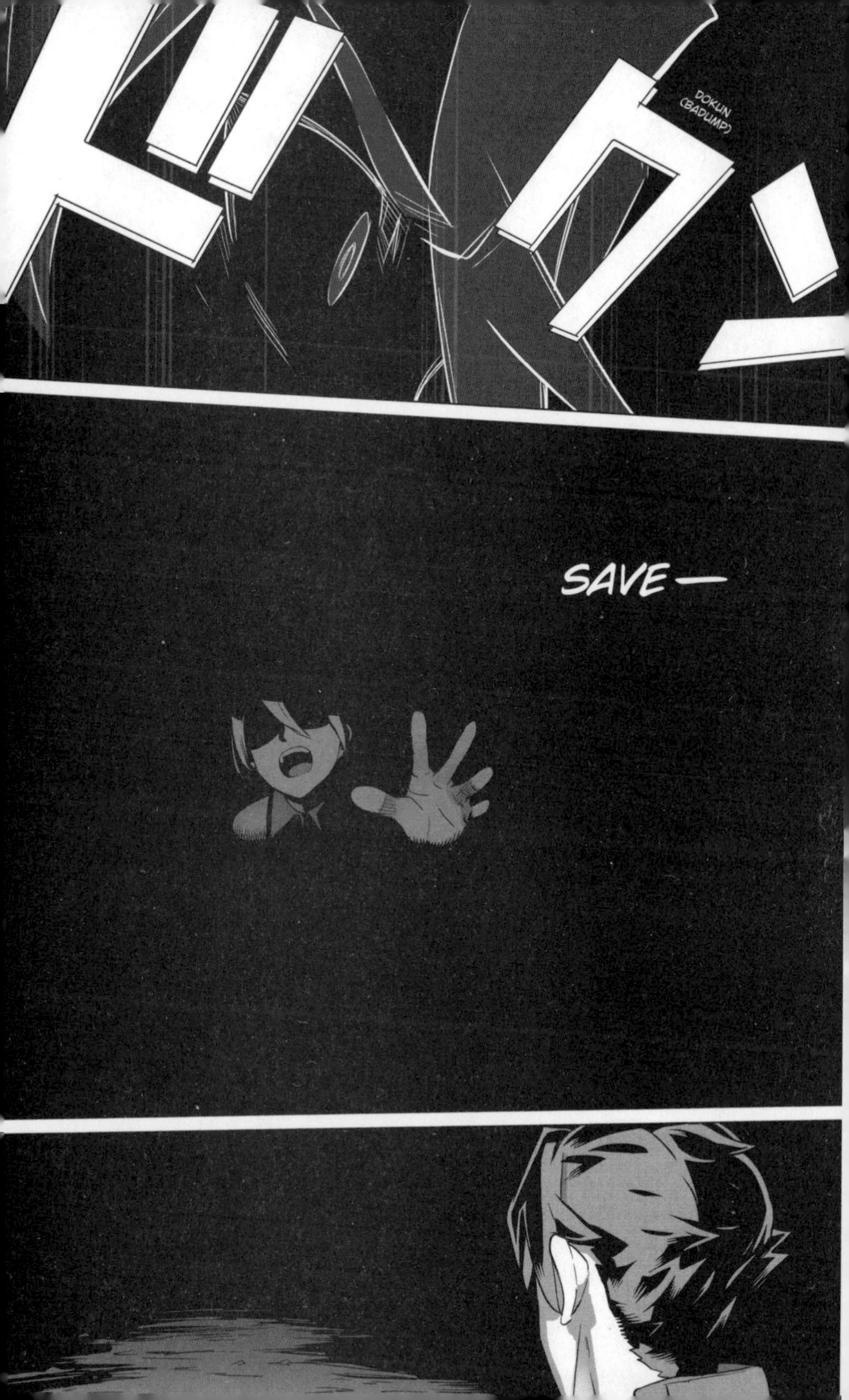
DOKUN
(BADUMP)
SAVE—

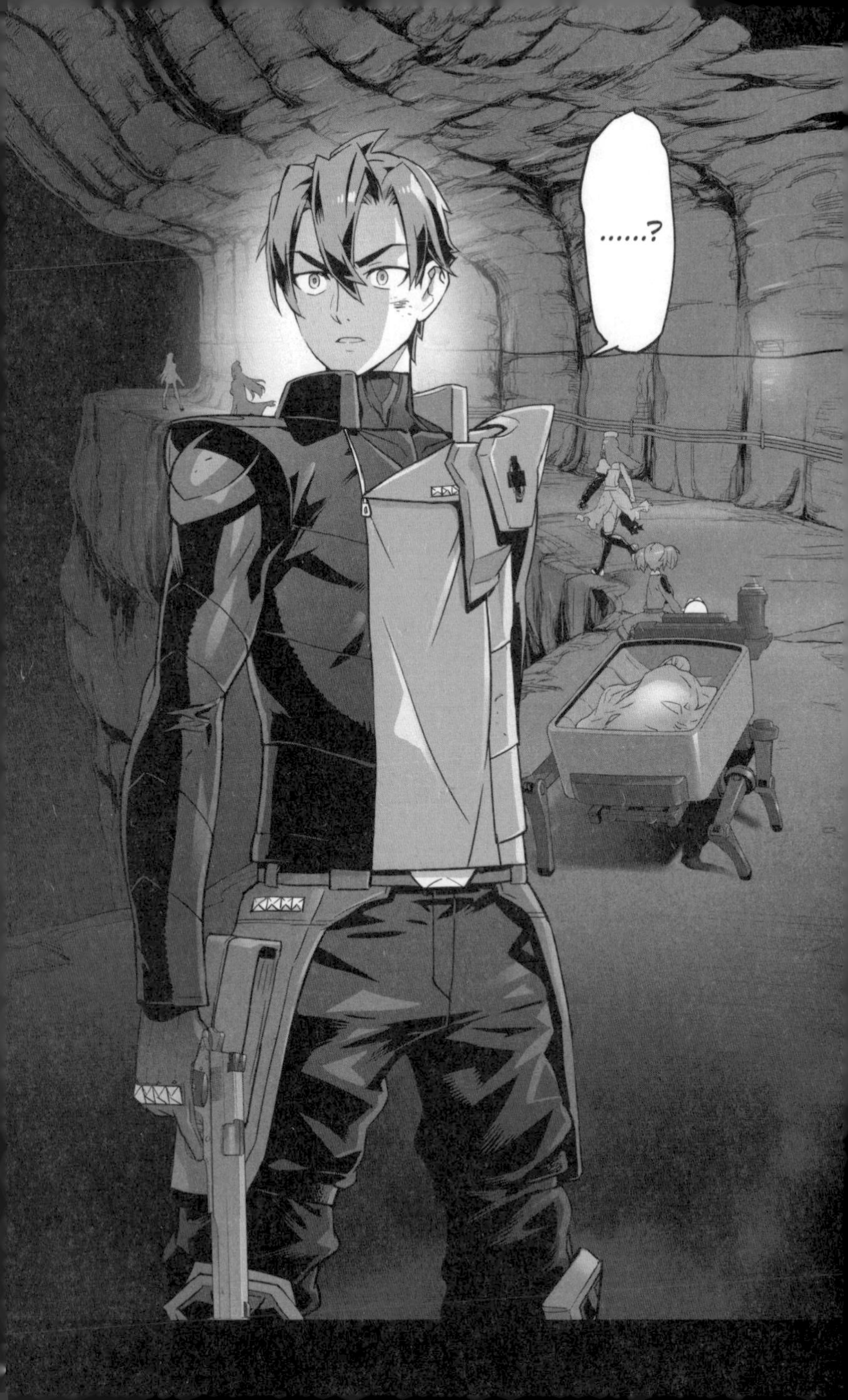
......?

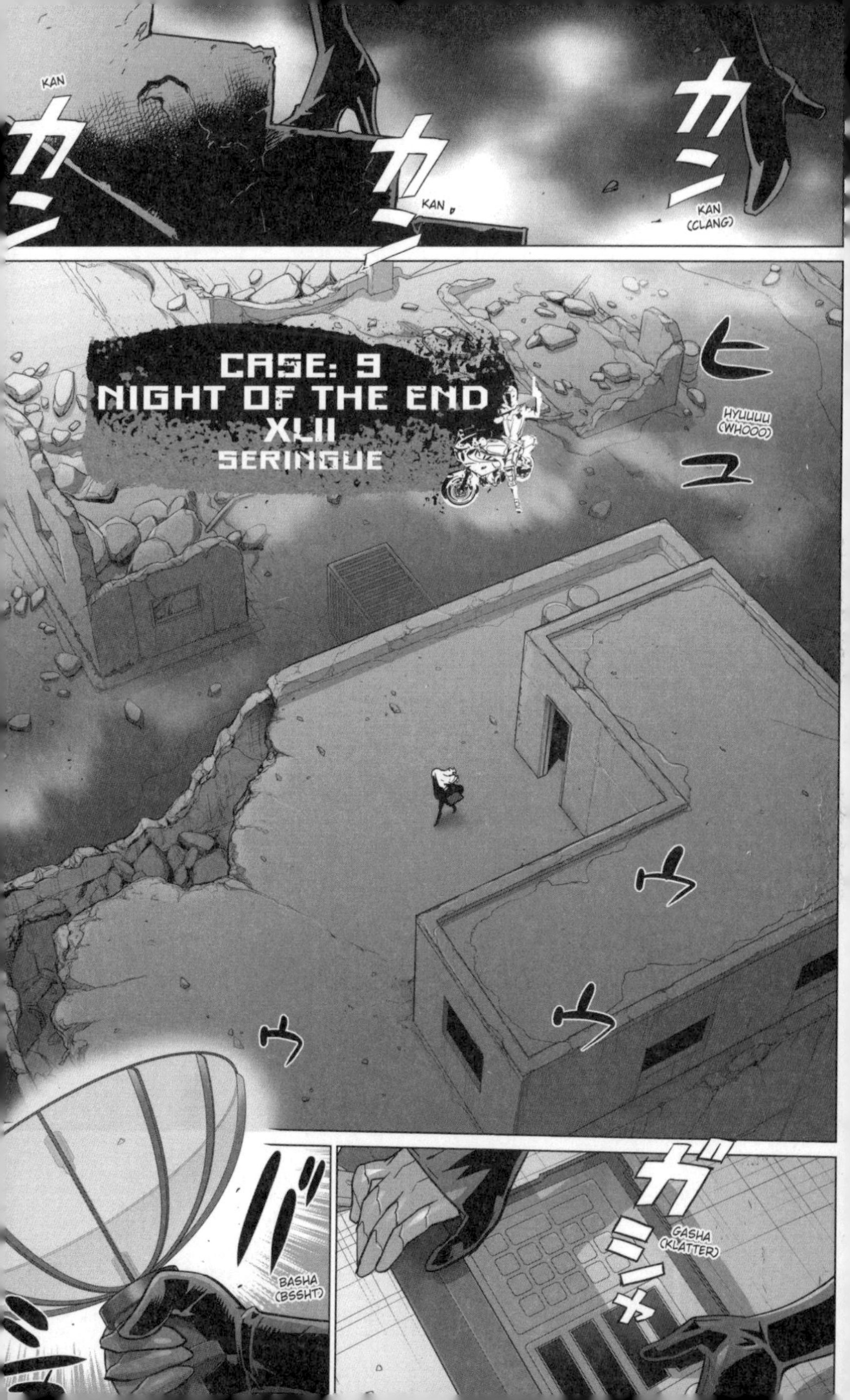
KAN (CLANG)
KAN
KAN
CASE: 9
NIGHT OF THE END
XLII
SERINGUE
HYUUUU (WHOOO)
GASHA (KLATTER)
BASHA (BSSHT)

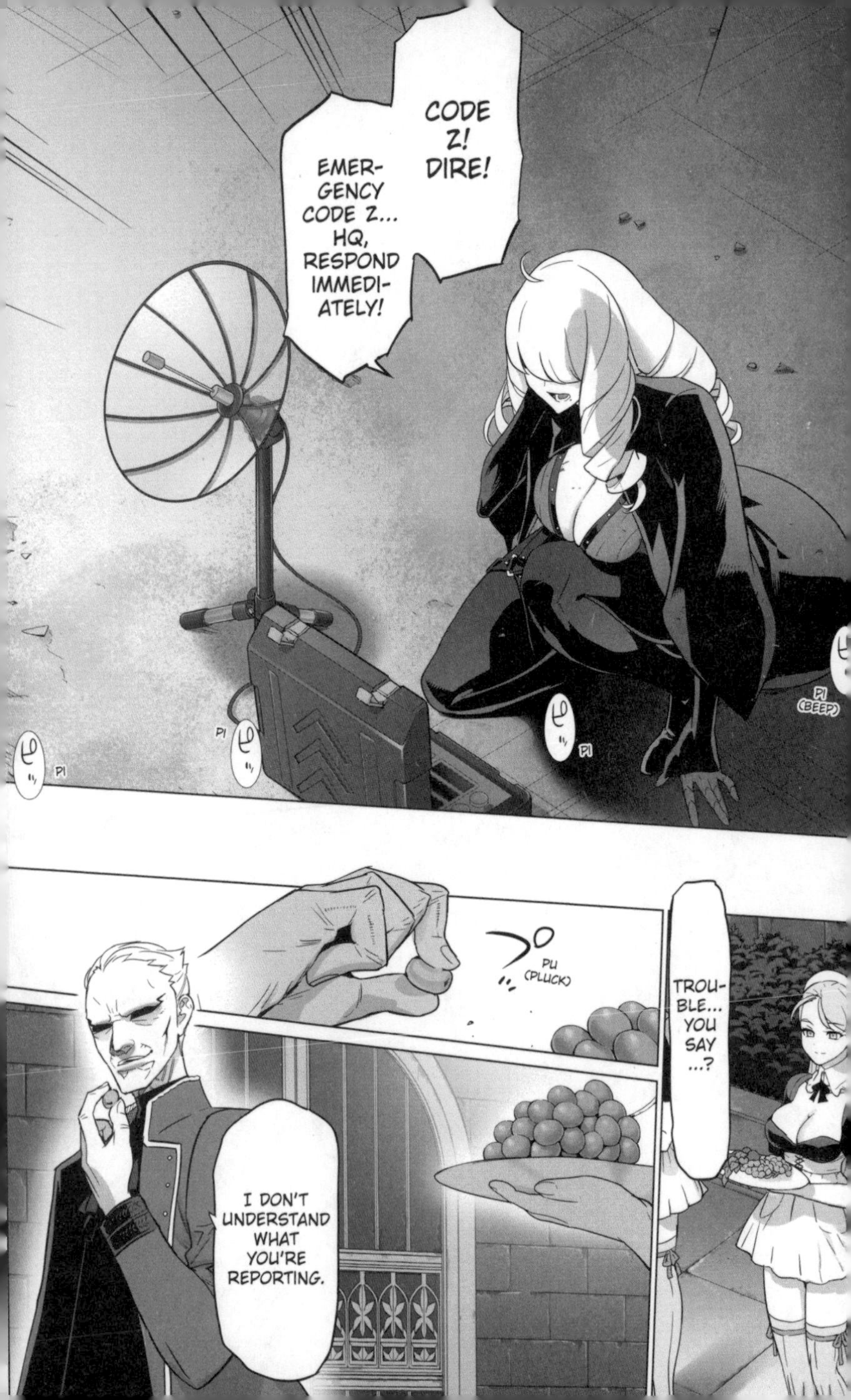
CODE Z! DIRE!
EMER-GENCY CODE Z... HQ, RESPOND IMMEDI-ATELY!
PI (BEEP)
PI
PI
PI
TROU-BLE... YOU SAY ...?
PU (PLUCK)
I DON'T UNDERSTAND WHAT YOU'RE REPORTING.

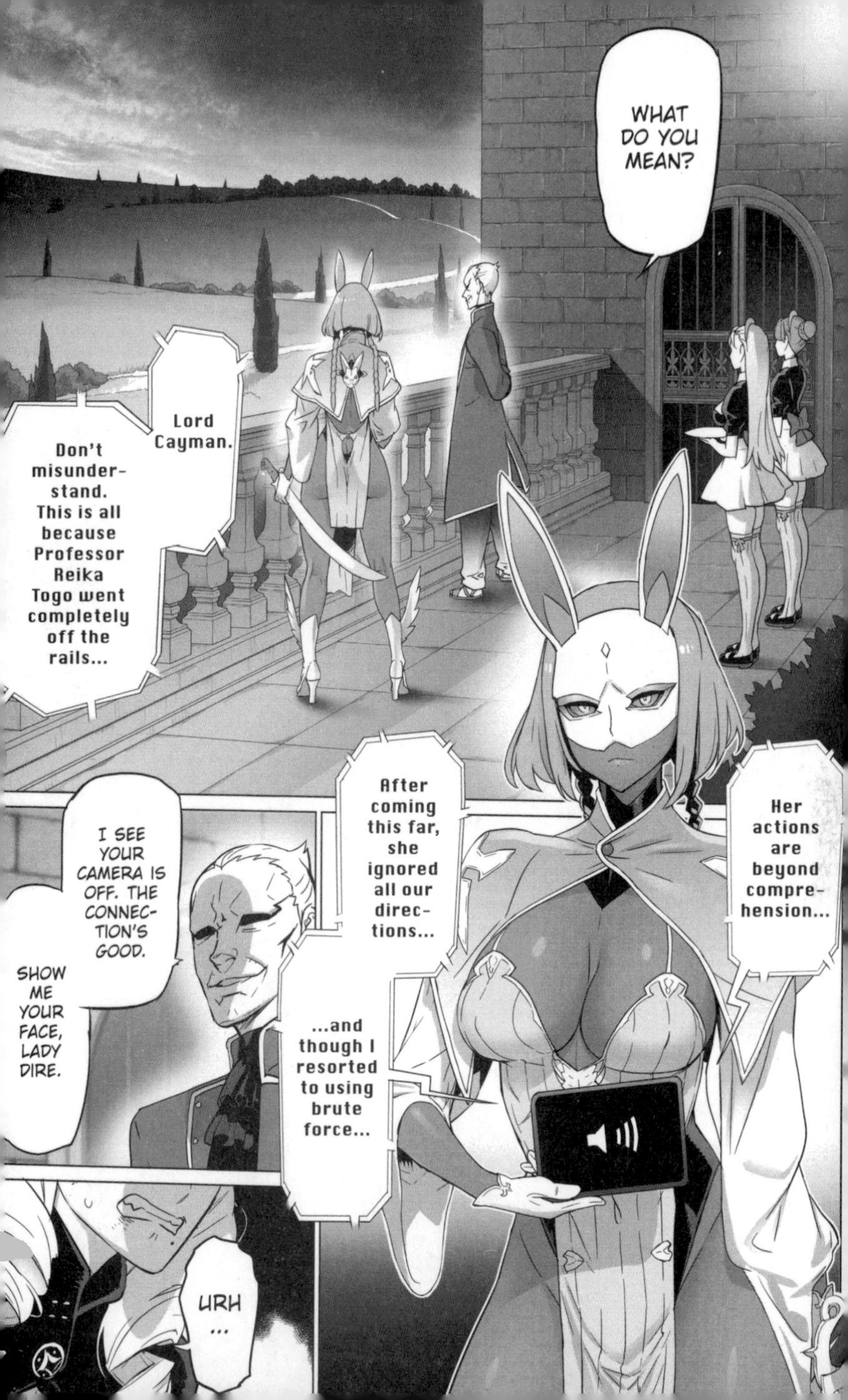
WHAT DO YOU MEAN?
Lord Cayman.
Don't misunderstand. This is all because Professor Reika Togo went completely off the rails...
Her actions are beyond comprehension...
After coming this far, she ignored all our directions...
...and though I resorted to using brute force...
I SEE YOUR CAMERA IS OFF. THE CONNECTION'S GOOD.
SHOW ME YOUR FACE, LADY DIRE.
URH ...

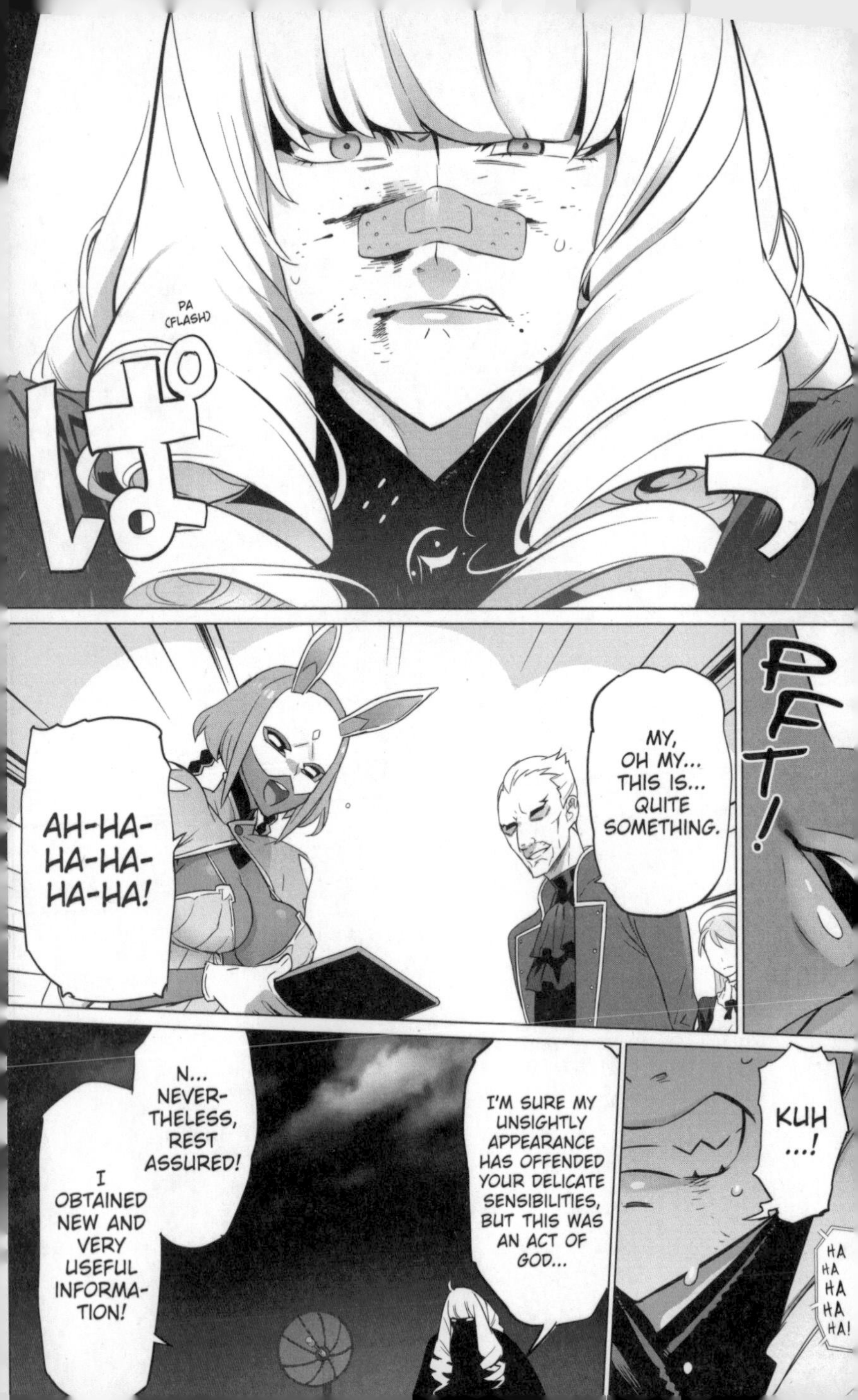
PA (FLASH)
ぱっ
PFFT!
MY, OH MY... THIS IS... QUITE SOMETHING.
AH-HA-HA-HA-HA-HA!
KUH ...!
HA HA HA HA HA HA!
I'M SURE MY UNSIGHTLY APPEARANCE HAS OFFENDED YOUR DELICATE SENSIBILITIES, BUT THIS WAS AN ACT OF GOD...
N... NEVER-THELESS, REST ASSURED!
I OBTAINED NEW AND VERY USEFUL INFORMA-TION!

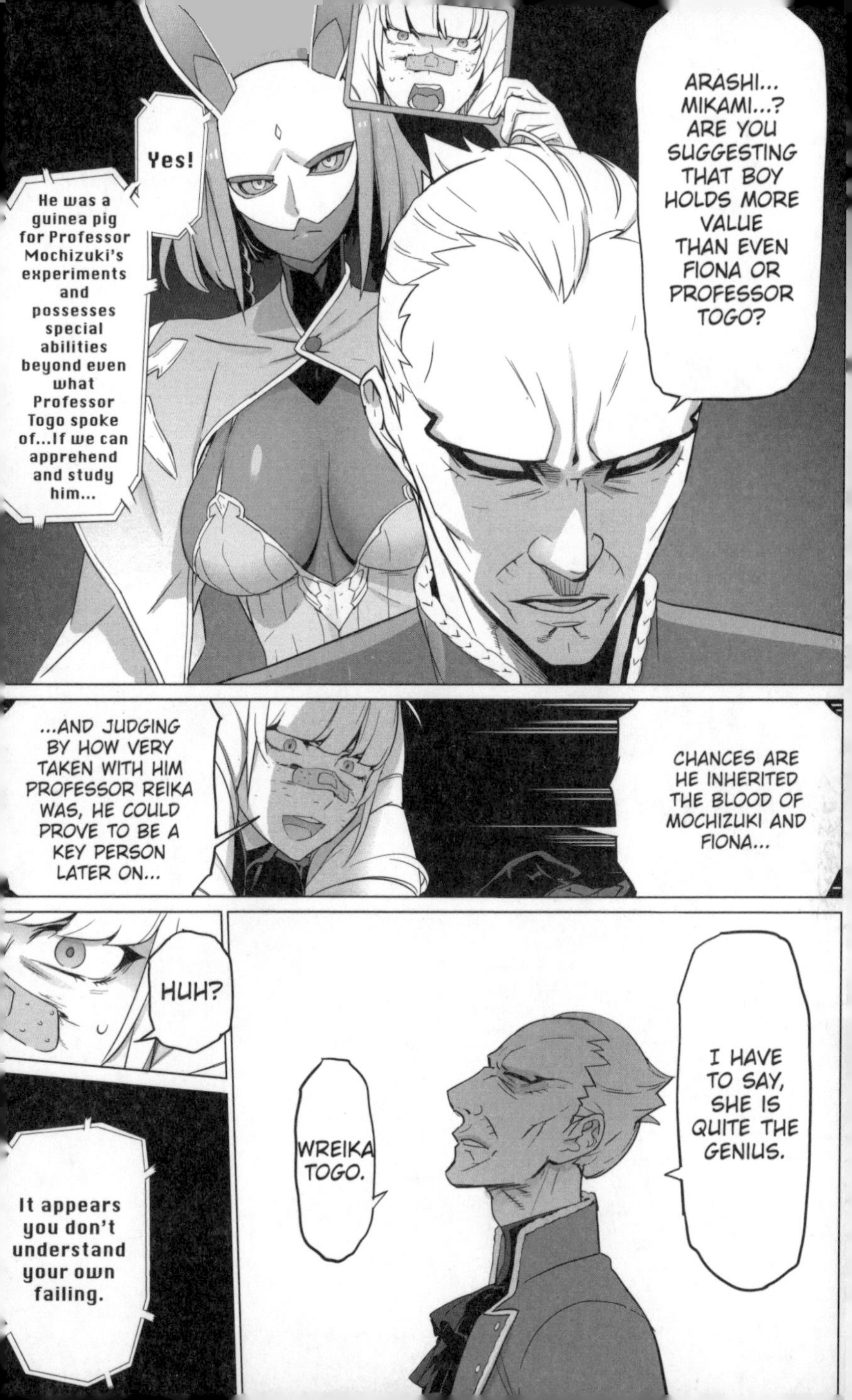
ARASHI... MIKAMI...? ARE YOU SUGGESTING THAT BOY HOLDS MORE VALUE THAN EVEN FIONA OR PROFESSOR TOGO?
Yes!
He was a guinea pig for Professor Mochizuki's experiments and possesses special abilities beyond even what Professor Togo spoke of...If we can apprehend and study him...
CHANCES ARE HE INHERITED THE BLOOD OF MOCHIZUKI AND FIONA...
...AND JUDGING BY HOW VERY TAKEN WITH HIM PROFESSOR REIKA WAS, HE COULD PROVE TO BE A KEY PERSON LATER ON...
I HAVE TO SAY, SHE IS QUITE THE GENIUS.
WREIKA TOGO.
HUH?
It appears you don't understand your own failing.

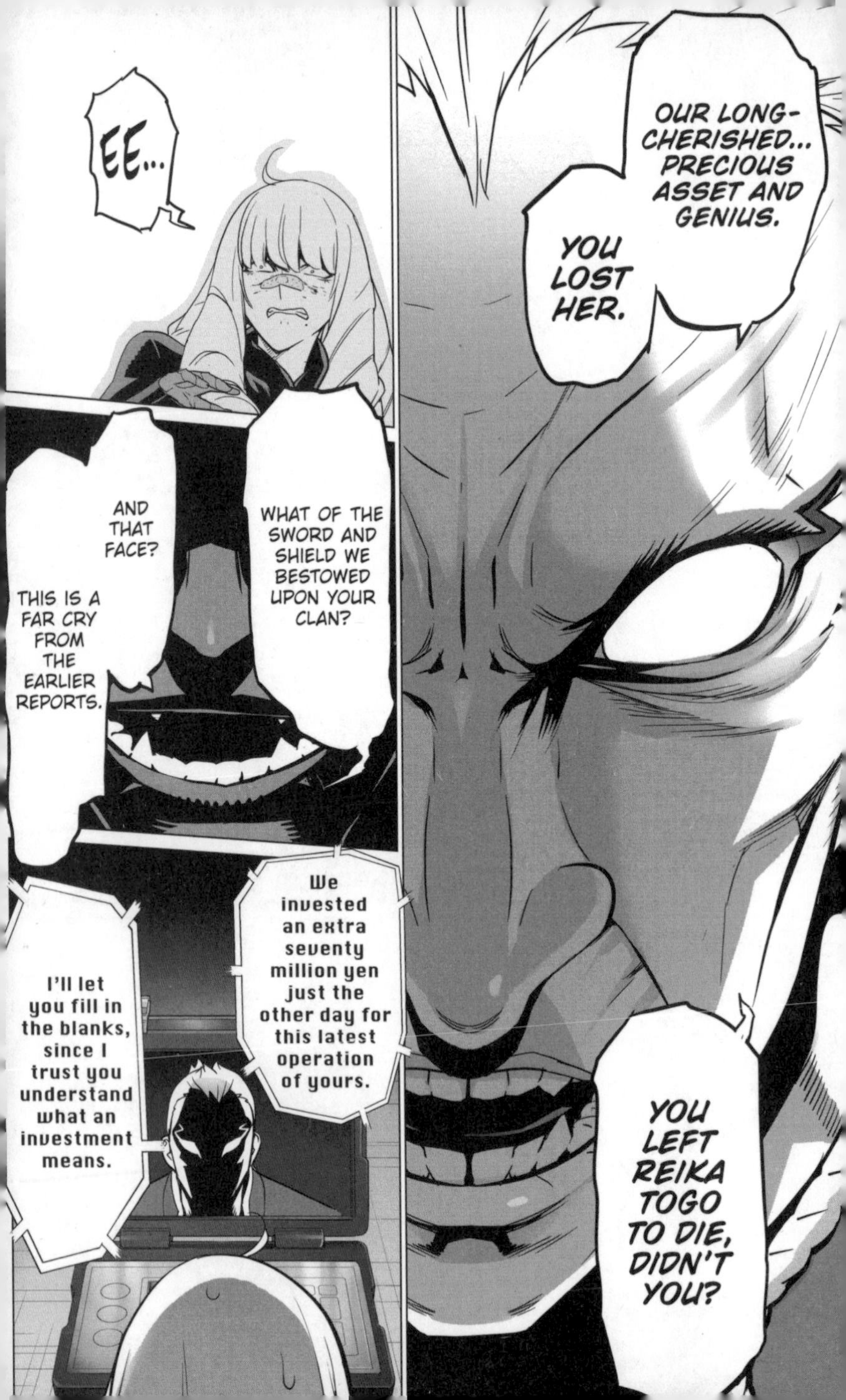
OUR LONG-CHERISHED... PRECIOUS ASSET AND GENIUS.
YOU LOST HER.
YOU LEFT REIKA TOGO TO DIE, DIDN'T YOU?
EE...
WHAT OF THE SWORD AND SHIELD WE BESTOWED UPON YOUR CLAN?
AND THAT FACE?
THIS IS A FAR CRY FROM THE EARLIER REPORTS.
We invested an extra seventy million yen just the other day for this latest operation of yours.
I'll let you fill in the blanks, since I trust you understand what an investment means.

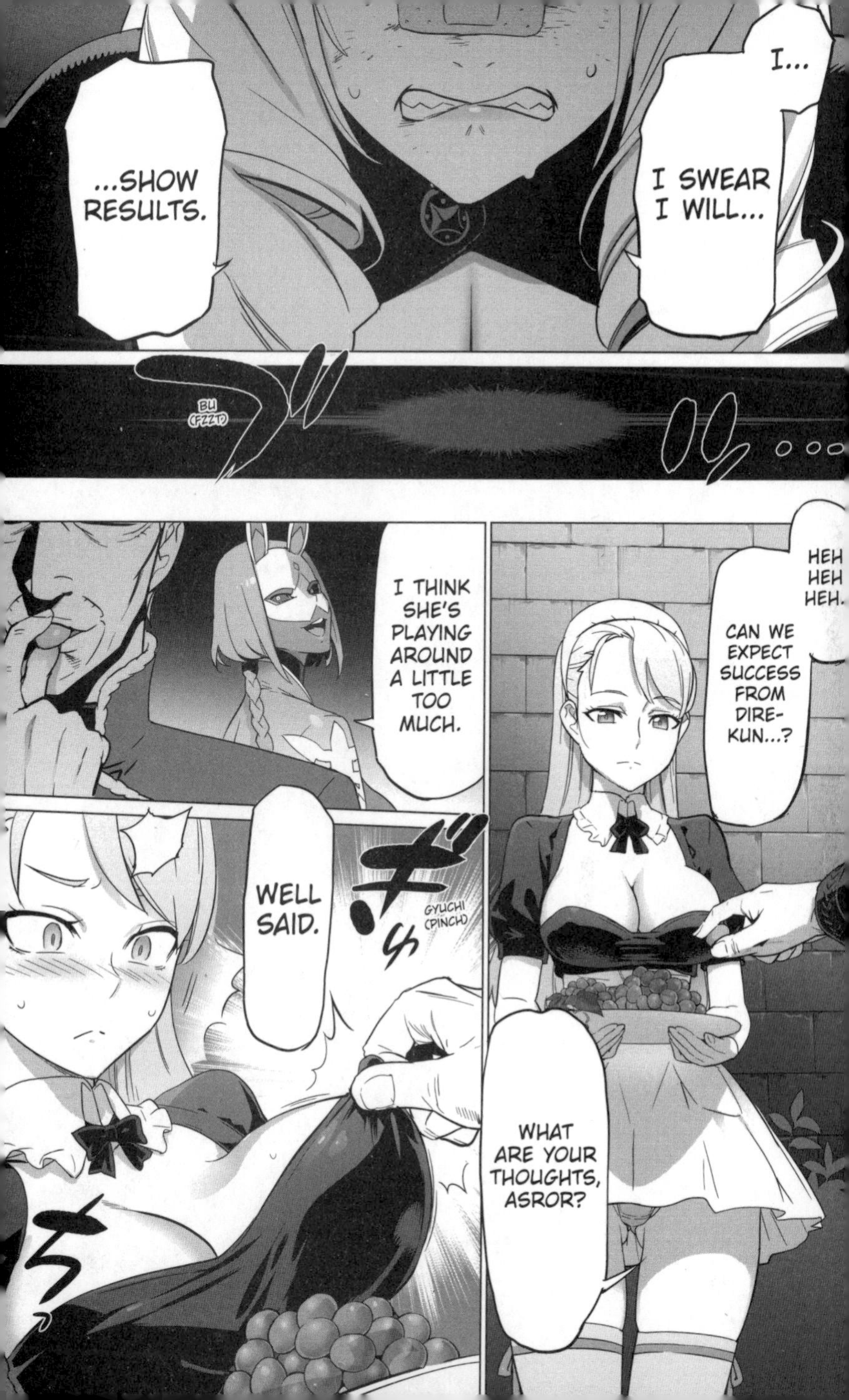
I...
I SWEAR I WILL...
...SHOW RESULTS.
BU (FZZT)
HEH HEH HEH.
CAN WE EXPECT SUCCESS FROM DIRE-KUN...?
WHAT ARE YOUR THOUGHTS, ASROR?
I THINK SHE'S PLAYING AROUND A LITTLE TOO MUCH.
WELL SAID.
GYUCHI (PINCH)

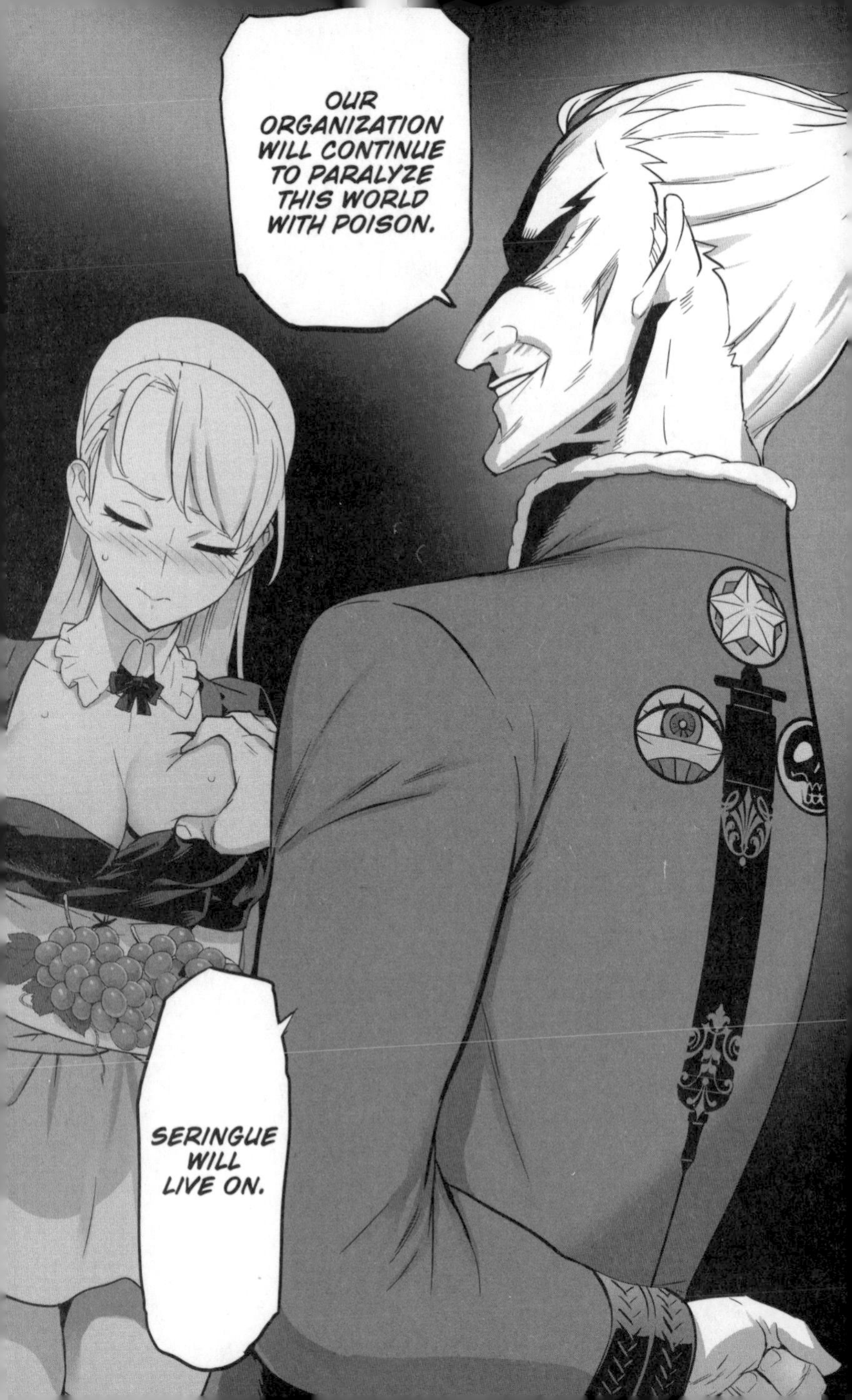
OUR ORGANIZATION WILL CONTINUE TO PARALYZE THIS WORLD WITH POISON.
SERINGUE WILL LIVE ON.

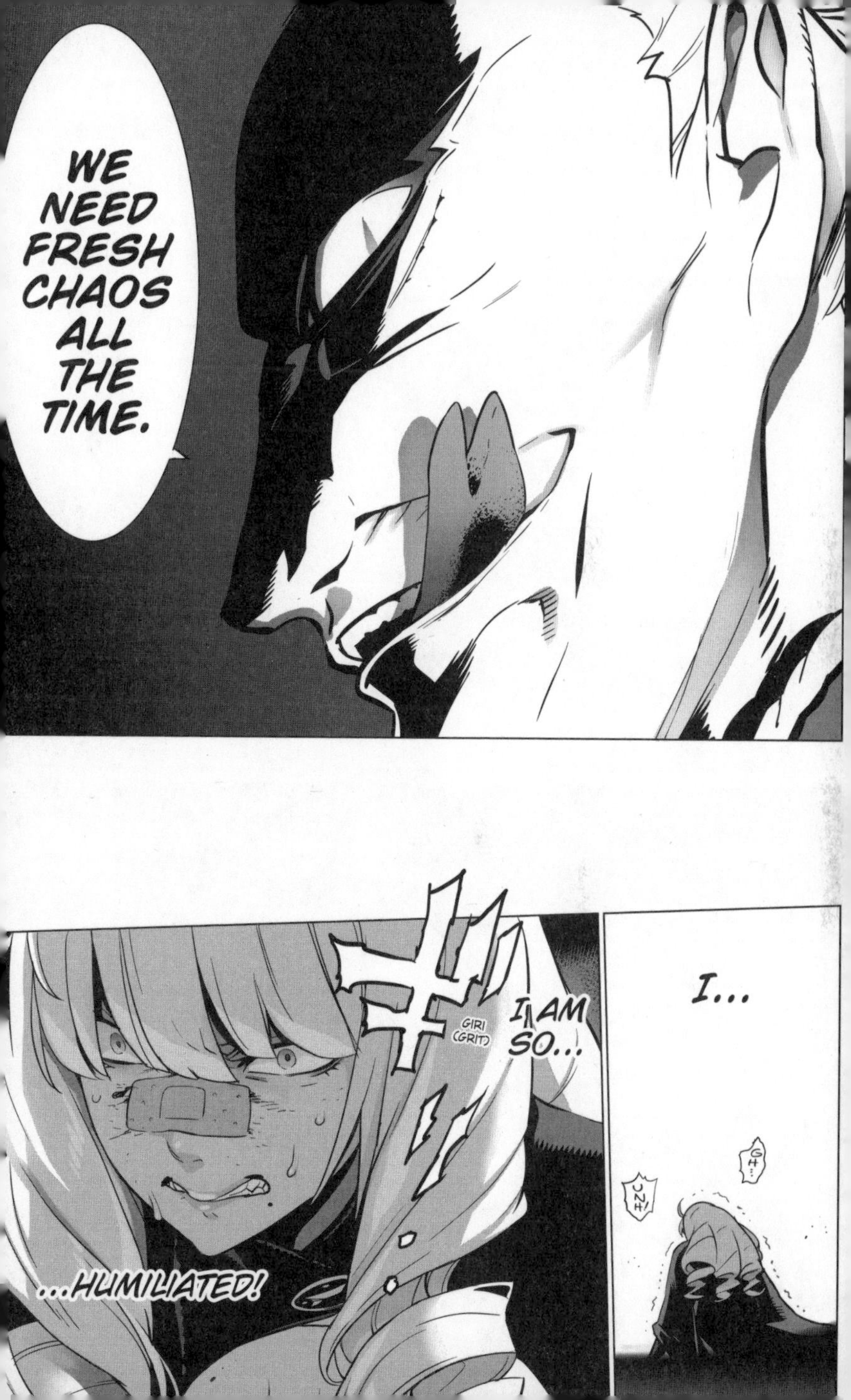
WE NEED FRESH CHAOS ALL THE TIME.
I...
GH...
UNH!
I AM SO...
GIRI (GRIT)
...HUMILIATED!

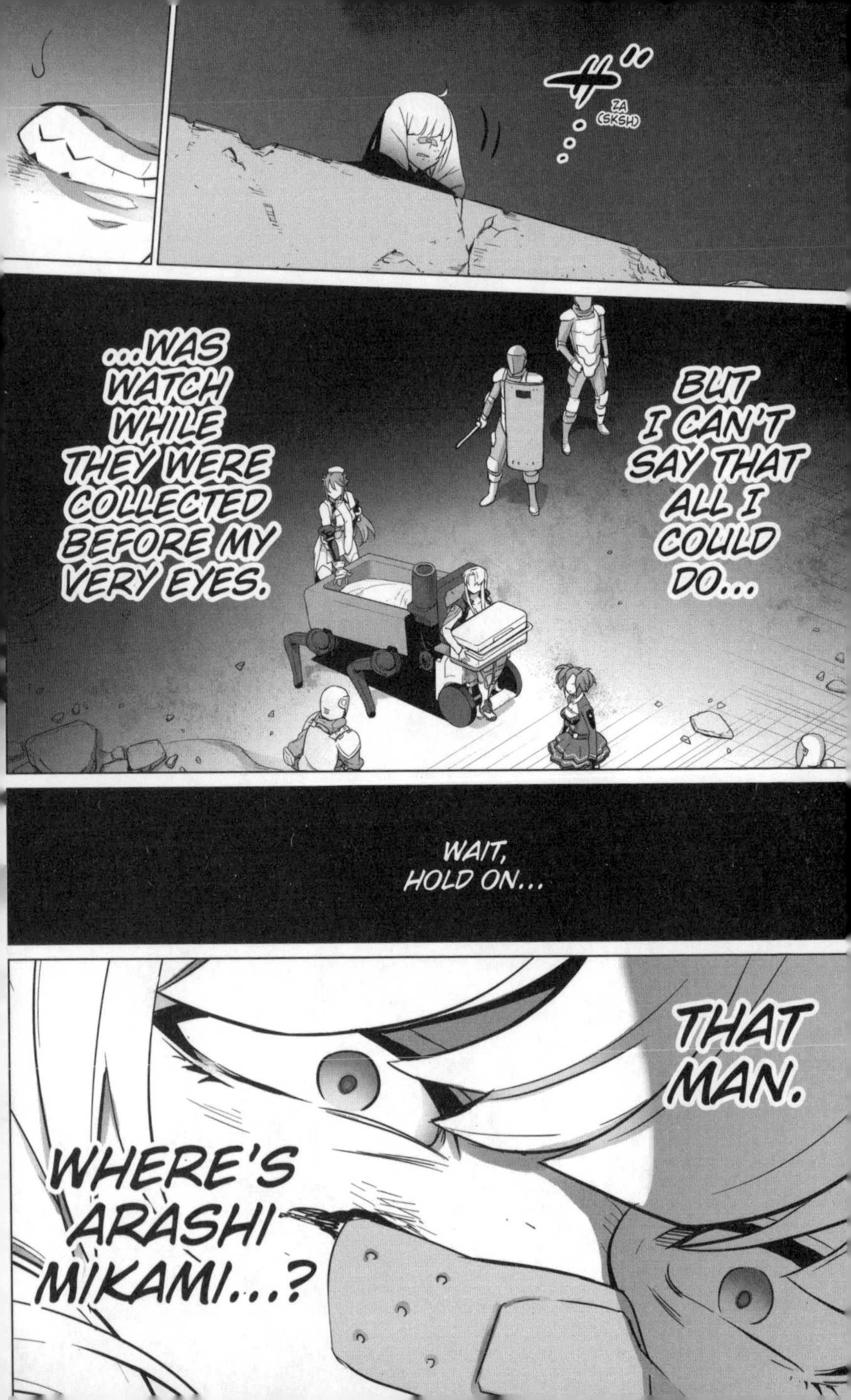
ZA (SKSH)
BUT I CAN'T SAY THAT ALL I COULD DO...
...WAS WATCH WHILE THEY WERE COLLECTED BEFORE MY VERY EYES.
WAIT, HOLD ON...
THAT MAN.
WHERE'S ARASHI MIKAMI...?

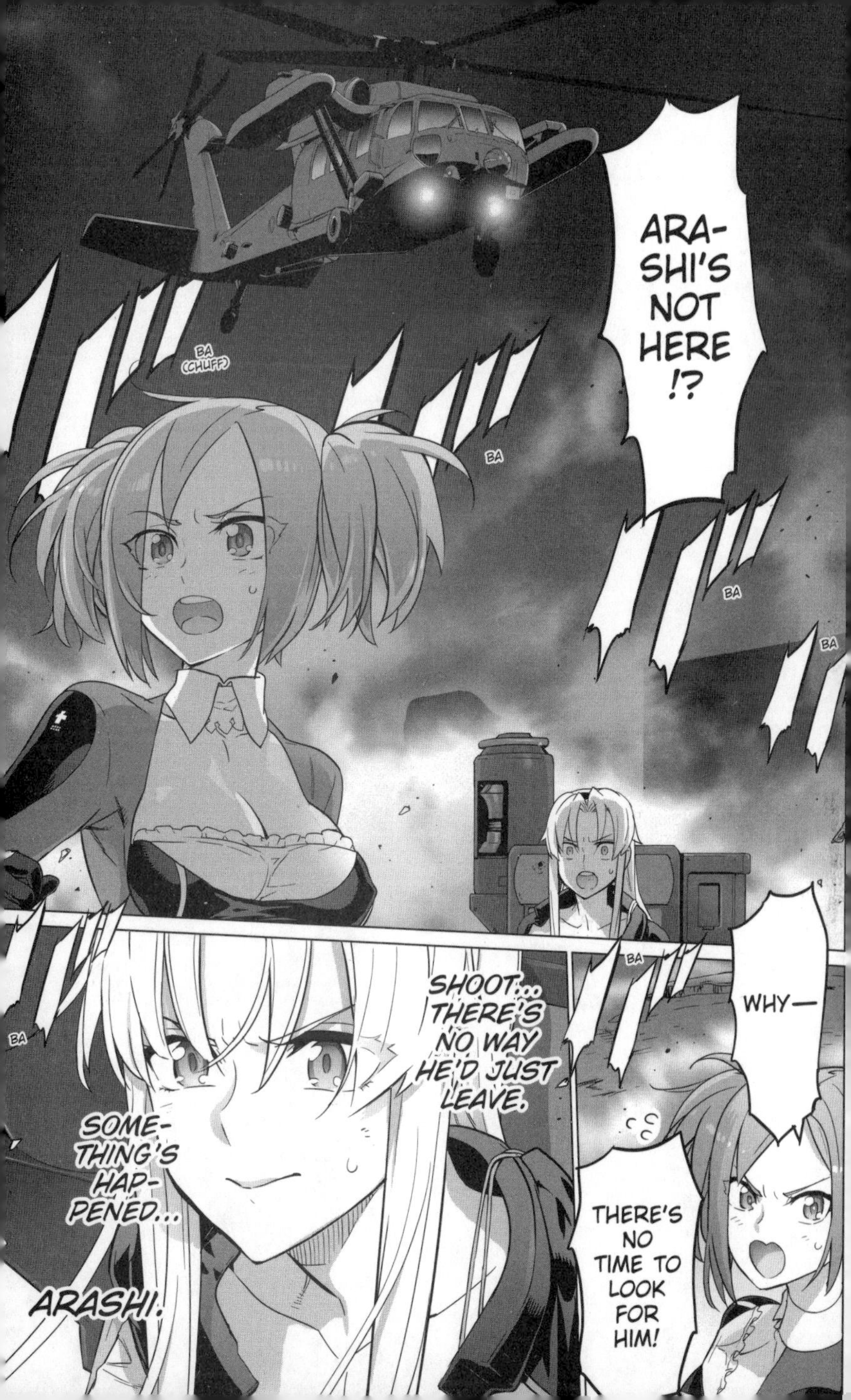
ARASHI'S NOT HERE!?
BA
BA
BA
BA (CHUFF)
WHY—
THERE'S NO TIME TO LOOK FOR HIM!
BA
SHOOT... THERE'S NO WAY HE'D JUST LEAVE.
SOMETHING'S HAPPENED...
ARASHI.
BA

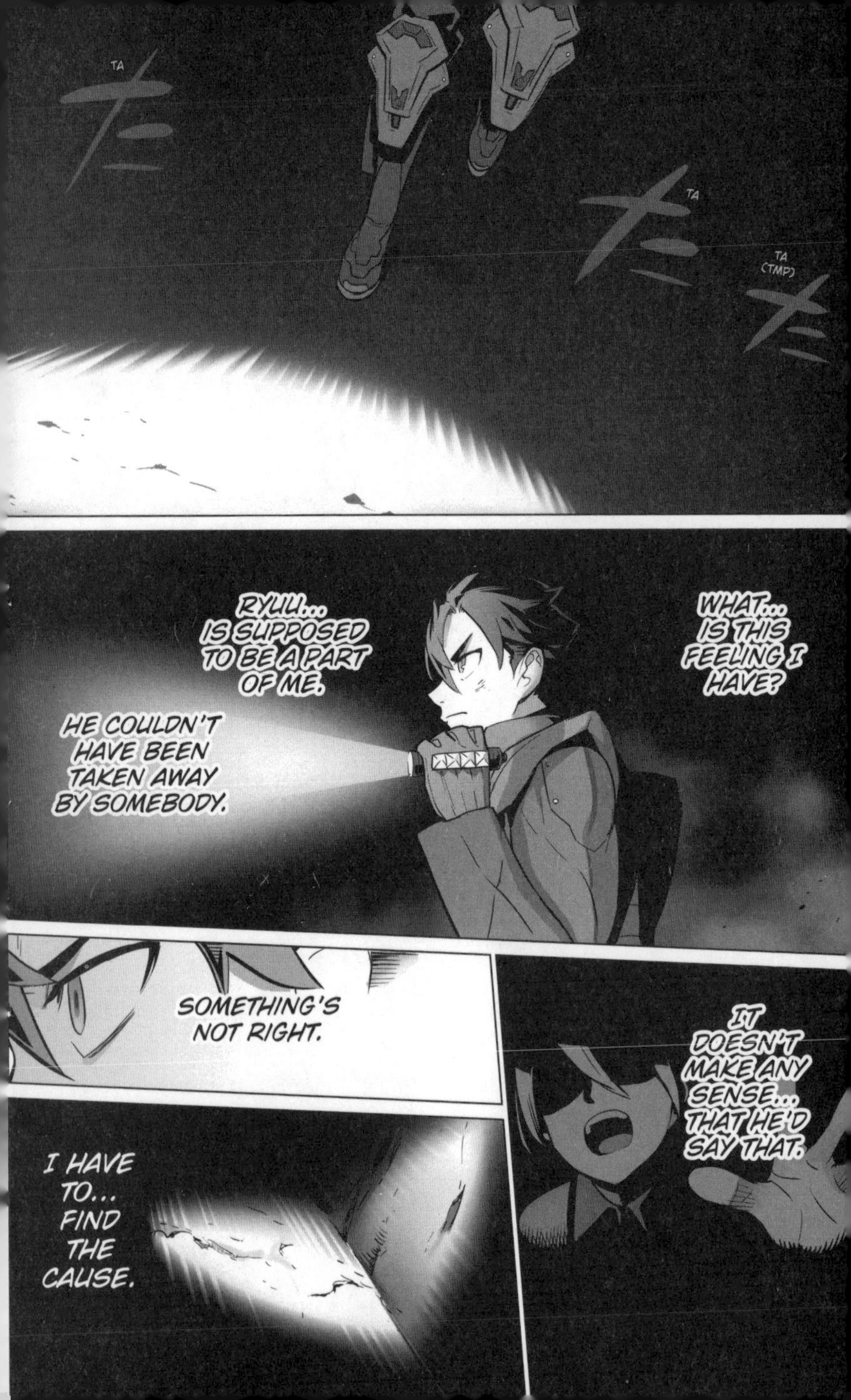
TA (TMP)
TA
TA
WHAT... IS THIS FEELING I HAVE?
RYUU... IS SUPPOSED TO BE A PART OF ME.
HE COULDN'T HAVE BEEN TAKEN AWAY BY SOMEBODY.
IT DOESN'T MAKE ANY SENSE... THAT HE'D SAY THAT.
SOMETHING'S NOT RIGHT.
I HAVE TO... FIND THE CAUSE.

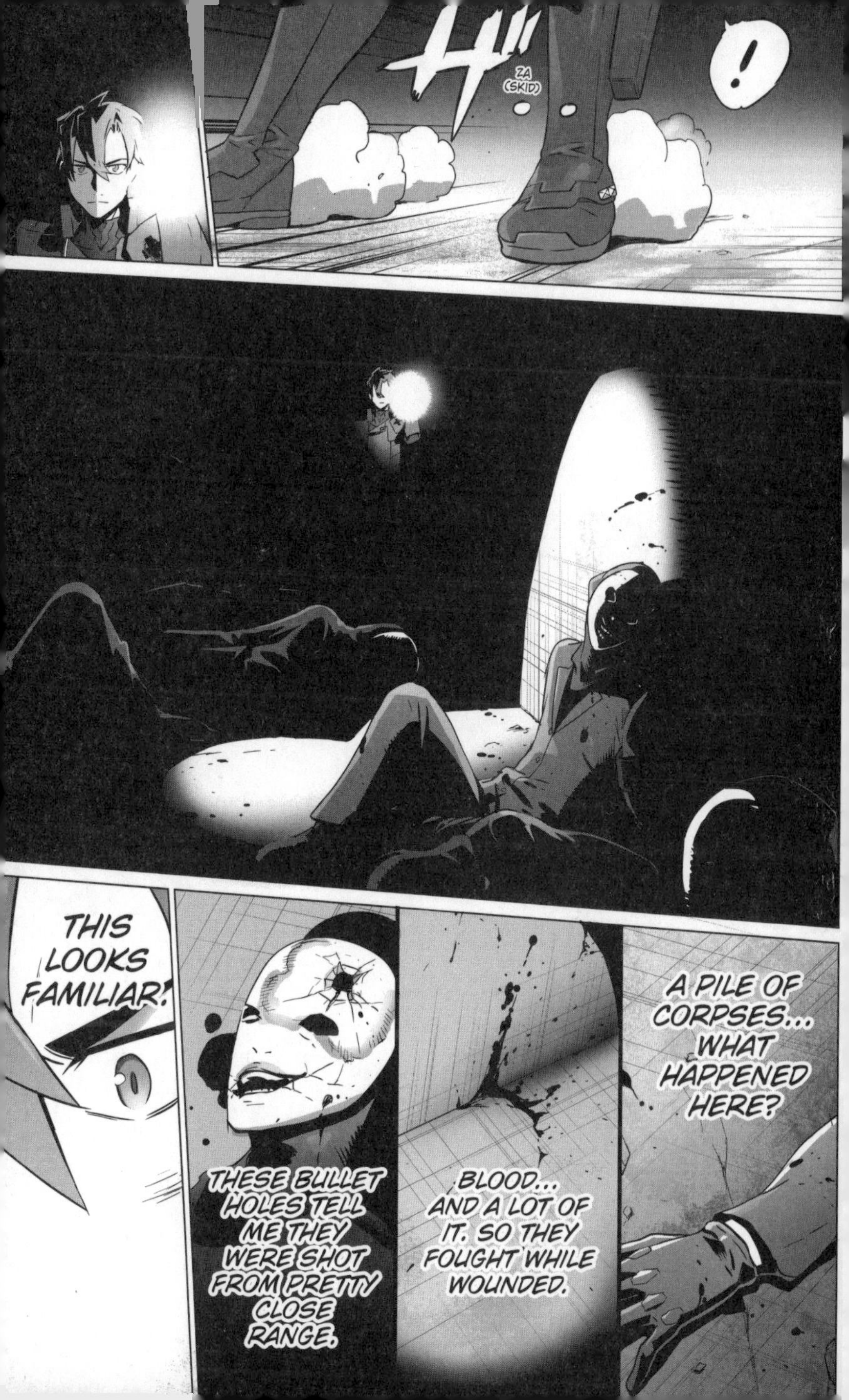
!
ZA (SKID)
A PILE OF CORPSES... WHAT HAPPENED HERE?
BLOOD... AND A LOT OF IT. SO THEY FOUGHT WHILE WOUNDED.
THESE BULLET HOLES TELL ME THEY WERE SHOT FROM PRETTY CLOSE RANGE.
THIS LOOKS FAMILIAR?!

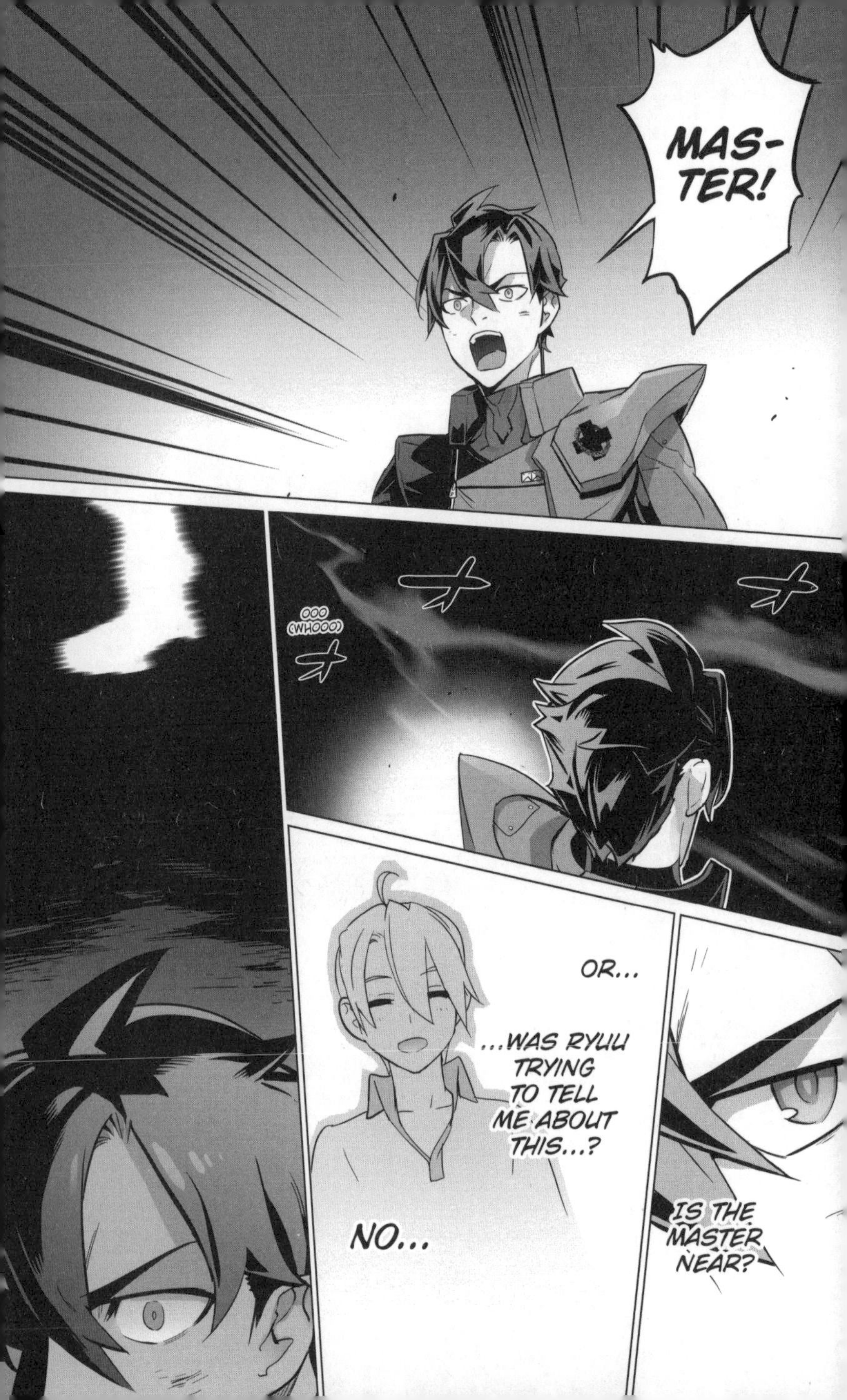
MAS-
TER!
OOO
(WHOOO)
OR...
...WAS RYUU TRYING TO TELL ME ABOUT THIS...?
NO...
IS THE MASTER NEAR?

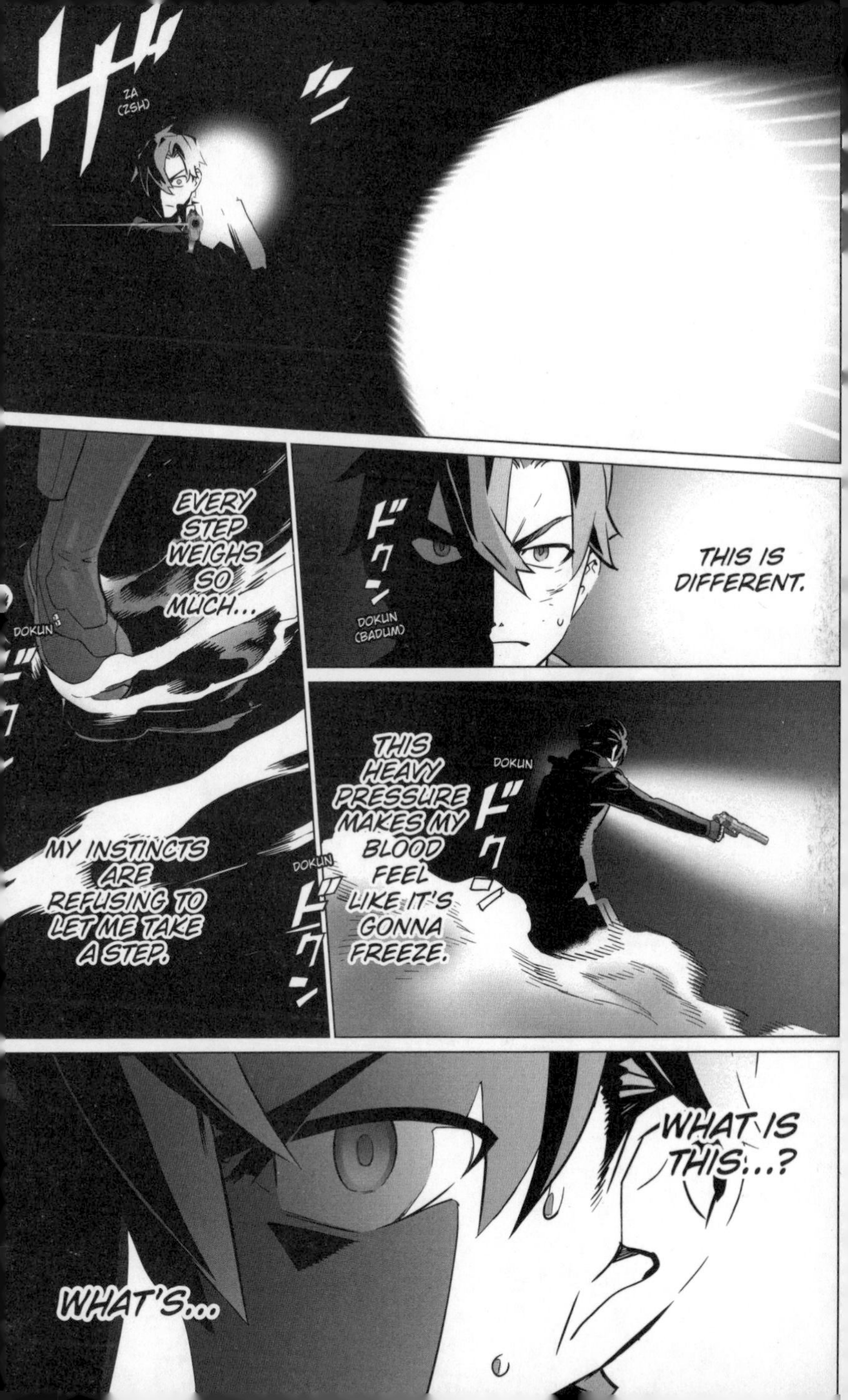
ZA
(ZSH)
THIS IS DIFFERENT.
DOKUN
(BADUM)
THIS HEAVY PRESSURE MAKES MY BLOOD FEEL LIKE IT'S GONNA FREEZE.
DOKUN
DOKUN
EVERY STEP WEIGHS SO MUCH...
DOKUN
MY INSTINCTS ARE REFUSING TO LET ME TAKE A STEP.
WHAT IS THIS...?
WHAT'S...

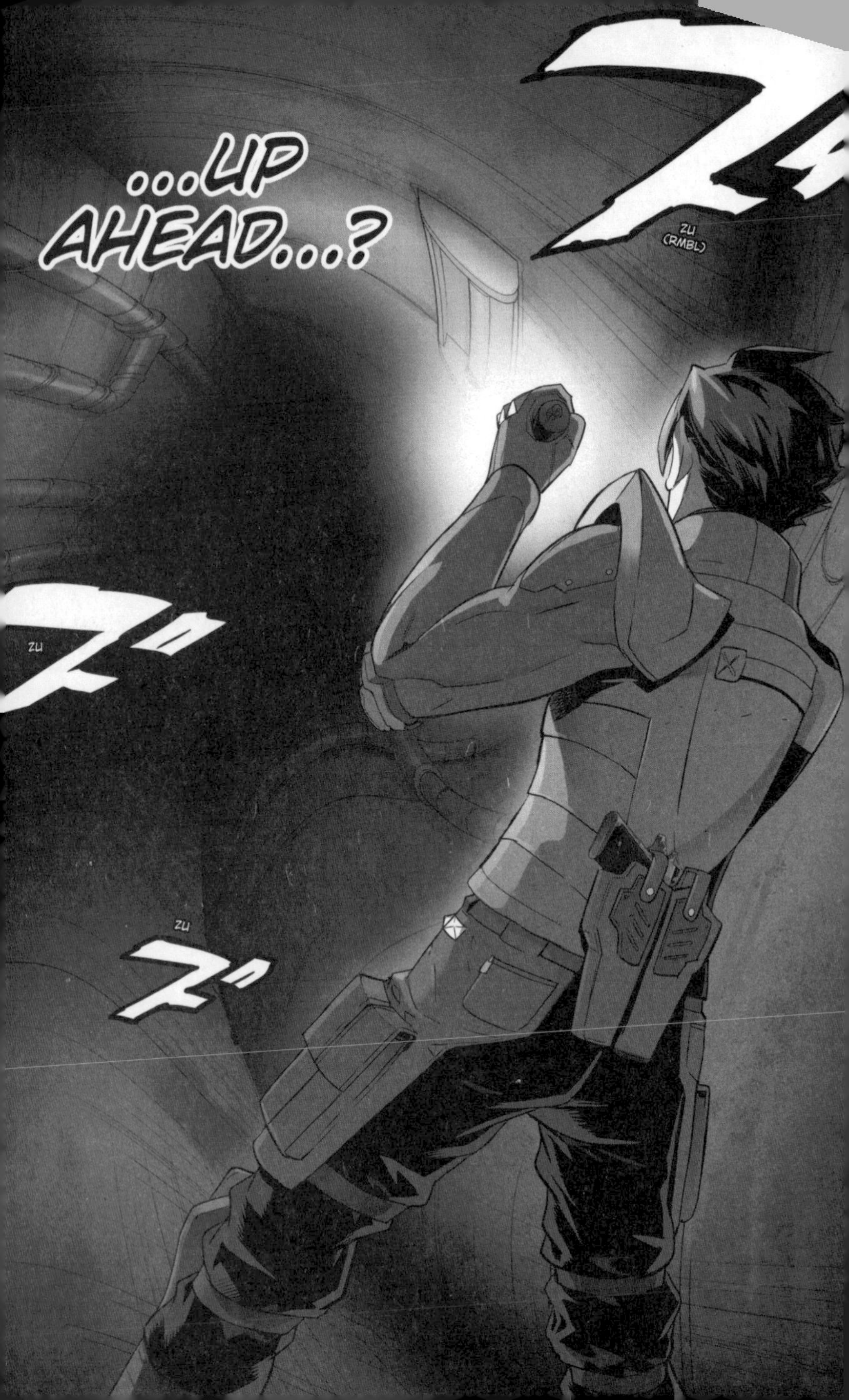
ZU (RMBL)
...UP AHEAD...?
ZU
ZU

TRIAGE X

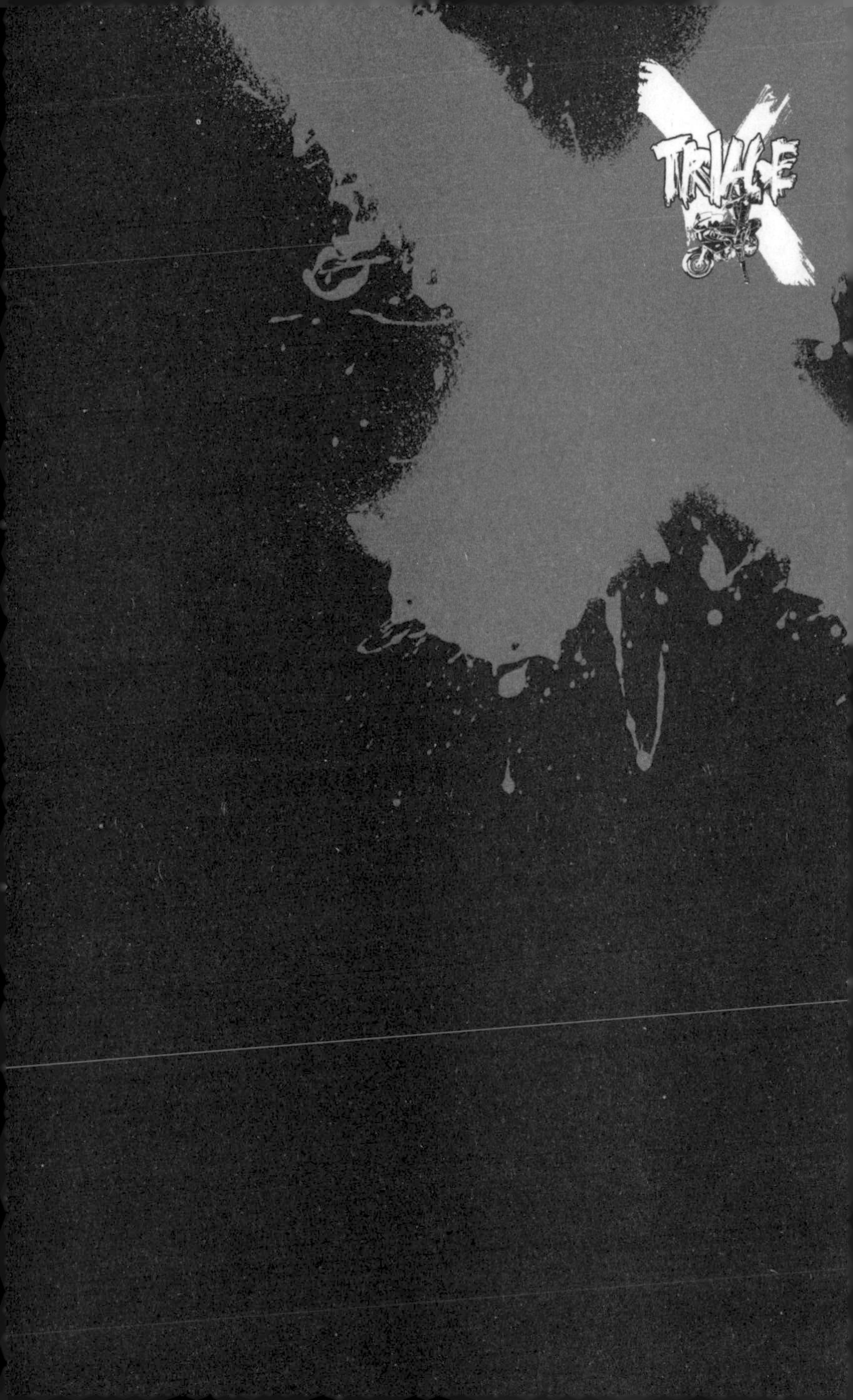
TRIAGE X

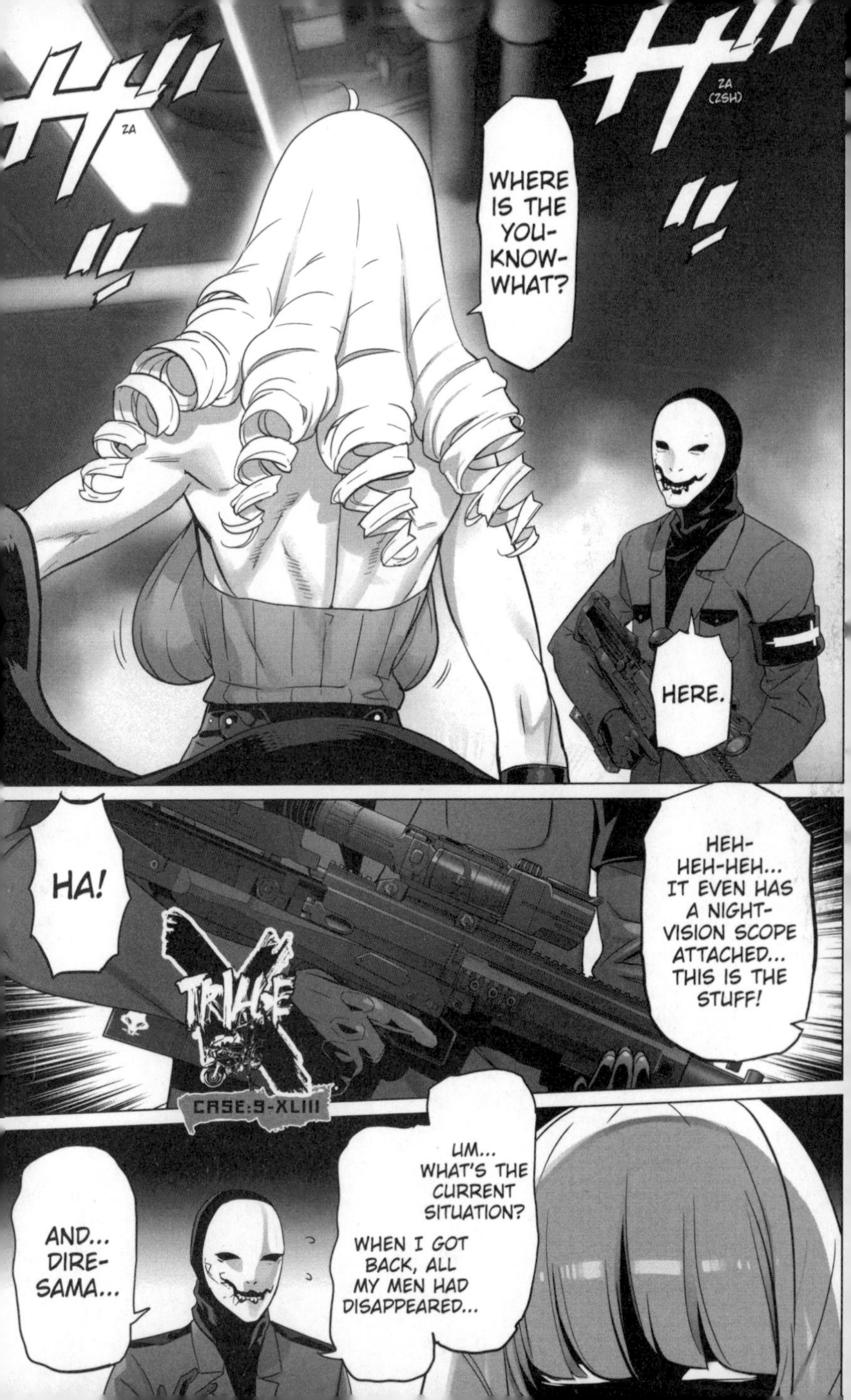
ZA (ZSH)
WHERE IS THE YOU-KNOW-WHAT?
ZA
HERE.
HEH-HEH-HEH... IT EVEN HAS A NIGHT-VISION SCOPE ATTACHED... THIS IS THE STUFF!
HA!
TRIAGE X
CASE:9-XLIII
UM... WHAT'S THE CURRENT SITUATION?
WHEN I GOT BACK, ALL MY MEN HAD DISAPPEARED...
AND... DIRE-SAMA...

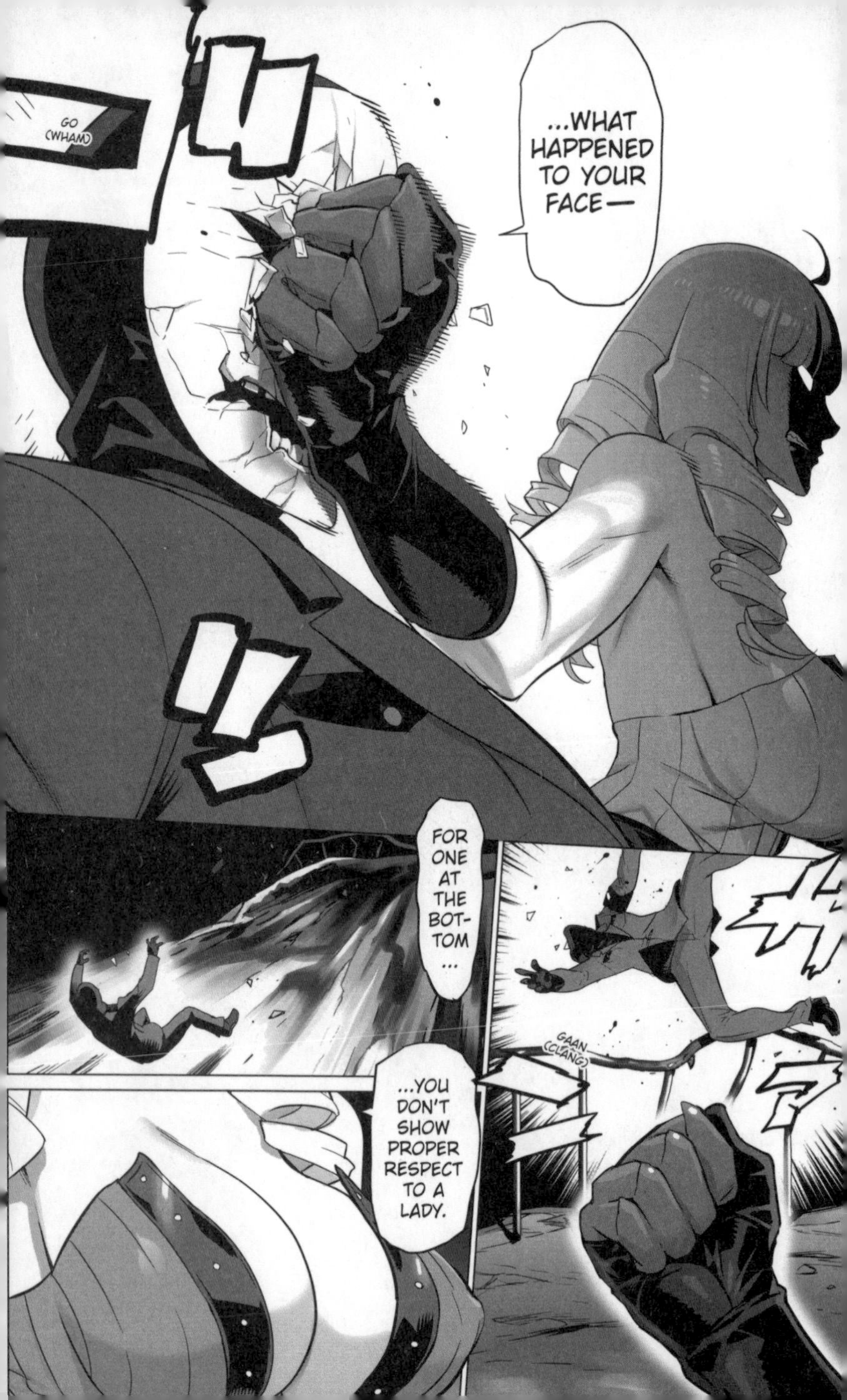
...WHAT HAPPENED TO YOUR FACE—
GO (WHAM)
GAAN (CLANG)
FOR ONE AT THE BOT-TOM ...
...YOU DON'T SHOW PROPER RESPECT TO A LADY.

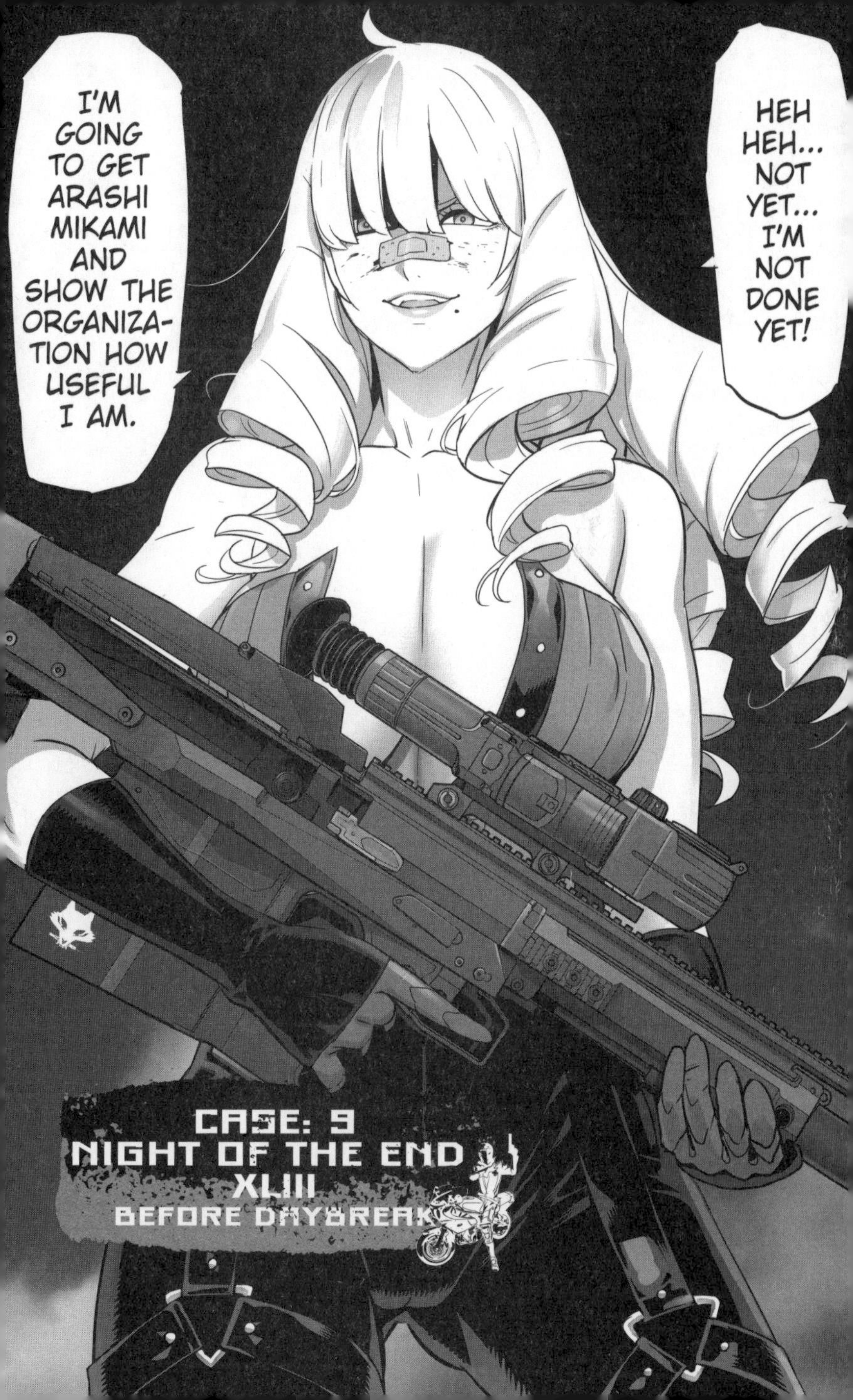
HEH HEH... NOT YET... I'M NOT DONE YET!
I'M GOING TO GET ARASHI MIKAMI AND SHOW THE ORGANIZA-TION HOW USEFUL I AM.
CASE: 9
NIGHT OF THE END
XLIII
BEFORE DAYBREAK

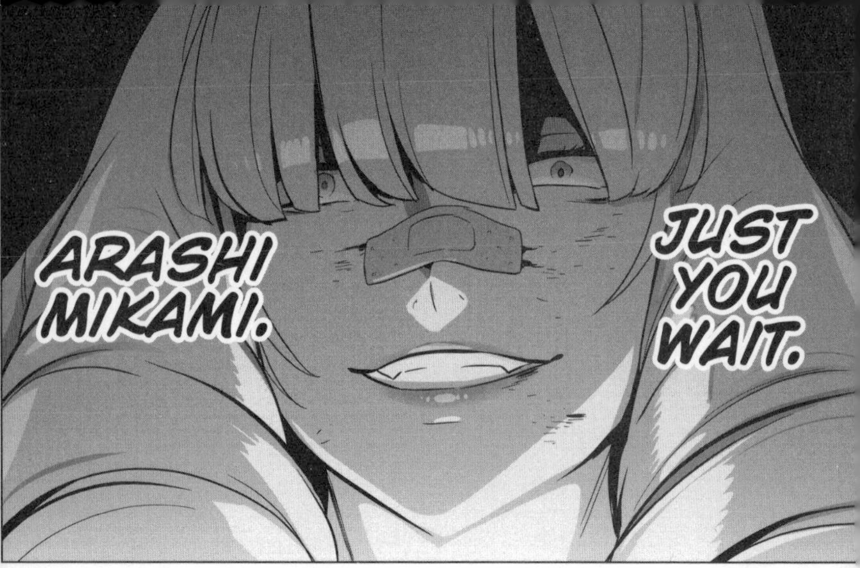
JUST YOU WAIT.
ARASHI MIKAMI.

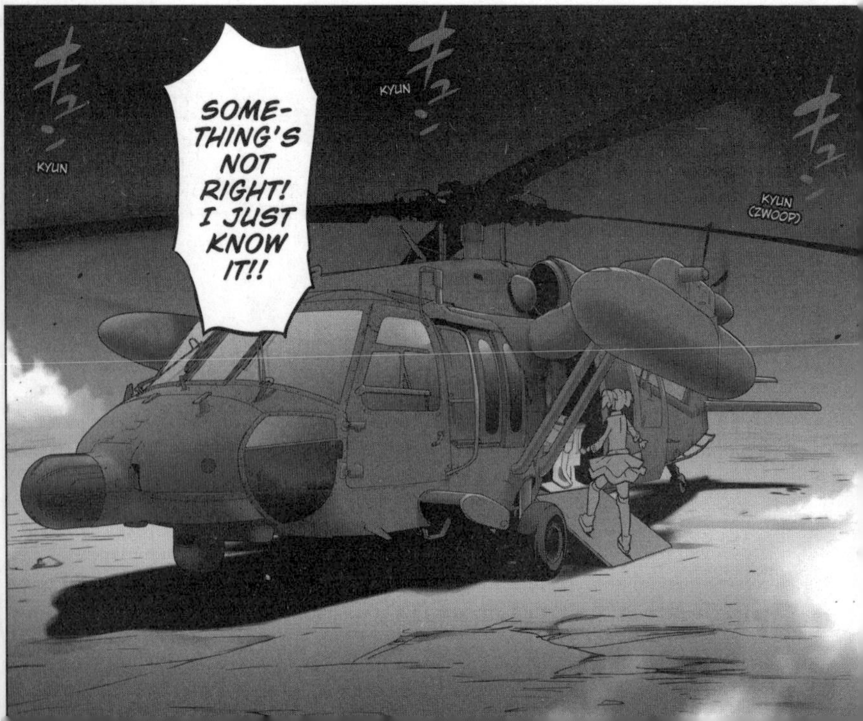
KYUN (ZWOOP)
KYUN
SOMETHING'S NOT RIGHT! I JUST KNOW IT!!
KYUN

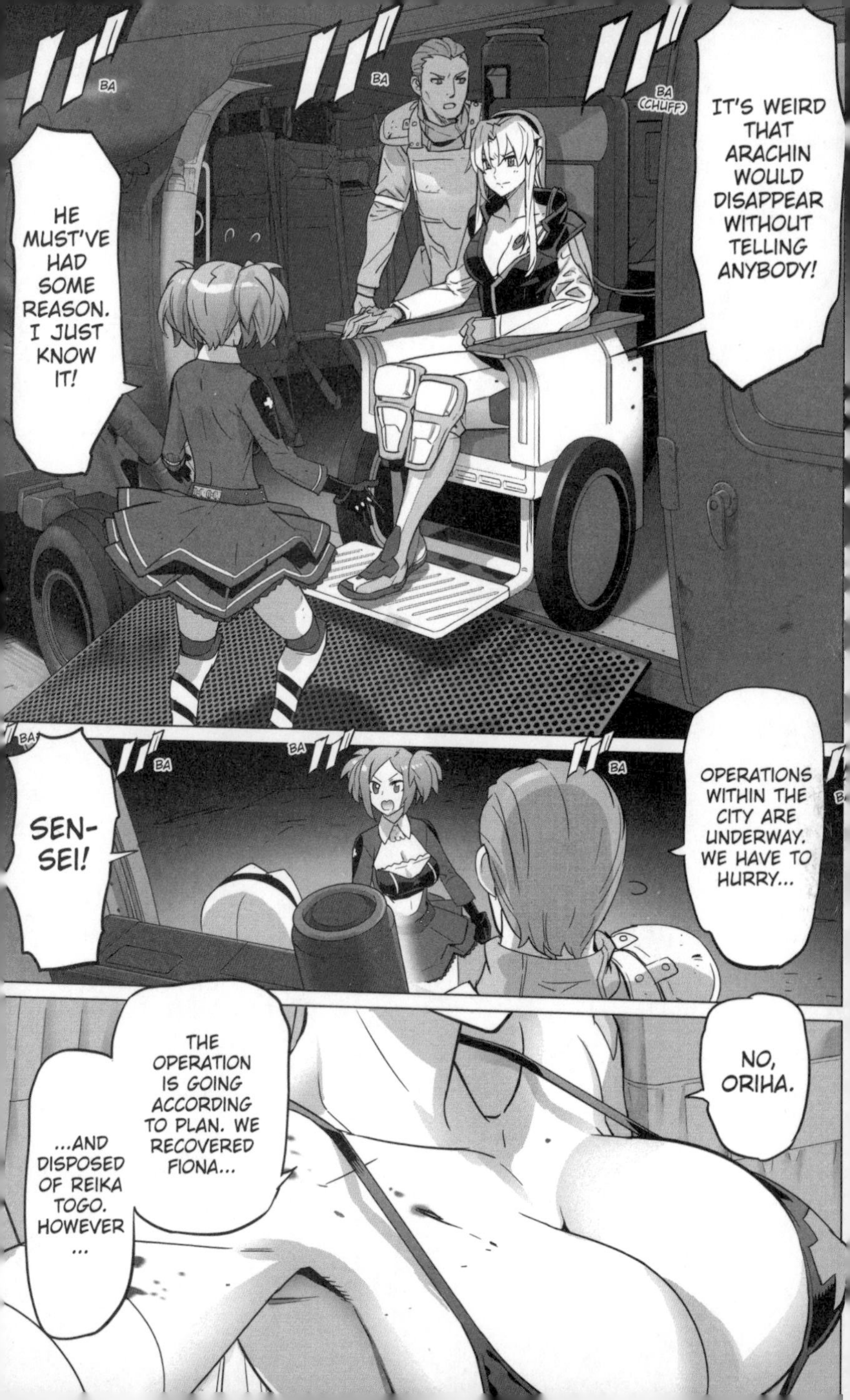
BA (CHUFF)
BA
BA
IT'S WEIRD THAT ARACHIN WOULD DISAPPEAR WITHOUT TELLING ANYBODY!
HE MUST'VE HAD SOME REASON. I JUST KNOW IT!
BA
BA
BA
BA
OPERATIONS WITHIN THE CITY ARE UNDERWAY. WE HAVE TO HURRY...
SEN-SEI!
NO, ORIHA.
THE OPERATION IS GOING ACCORDING TO PLAN. WE RECOVERED FIONA...
...AND DISPOSED OF REIKA TOGO. HOWEVER ...

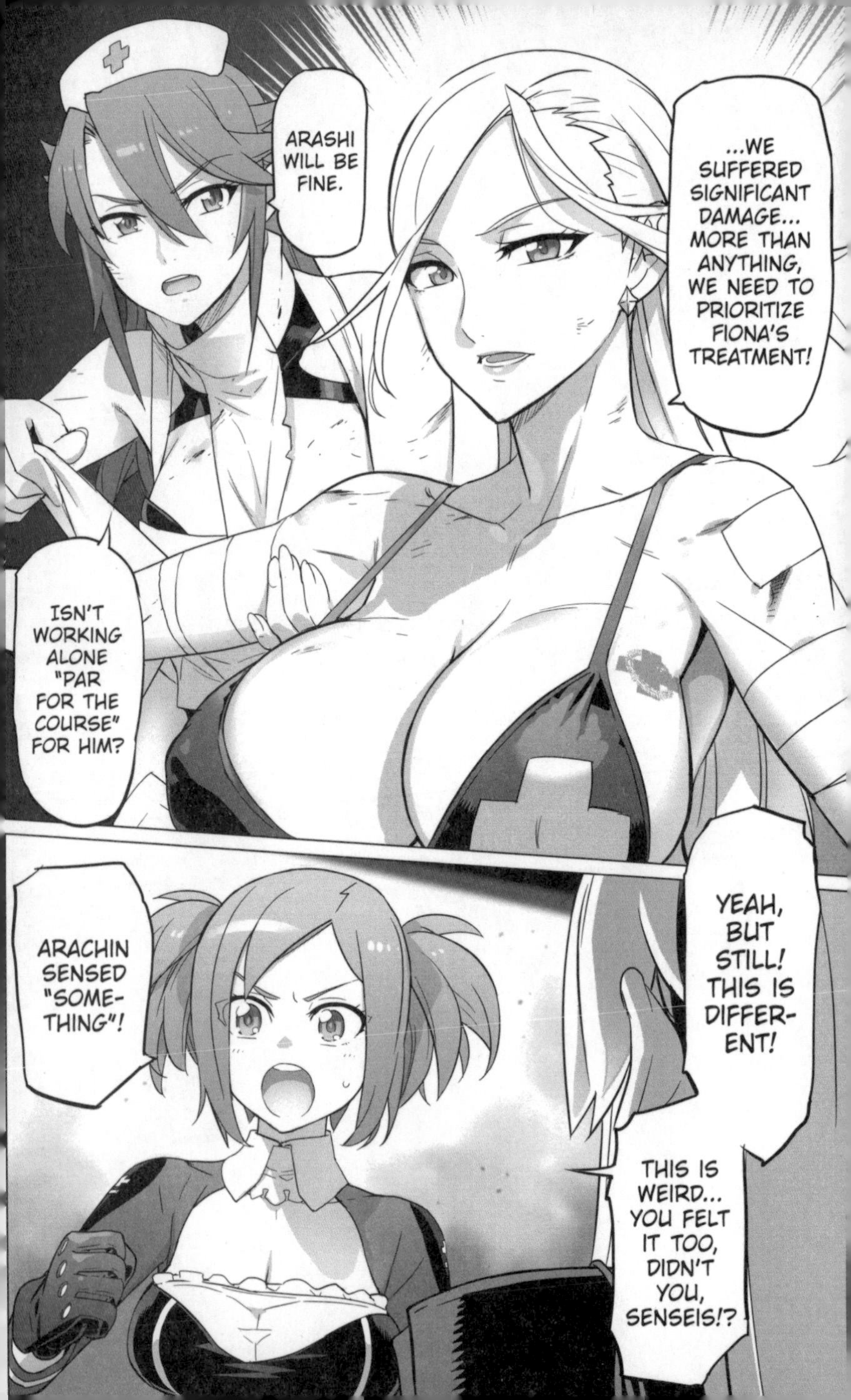
...WE SUFFERED SIGNIFICANT DAMAGE... MORE THAN ANYTHING, WE NEED TO PRIORITIZE FIONA'S TREATMENT!
ARASHI WILL BE FINE.
ISN'T WORKING ALONE "PAR FOR THE COURSE" FOR HIM?
YEAH, BUT STILL! THIS IS DIFFER-ENT!
ARACHIN SENSED "SOME-THING"!
THIS IS WEIRD... YOU FELT IT TOO, DIDN'T YOU, SENSEIS!?

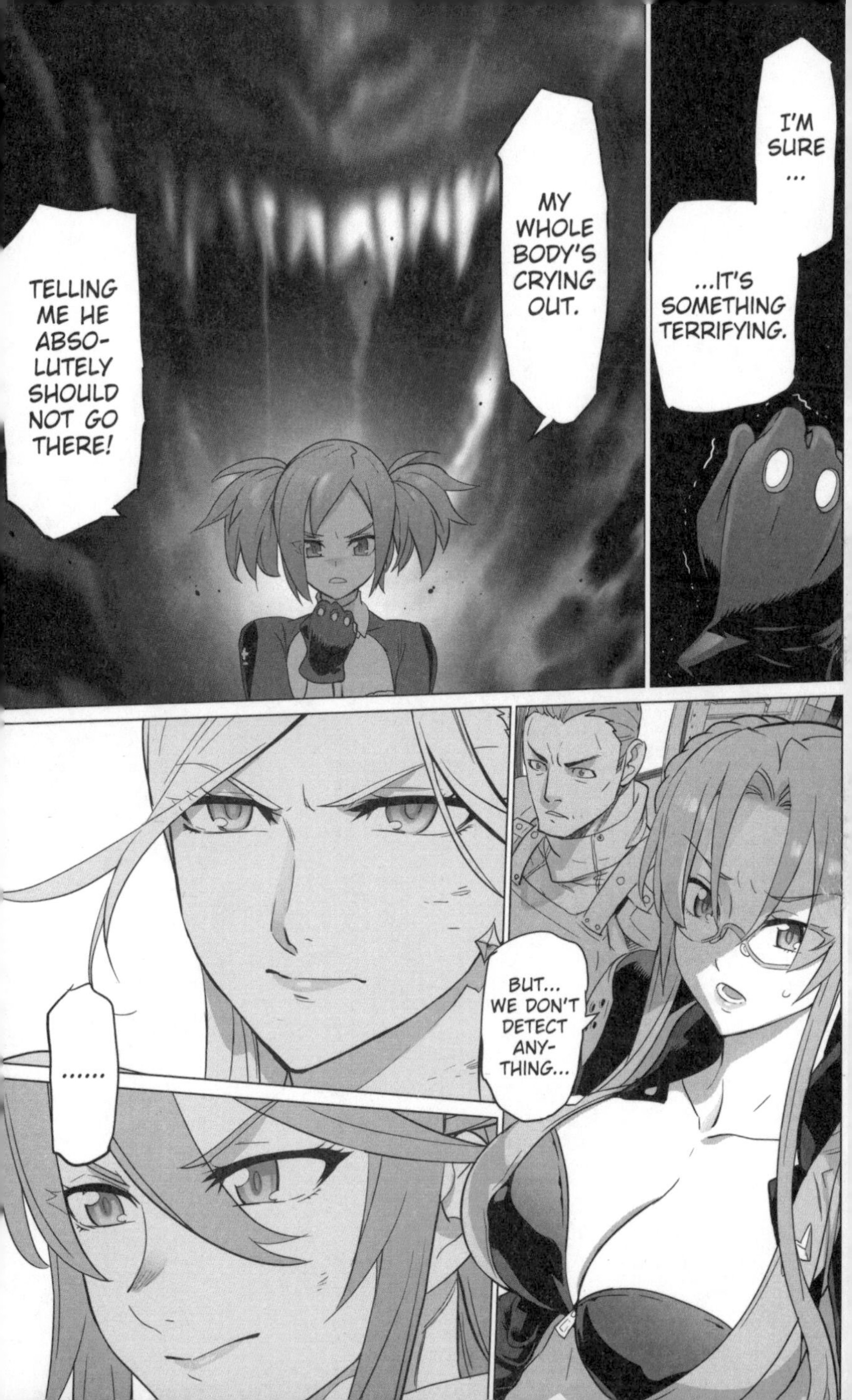
I'M SURE...
...IT'S SOMETHING TERRIFYING.
MY WHOLE BODY'S CRYING OUT.
TELLING ME HE ABSOLUTELY SHOULD NOT GO THERE!
BUT... WE DON'T DETECT ANYTHING...
......

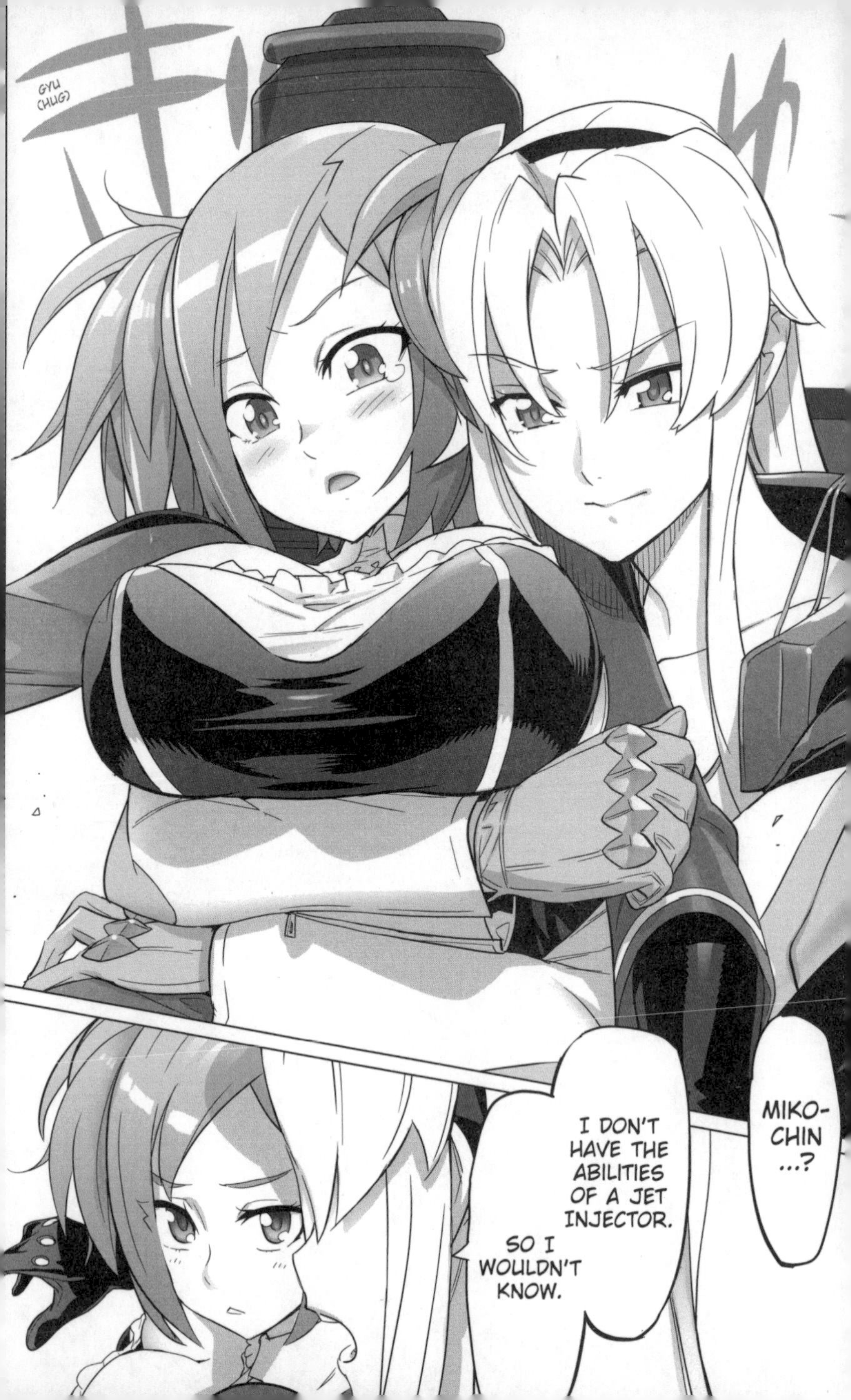
GYU (HUG)
MIKO-CHIN ...?
I DON'T HAVE THE ABILITIES OF A JET INJECTOR.
SO I WOULDN'T KNOW.

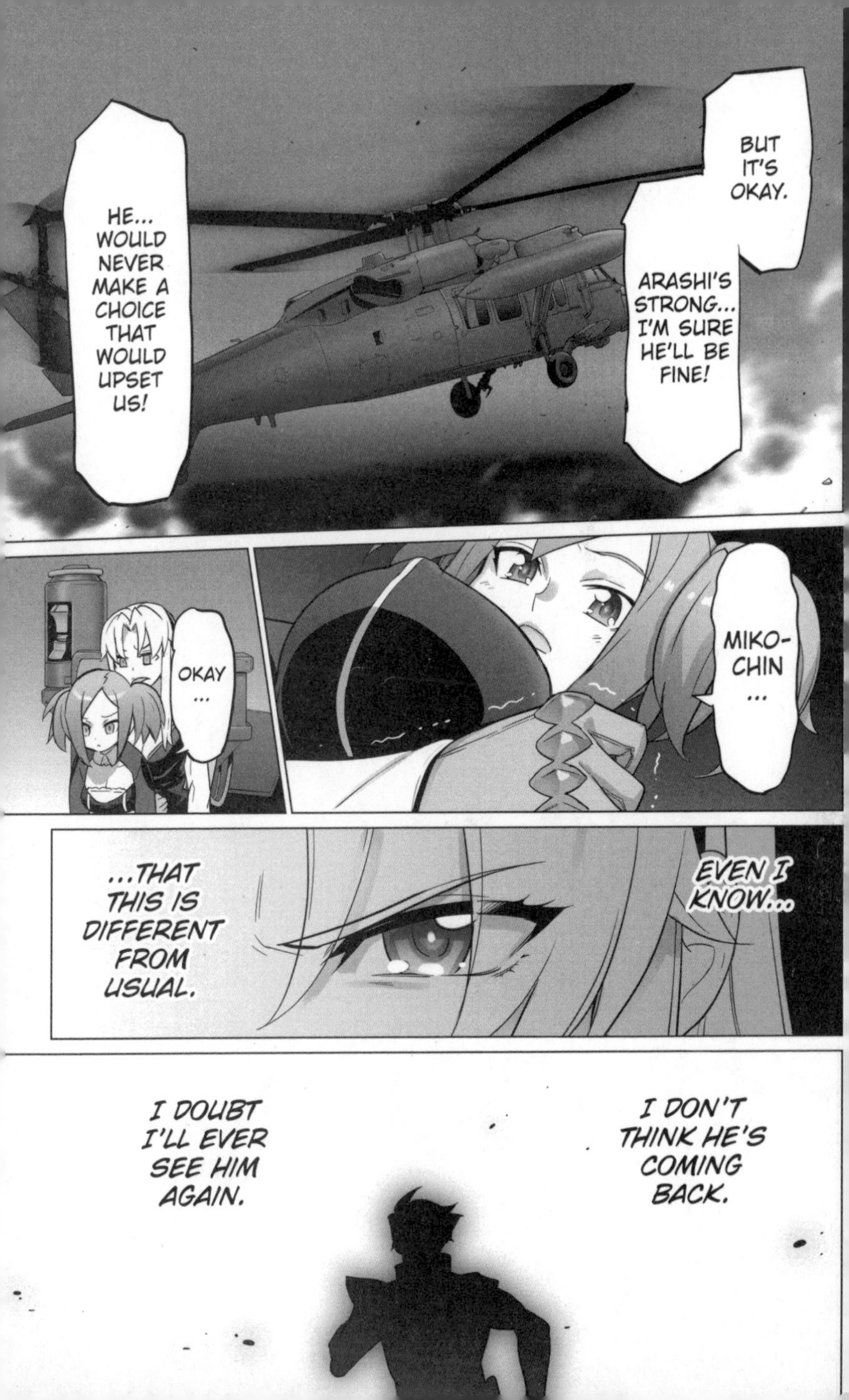
BUT IT'S OKAY.
ARASHI'S STRONG... I'M SURE HE'LL BE FINE!
HE... WOULD NEVER MAKE A CHOICE THAT WOULD UPSET US!
MIKO-CHIN...
OKAY...
EVEN I KNOW...
...THAT THIS IS DIFFERENT FROM USUAL.
I DON'T THINK HE'S COMING BACK.
I DOUBT I'LL EVER SEE HIM AGAIN.

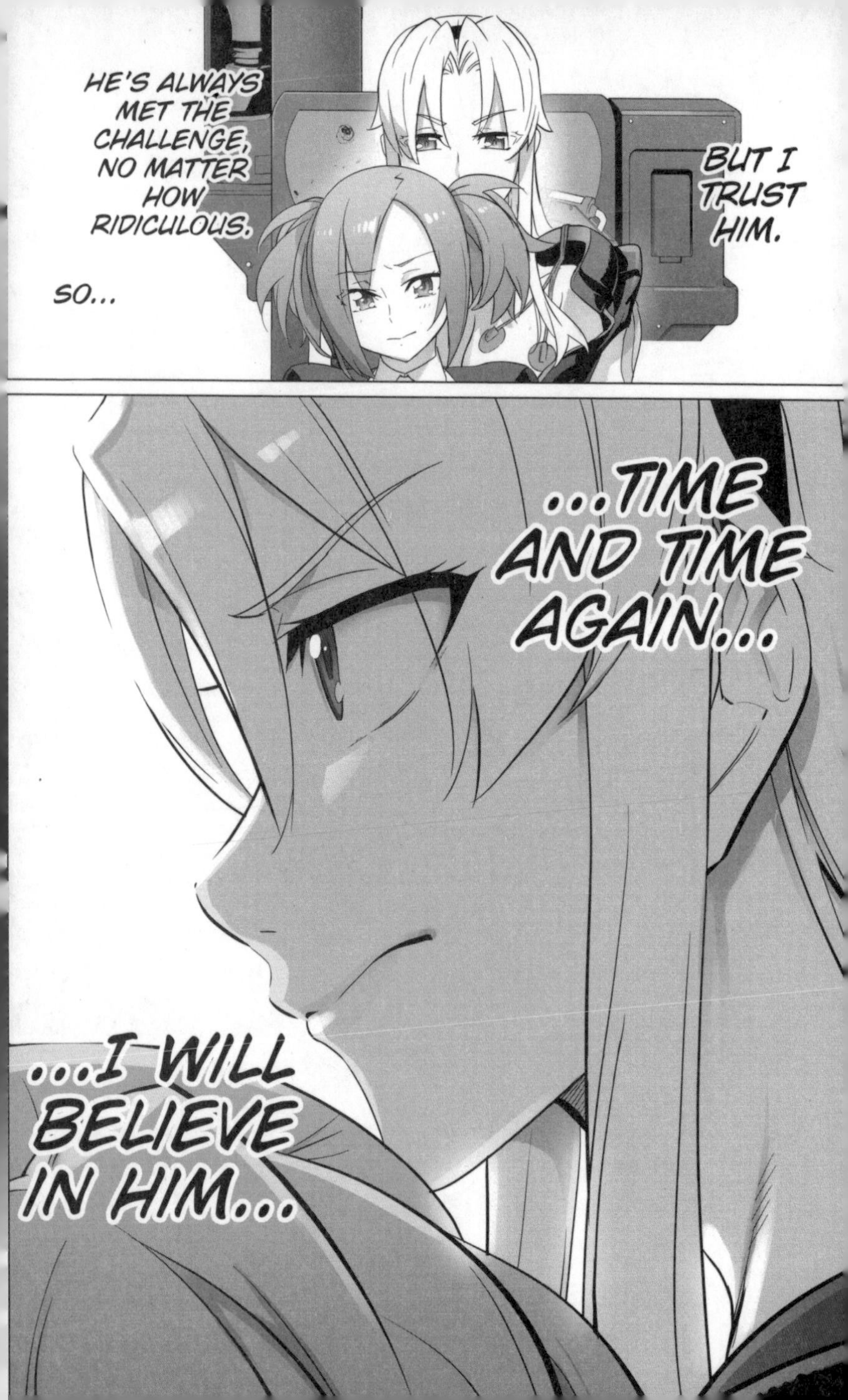
BUT I TRUST HIM.
HE'S ALWAYS MET THE CHALLENGE, NO MATTER HOW RIDICULOUS.
SO...
...TIME AND TIME AGAIN...
...I WILL BELIEVE IN HIM...

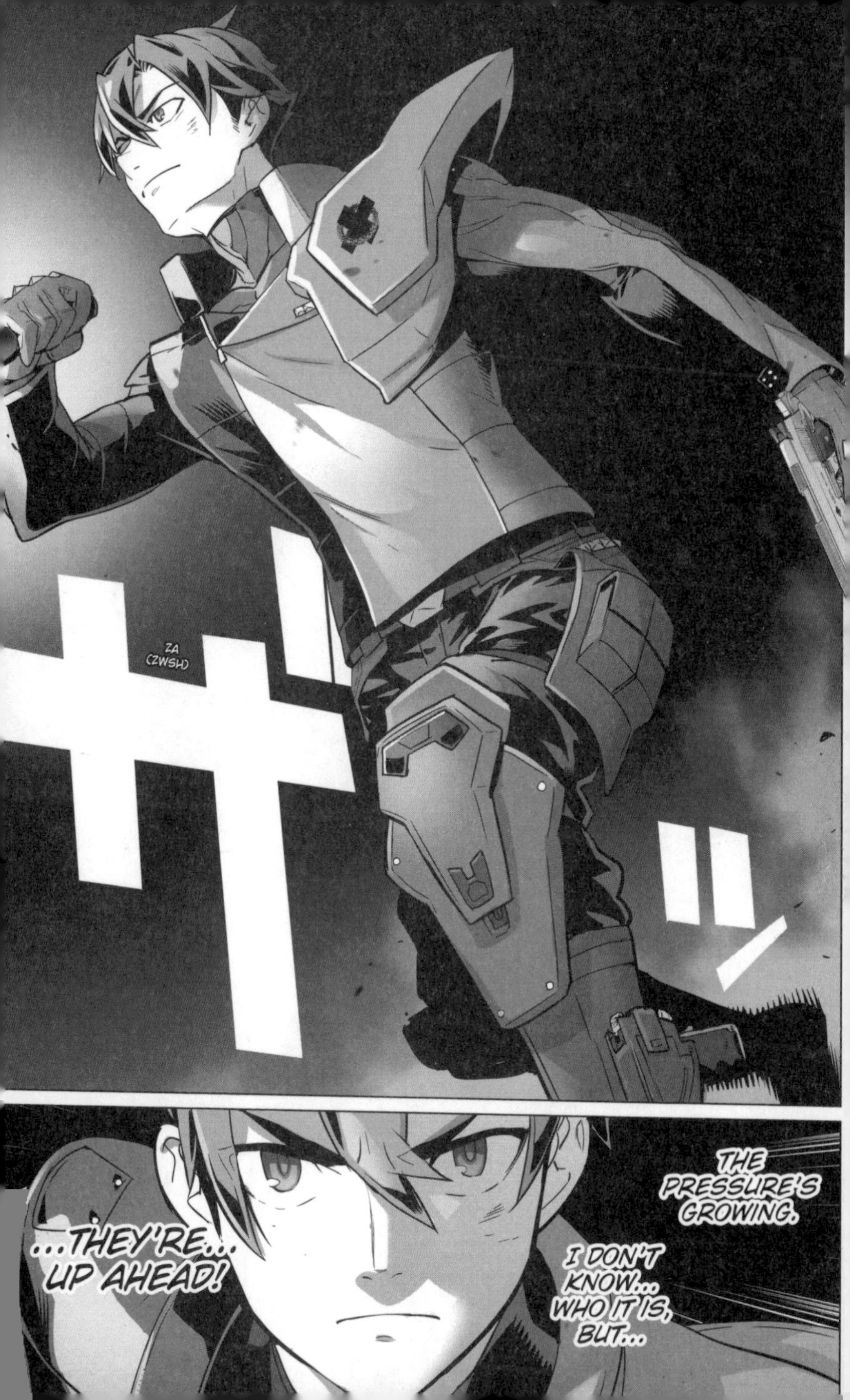
ザッ
ZA (ZWSH)
THE PRESSURE'S GROWING.
I DON'T KNOW... WHO IT IS, BUT...
...THEY'RE... UP AHEAD!

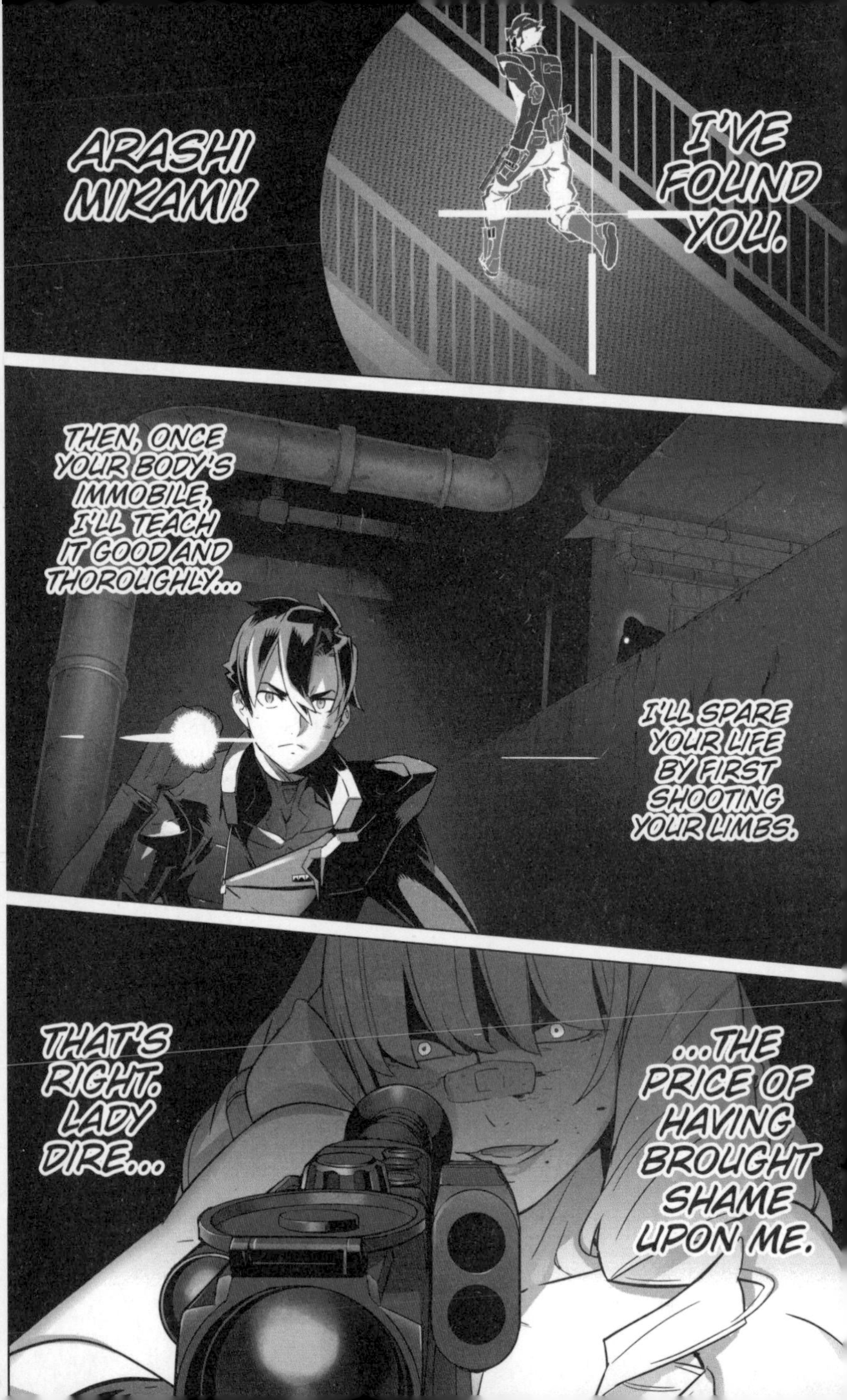
I'VE FOUND YOU.
ARASHI MIKAMI!
I'LL SPARE YOUR LIFE BY FIRST SHOOTING YOUR LIMBS.
THEN, ONCE YOUR BODY'S IMMOBILE, I'LL TEACH IT GOOD AND THOROUGHLY...
...THE PRICE OF HAVING BROUGHT SHAME UPON ME.
THAT'S RIGHT. LADY DIRE...

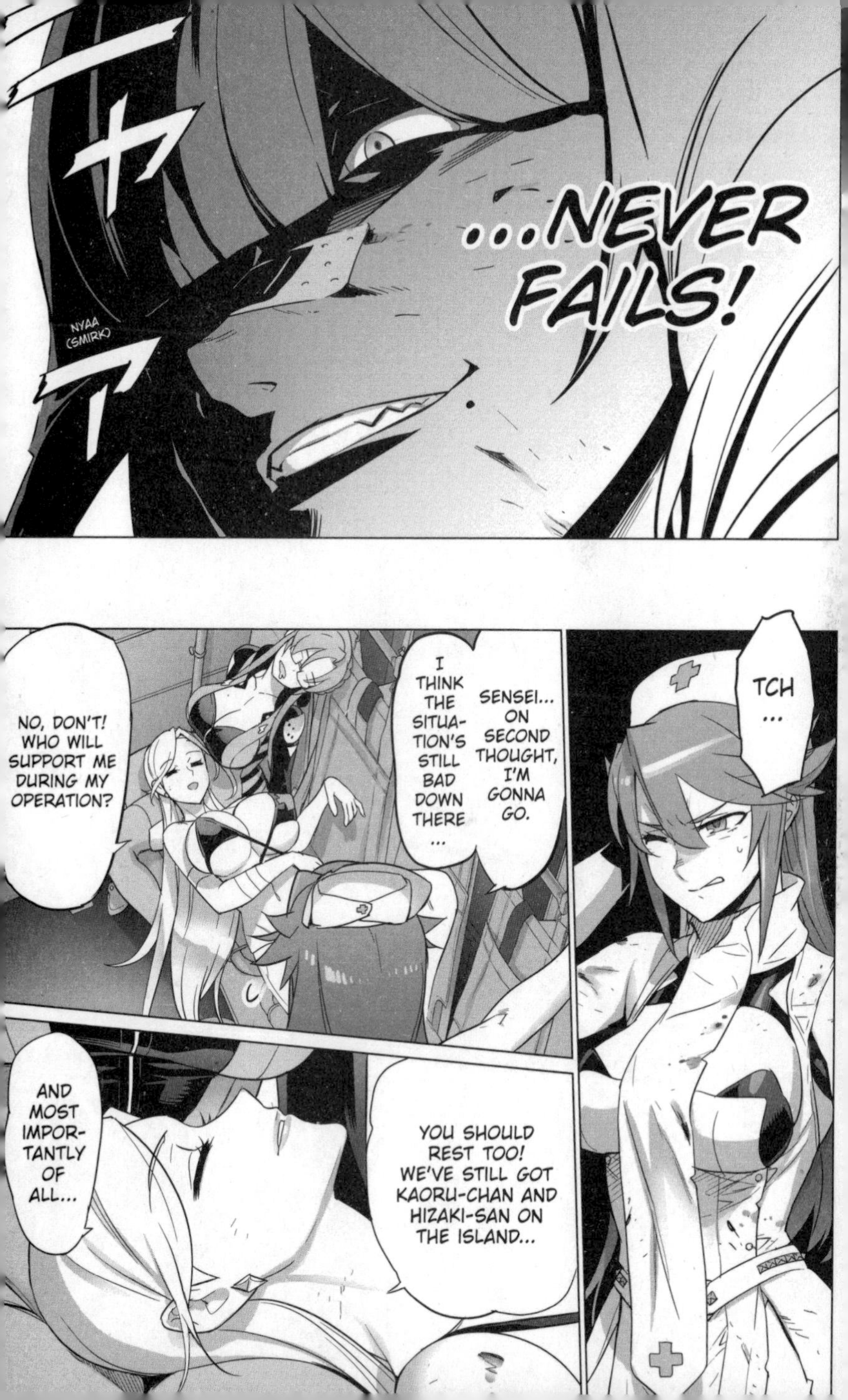
NYAA (SMIRK)
...NEVER FAILS!
TCH ...
SENSEI... ON SECOND THOUGHT, I'M GONNA GO.
I THINK THE SITUATION'S STILL BAD DOWN THERE ...
NO, DON'T! WHO WILL SUPPORT ME DURING MY OPERATION?
YOU SHOULD REST TOO! WE'VE STILL GOT KAORU-CHAN AND HIZAKI-SAN ON THE ISLAND...
AND MOST IMPORTANTLY OF ALL...

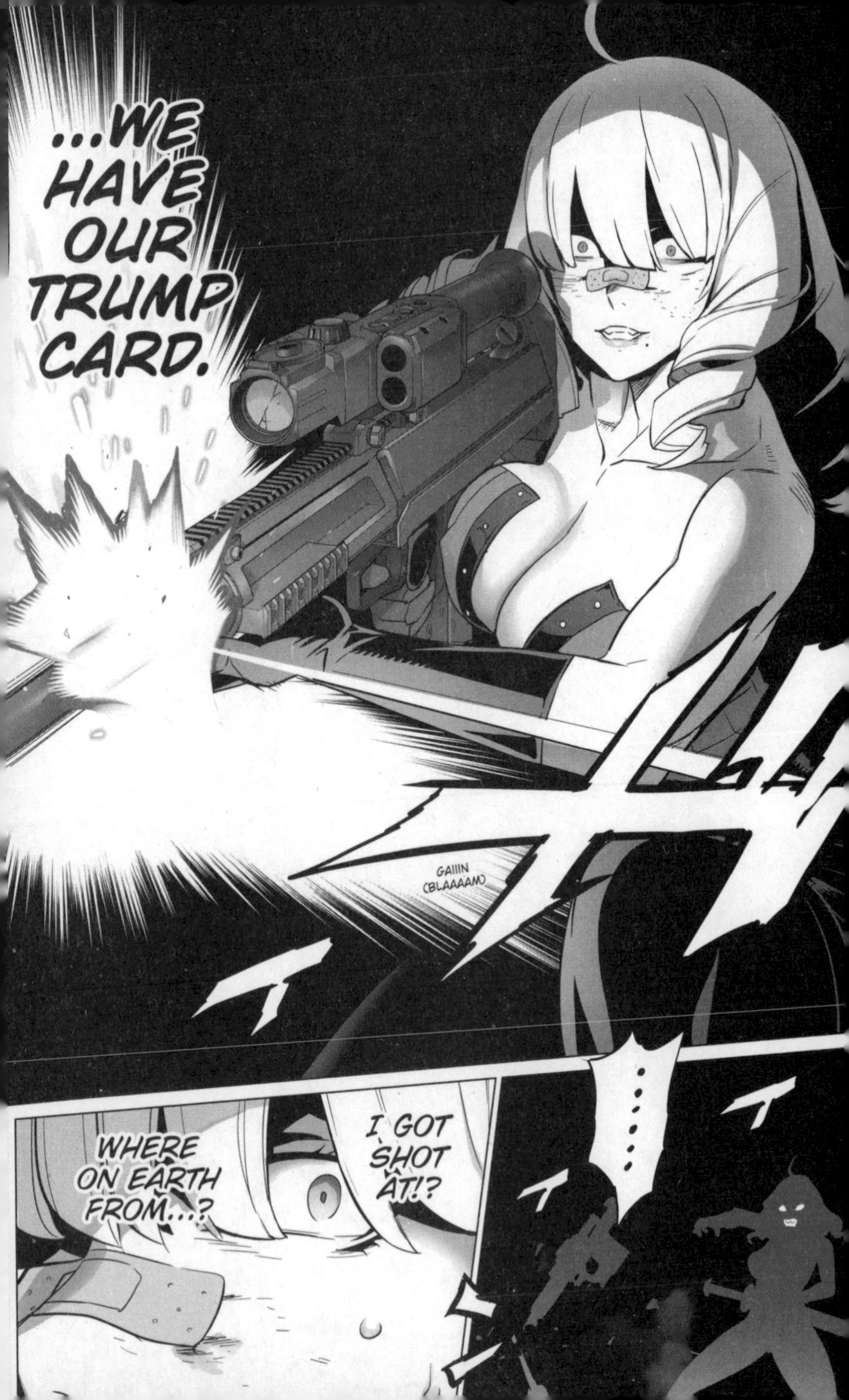
...WE HAVE OUR TRUMP CARD.
GAIIIN (BLAAAAM)
......
I GOT SHOT AT!?
WHERE ON EARTH FROM...?

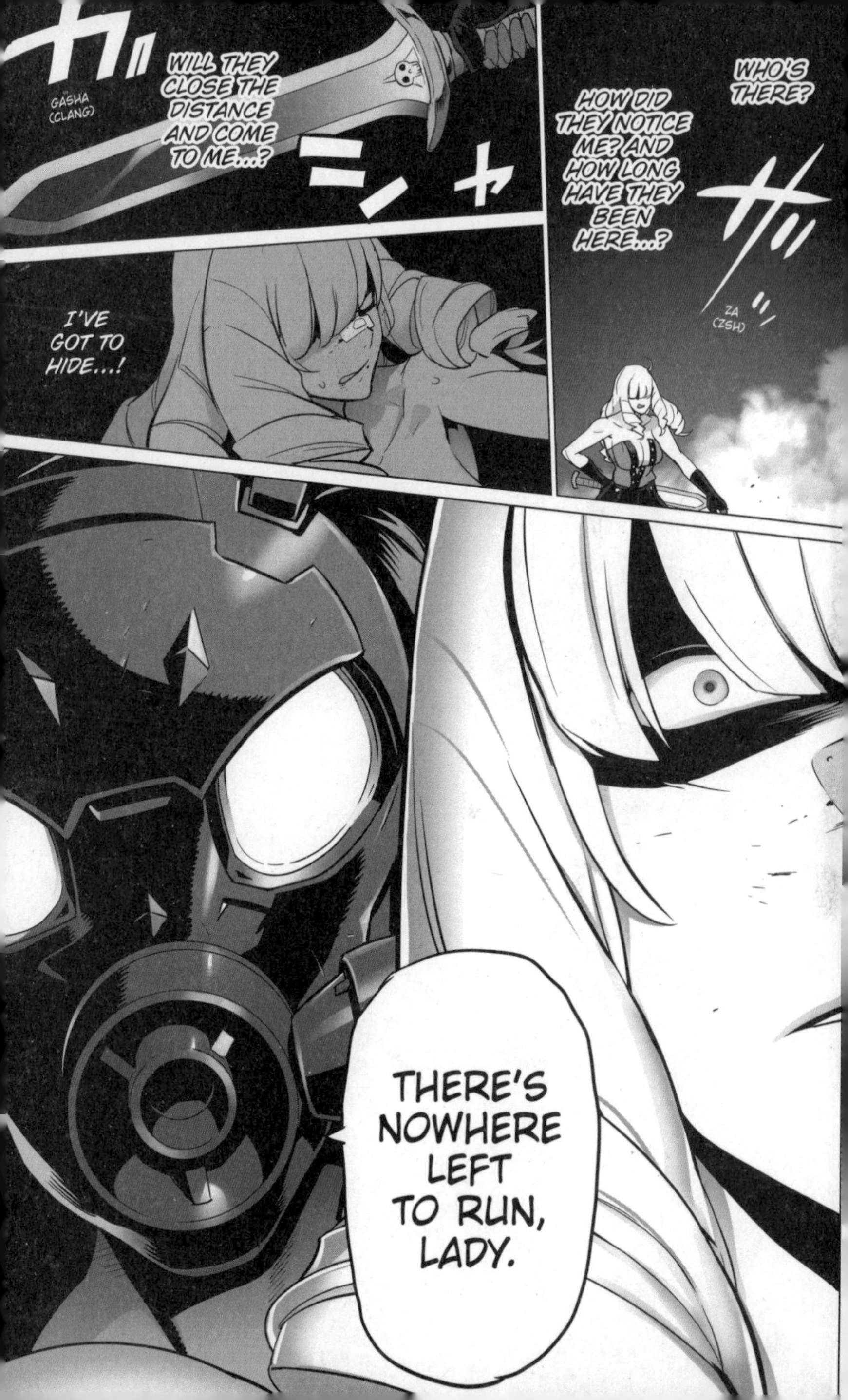
WHO'S THERE?
HOW DID THEY NOTICE ME? AND HOW LONG HAVE THEY BEEN HERE...?
ZA (ZSH)
WILL THEY CLOSE THE DISTANCE AND COME TO ME...?
GASHA (CLANG)
I'VE GOT TO HIDE...!
THERE'S NOWHERE LEFT TO RUN, LADY.

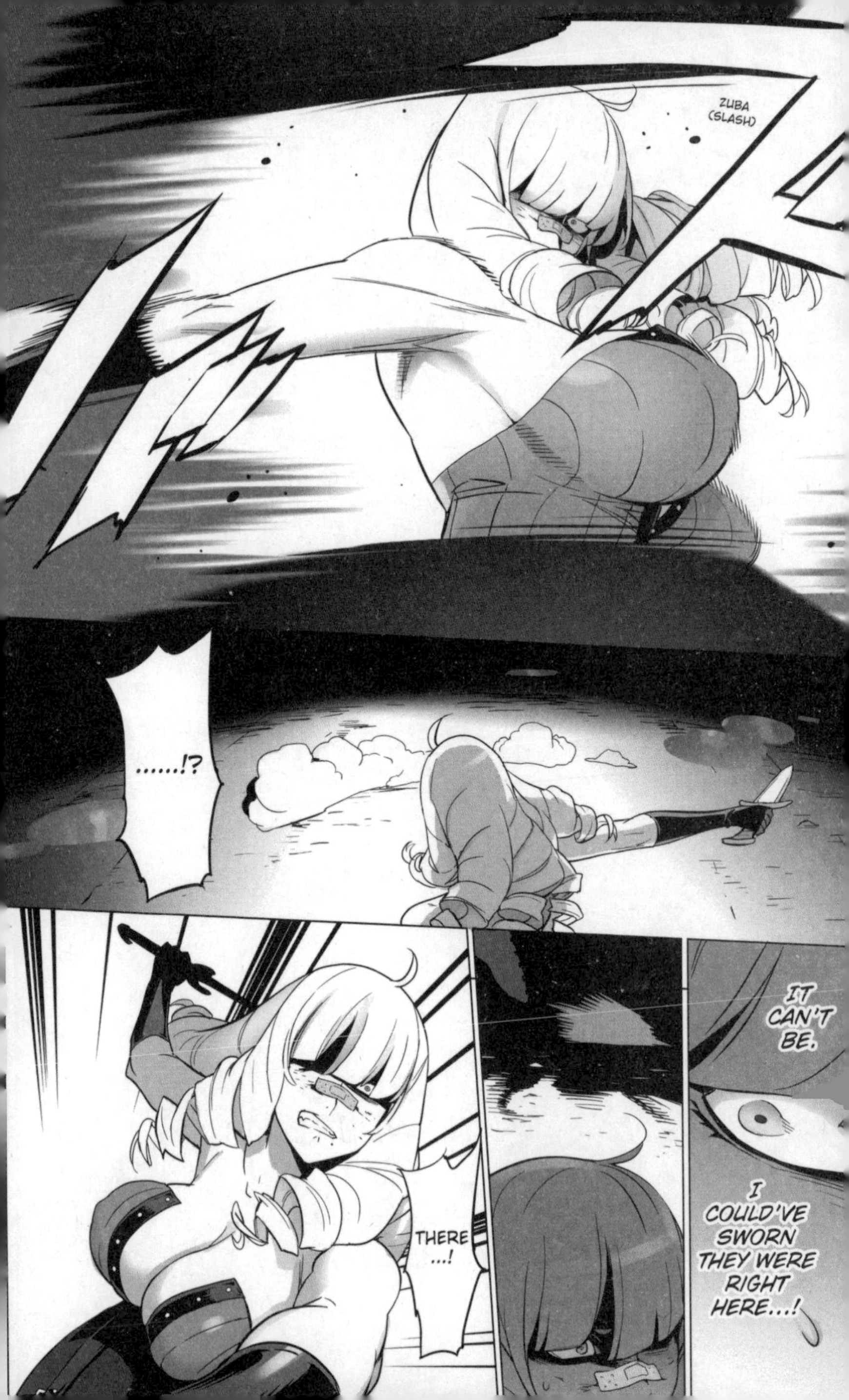
ZUBA (SLASH)
......!?
IT CAN'T BE.
I COULD'VE SWORN THEY WERE RIGHT HERE...!
THERE ...!

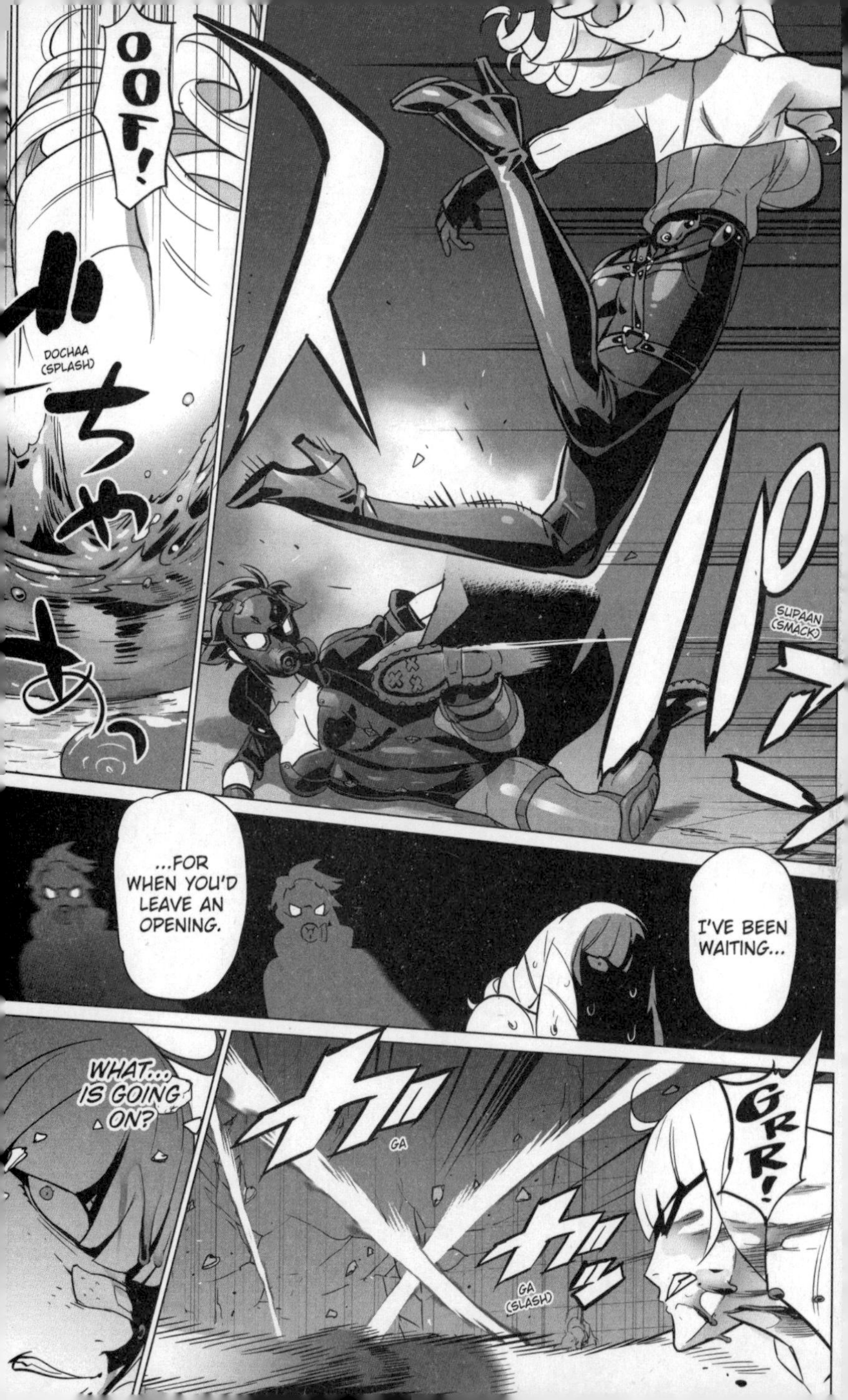
SUPAAN (SMACK)
OOF!
DOCHAA (SPLASH)
I'VE BEEN WAITING...
...FOR WHEN YOU'D LEAVE AN OPENING.
GRR!
GA (SLASH)
GA
WHAT... IS GOING ON?

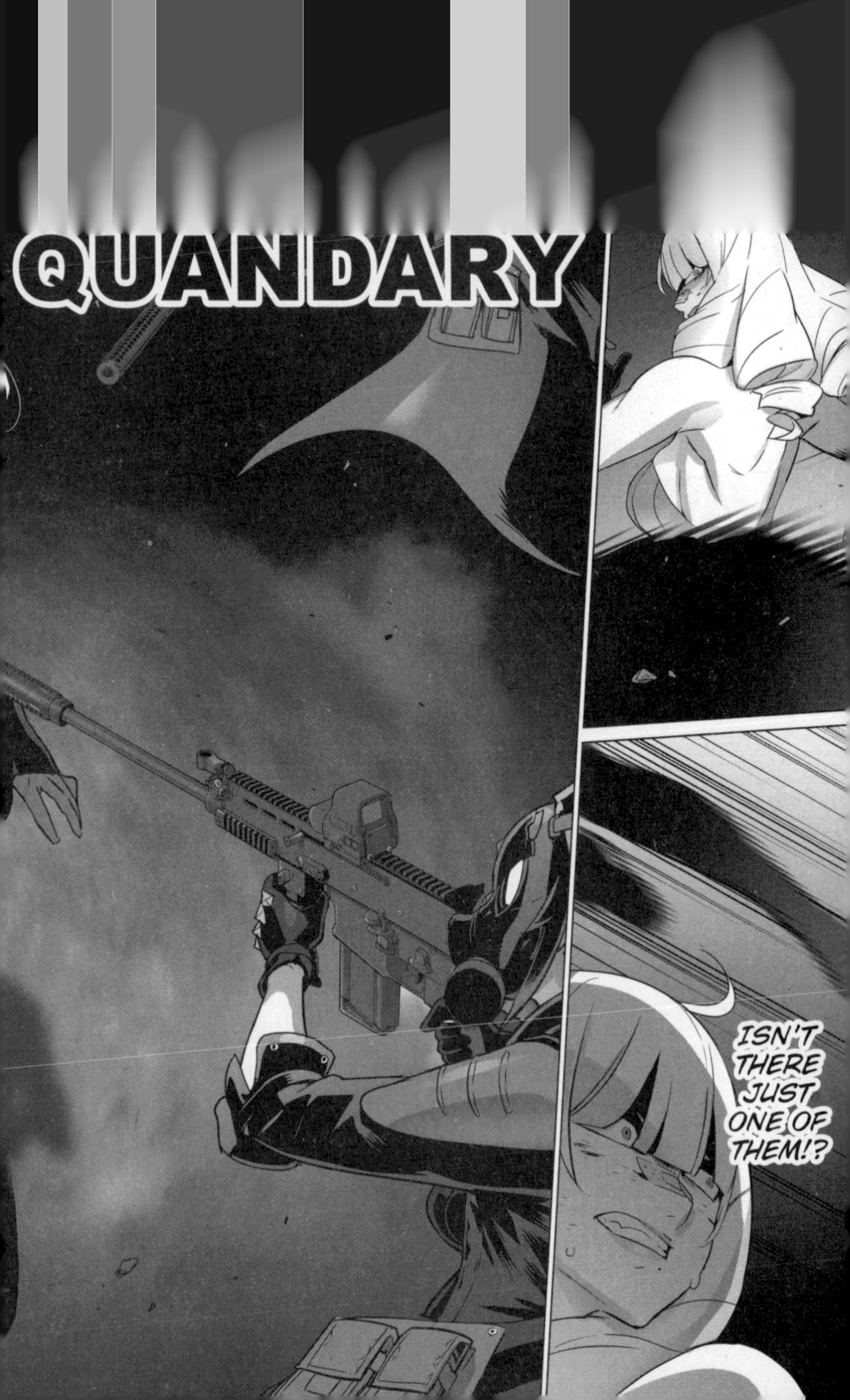
ISN'T THERE JUST ONE OF THEM!?
QUANDARY

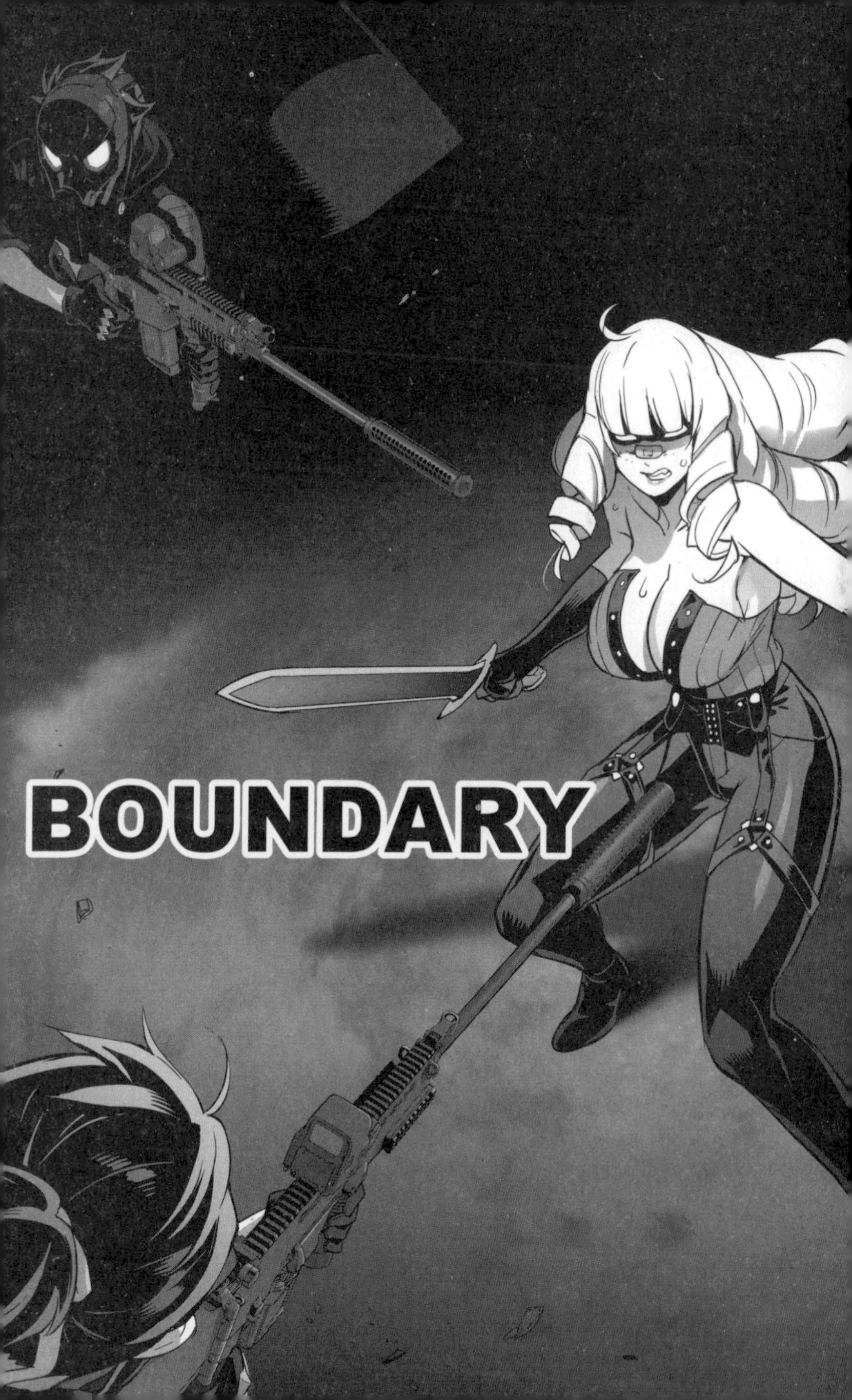
BOUNDARY

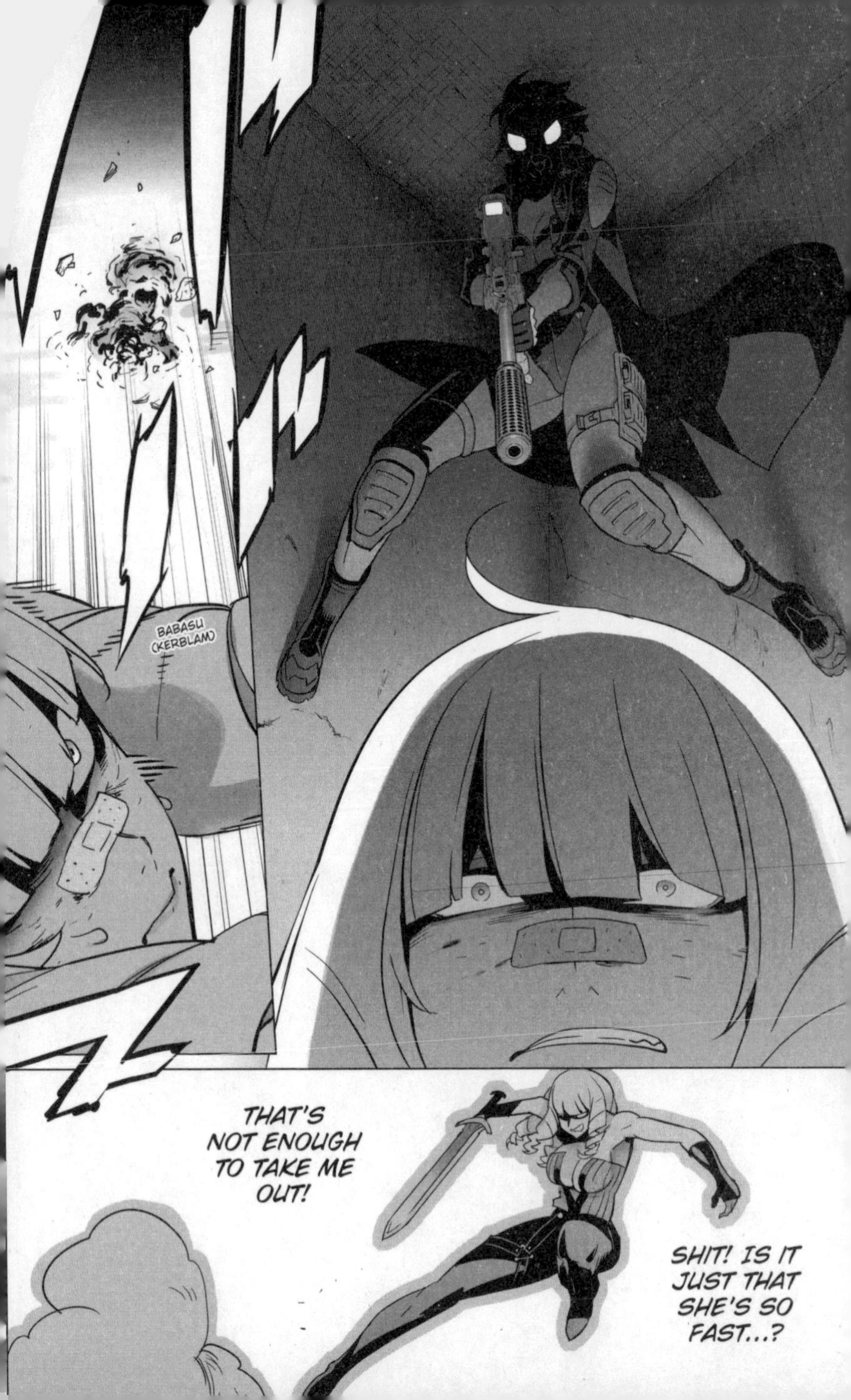
BABASU (KERBLAM)
THAT'S NOT ENOUGH TO TAKE ME OUT!
SHIT! IS IT JUST THAT SHE'S SO FAST...?

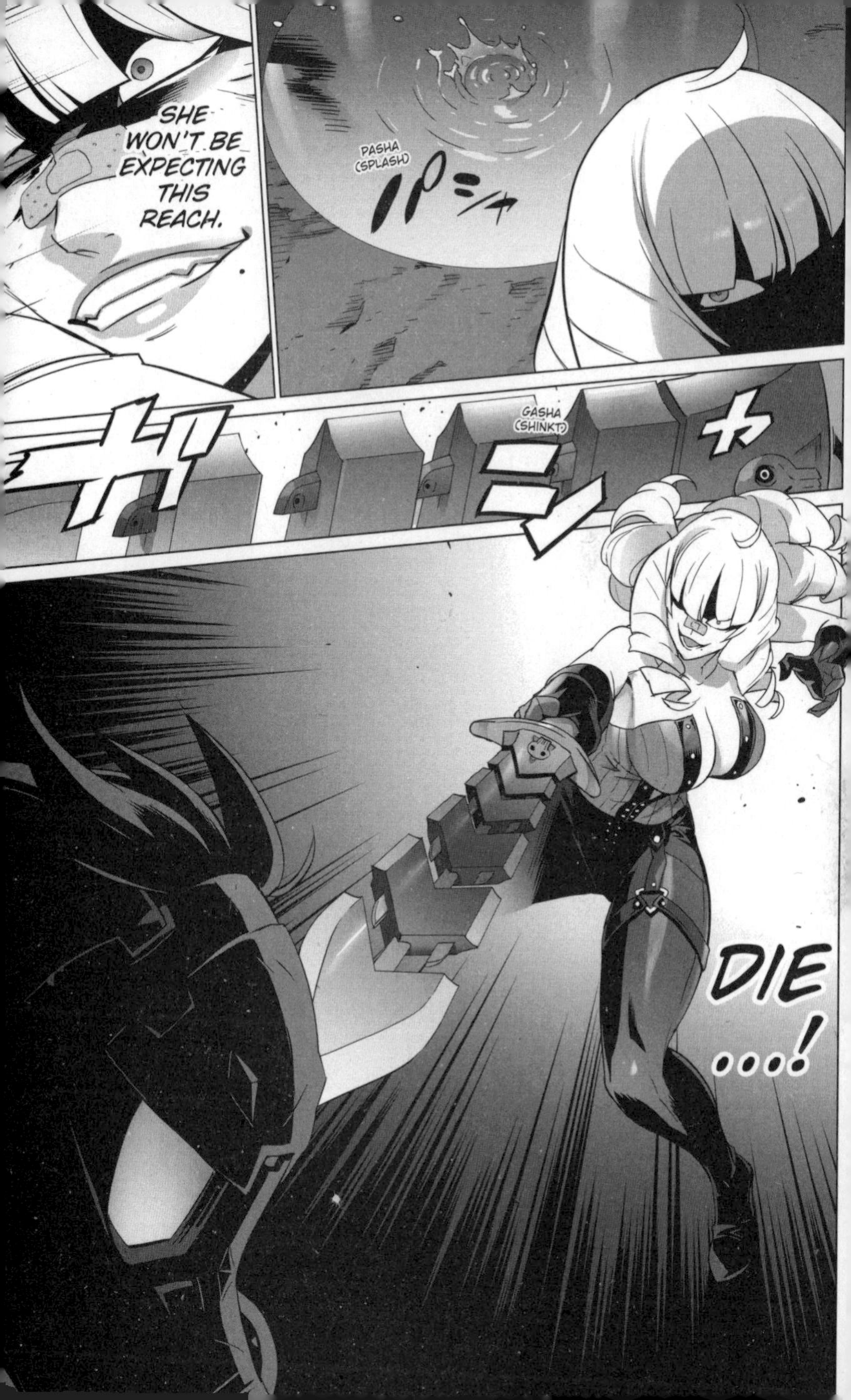
PASHA (SPLASH)
SHE WON'T BE EXPECTING THIS REACH.
GASHA (SHINKT)
DIE...!

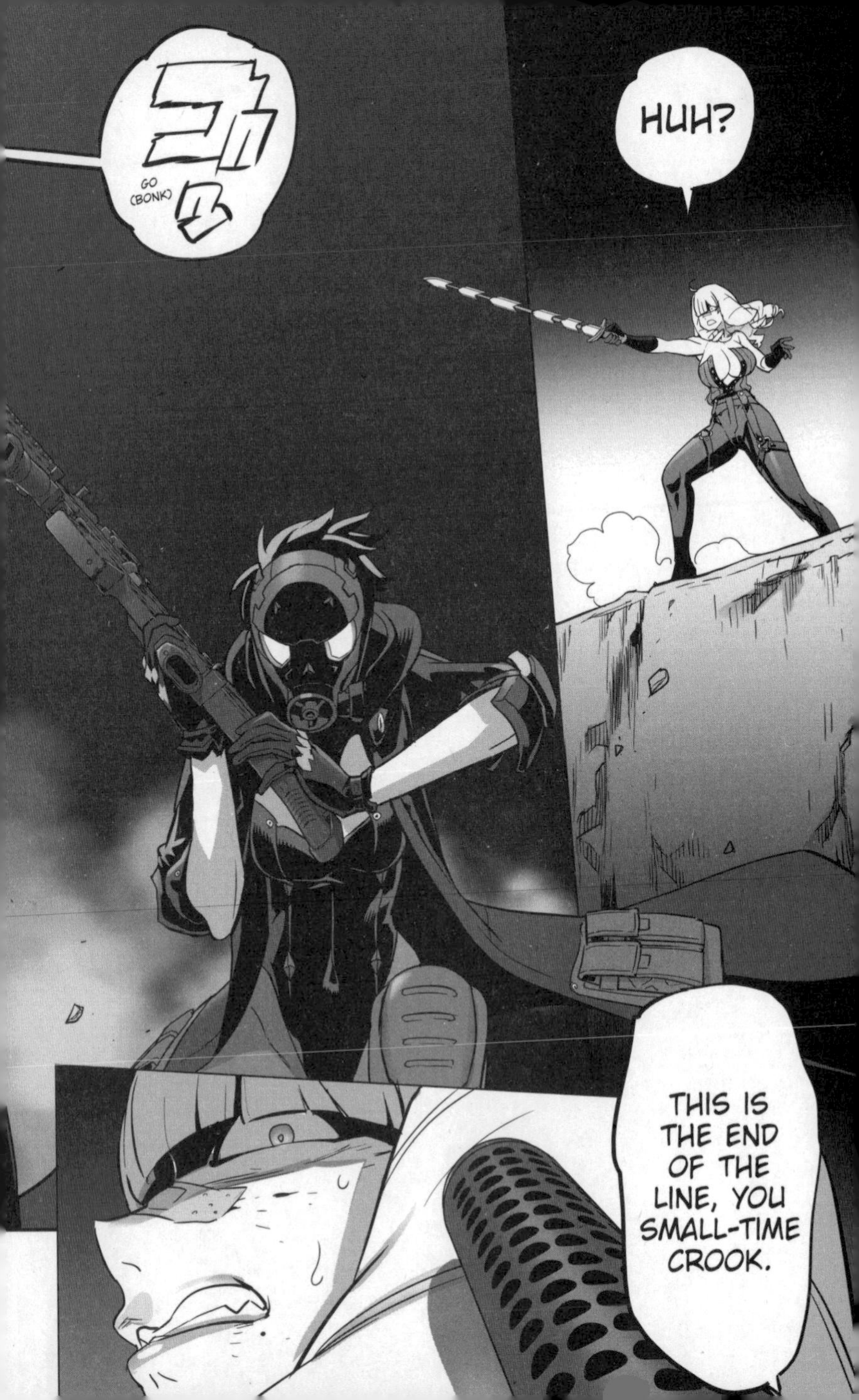
HUH?
ゴッ
GO (BONK)
THIS IS THE END OF THE LINE, YOU SMALL-TIME CROOK.

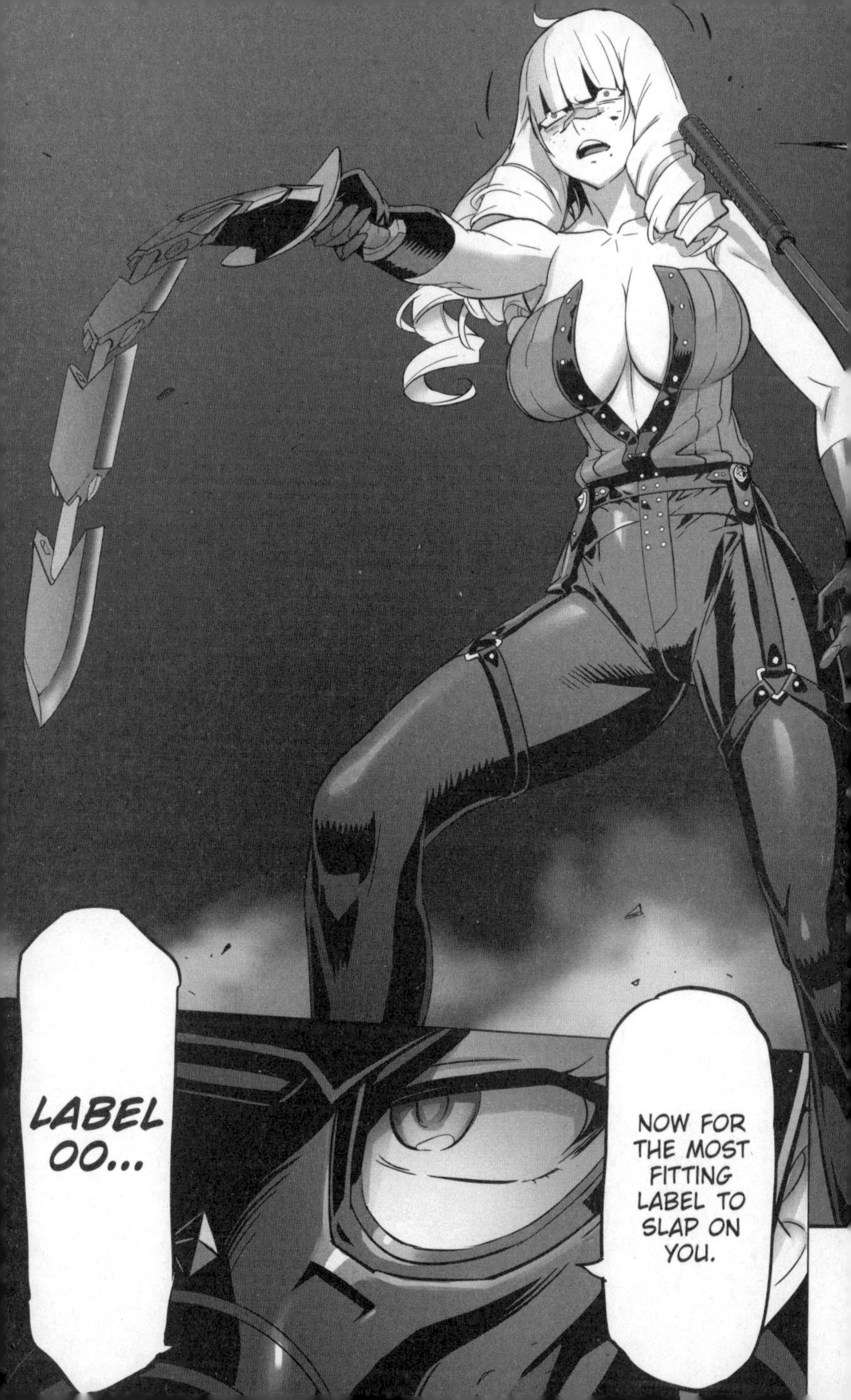
NOW FOR THE MOST FITTING LABEL TO SLAP ON YOU.
LABEL OO...

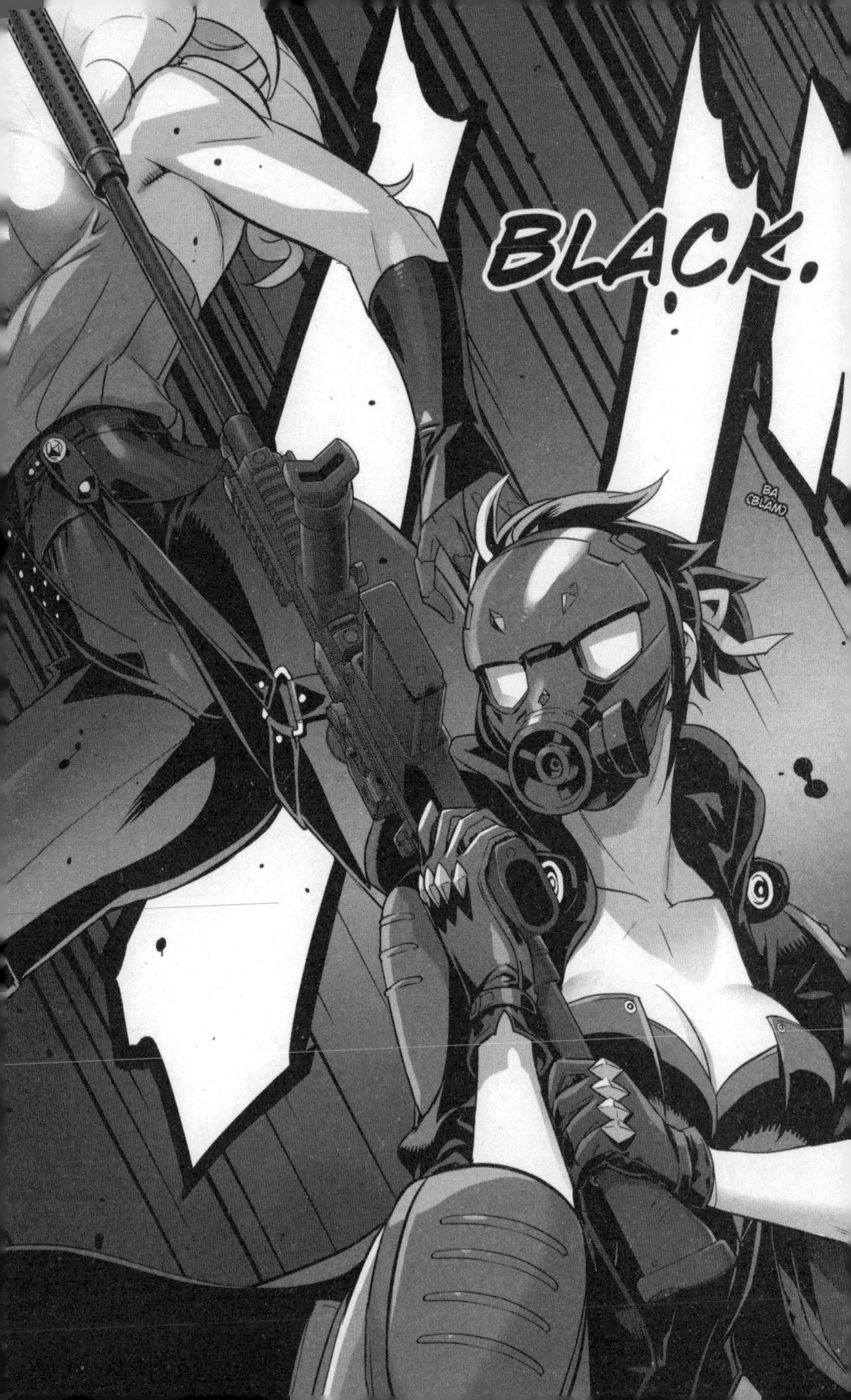
BLACK.
BA (BLAM)

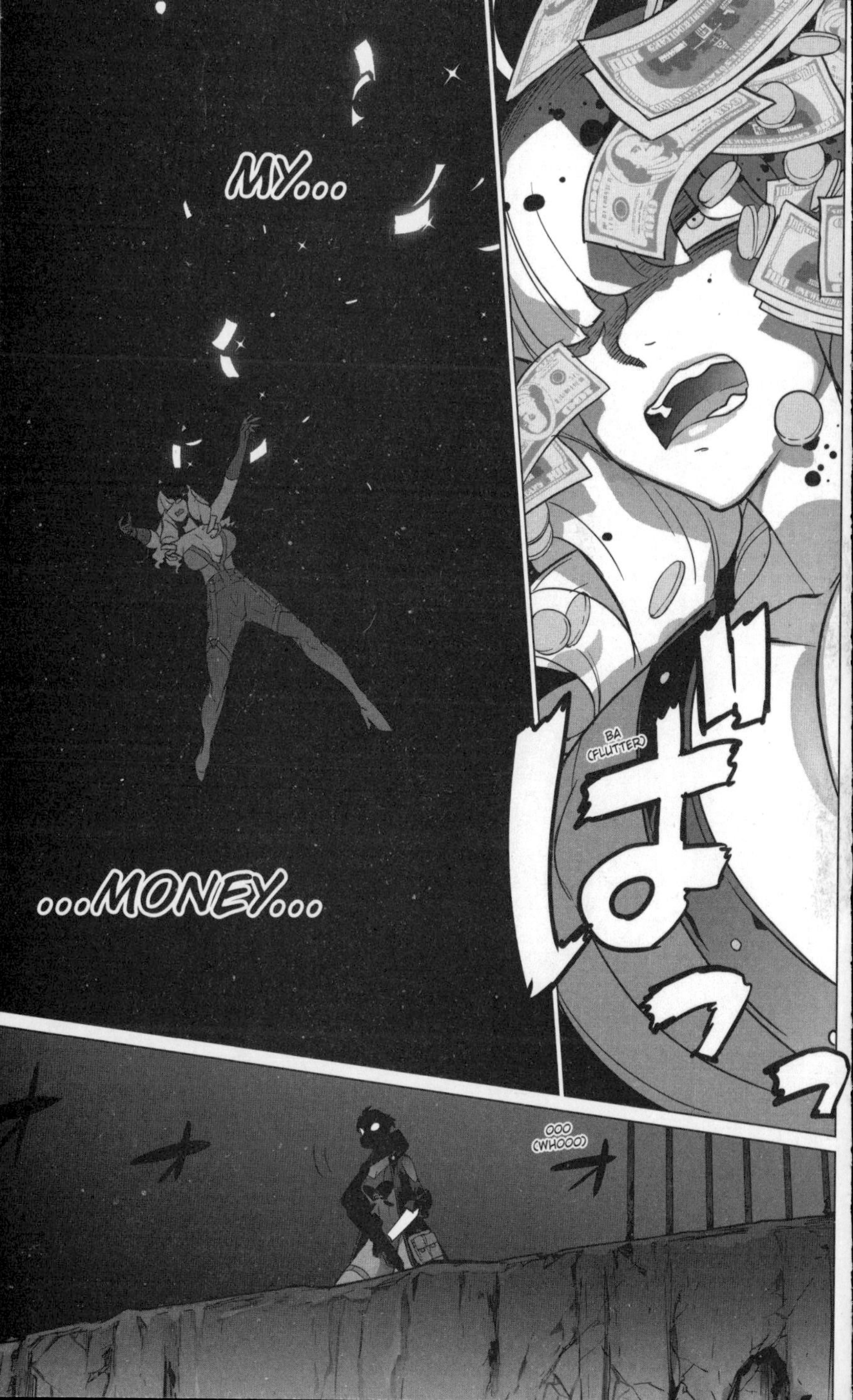
BA (FLUTTER)
MY...
...MONEY...
OOO (WHOOO)

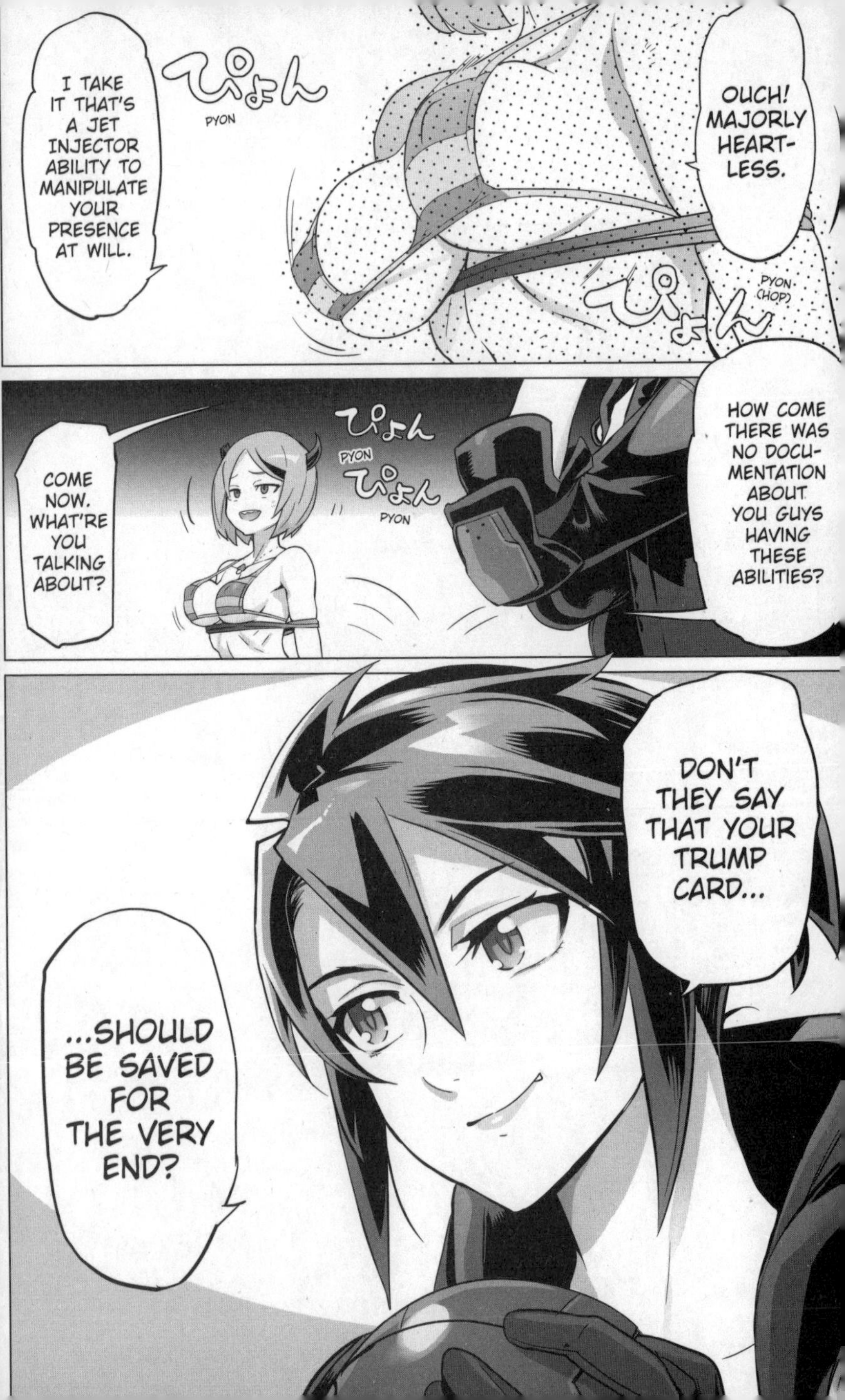
OUCH! MAJORLY HEART-LESS.
ぴょん
PYON (HOP)
I TAKE IT THAT'S A JET INJECTOR ABILITY TO MANIPULATE YOUR PRESENCE AT WILL.
ぴょん
PYON
HOW COME THERE WAS NO DOCU-MENTATION ABOUT YOU GUYS HAVING THESE ABILITIES?
ぴょん
PYON
ぴょん
PYON
COME NOW. WHAT'RE YOU TALKING ABOUT?
DON'T THEY SAY THAT YOUR TRUMP CARD...
...SHOULD BE SAVED FOR THE VERY END?

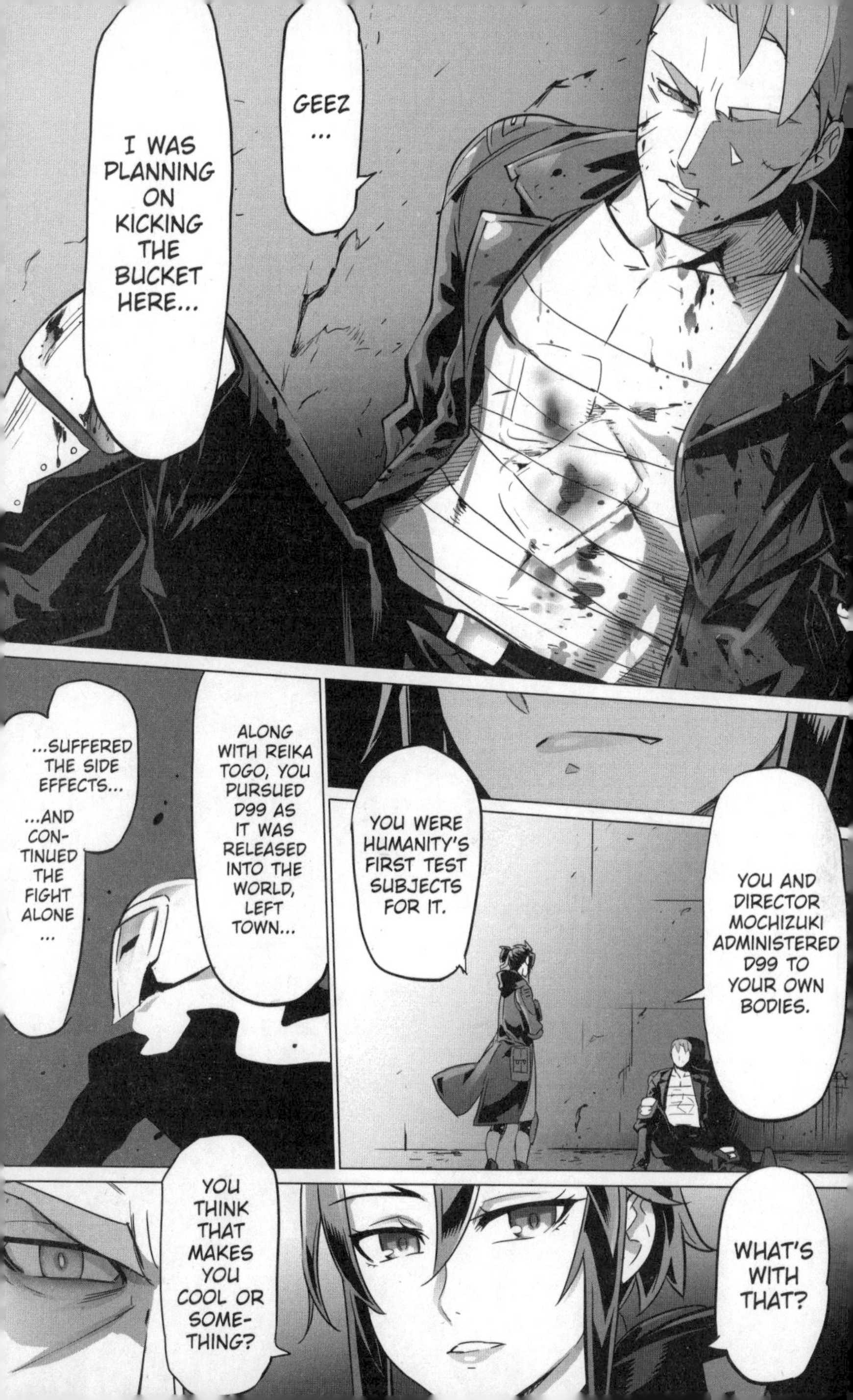
GEEZ ...
I WAS PLANNING ON KICKING THE BUCKET HERE...
YOU AND DIRECTOR MOCHIZUKI ADMINISTERED D99 TO YOUR OWN BODIES.
YOU WERE HUMANITY'S FIRST TEST SUBJECTS FOR IT.
ALONG WITH REIKA TOGO, YOU PURSUED D99 AS IT WAS RELEASED INTO THE WORLD, LEFT TOWN...
...SUFFERED THE SIDE EFFECTS...
...AND CON-TINUED THE FIGHT ALONE ...
WHAT'S WITH THAT?
YOU THINK THAT MAKES YOU COOL OR SOME-THING?

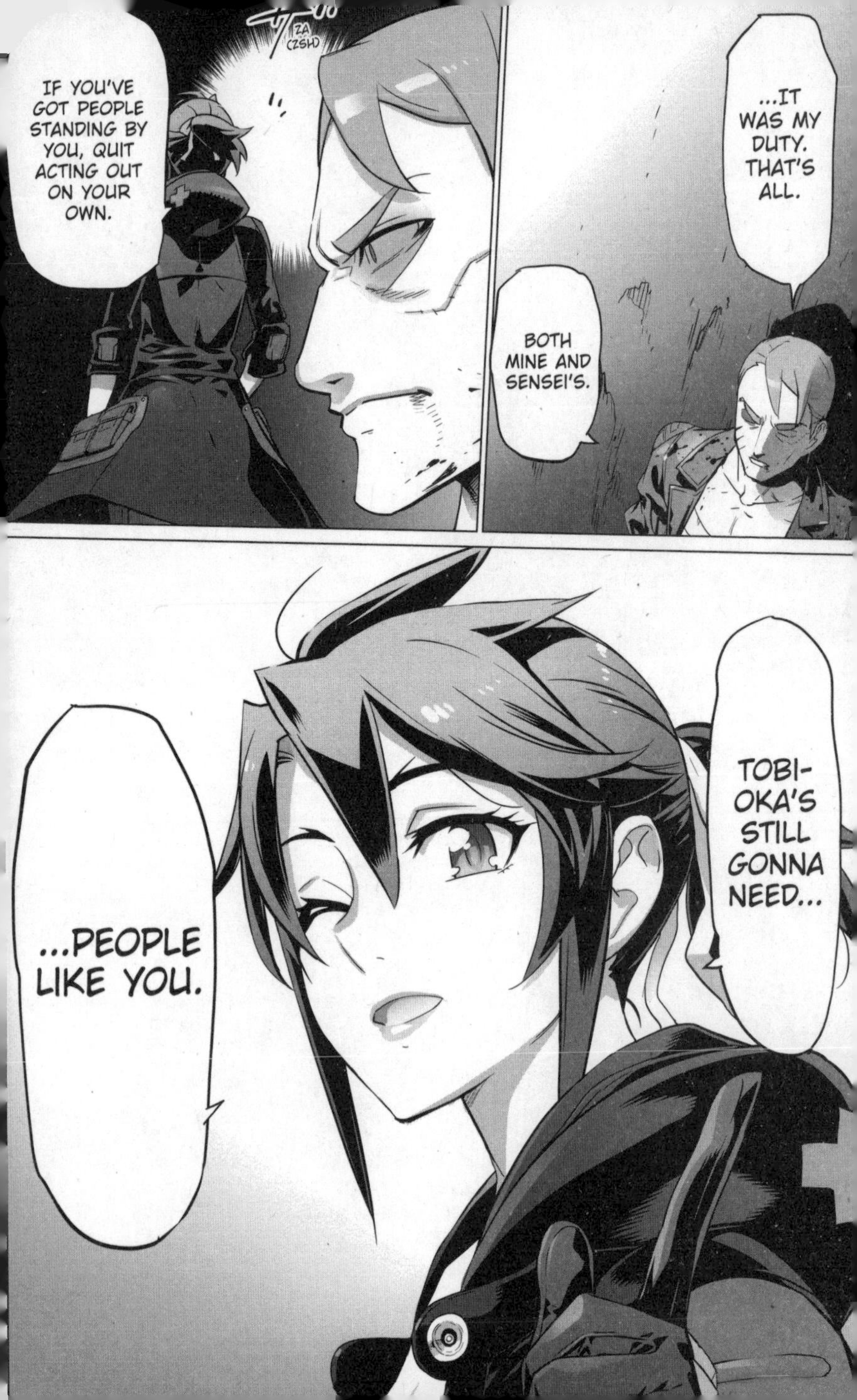
...IT WAS MY DUTY. THAT'S ALL.
BOTH MINE AND SENSEI'S.
ZA (ZSH)
IF YOU'VE GOT PEOPLE STANDING BY YOU, QUIT ACTING OUT ON YOUR OWN.
TOBI-OKA'S STILL GONNA NEED...
...PEOPLE LIKE YOU.

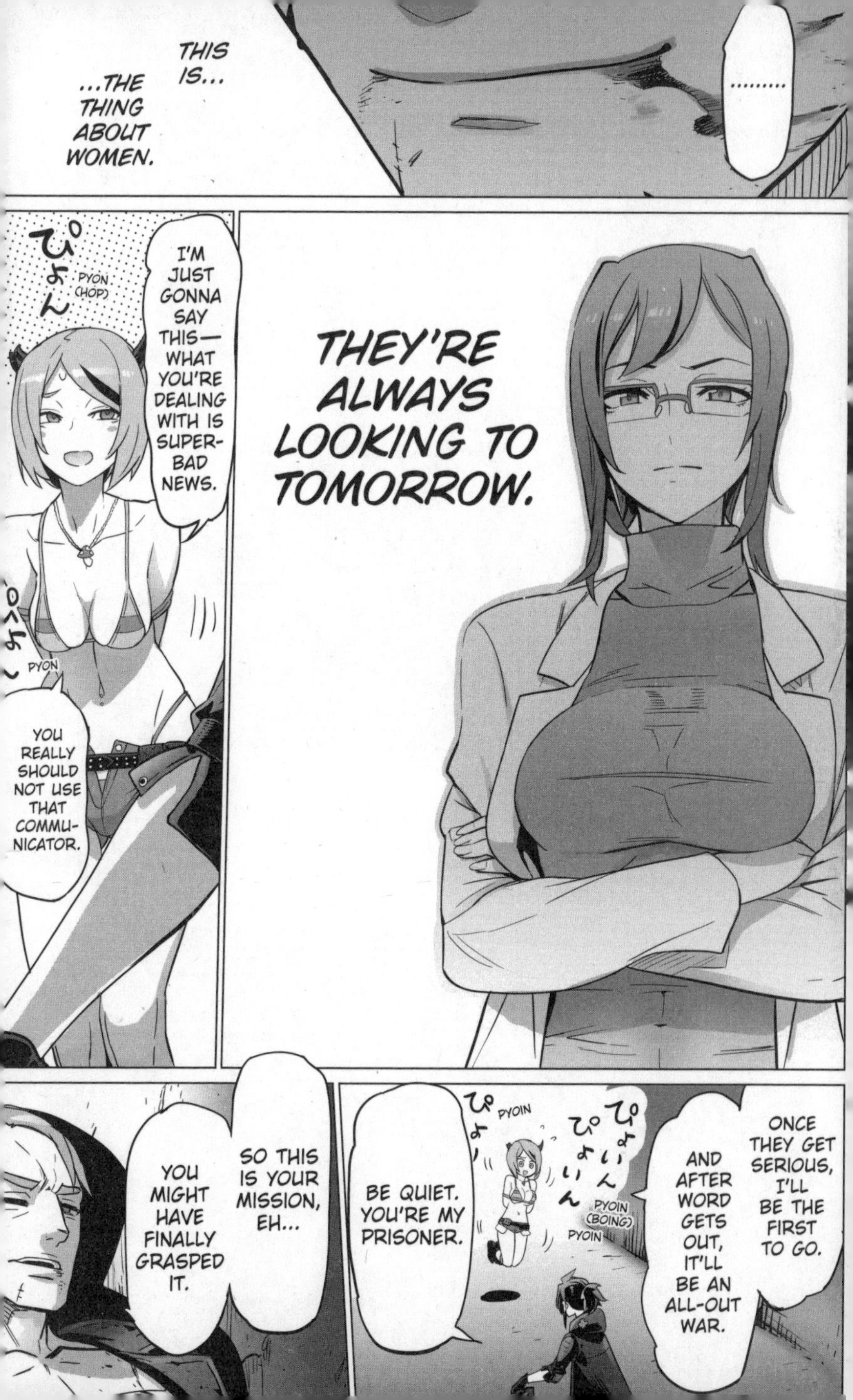
....
THIS IS...
...THE THING ABOUT WOMEN.
THEY'RE ALWAYS LOOKING TO TOMORROW.
ぴょん
PYON (HOP)
I'M JUST GONNA SAY THIS— WHAT YOU'RE DEALING WITH IS SUPER-BAD NEWS.
ぴょん
PYON
YOU REALLY SHOULD NOT USE THAT COMMUNICATOR.
ONCE THEY GET SERIOUS, I'LL BE THE FIRST TO GO.
AND AFTER WORD GETS OUT, IT'LL BE AN ALL-OUT WAR.
ぴょいん ぴょいん
PYOIN (BOING) PYOIN
ぴょ〜
PYOIN
BE QUIET. YOU'RE MY PRISONER.
SO THIS IS YOUR MISSION, EH...
YOU MIGHT HAVE FINALLY GRASPED IT.

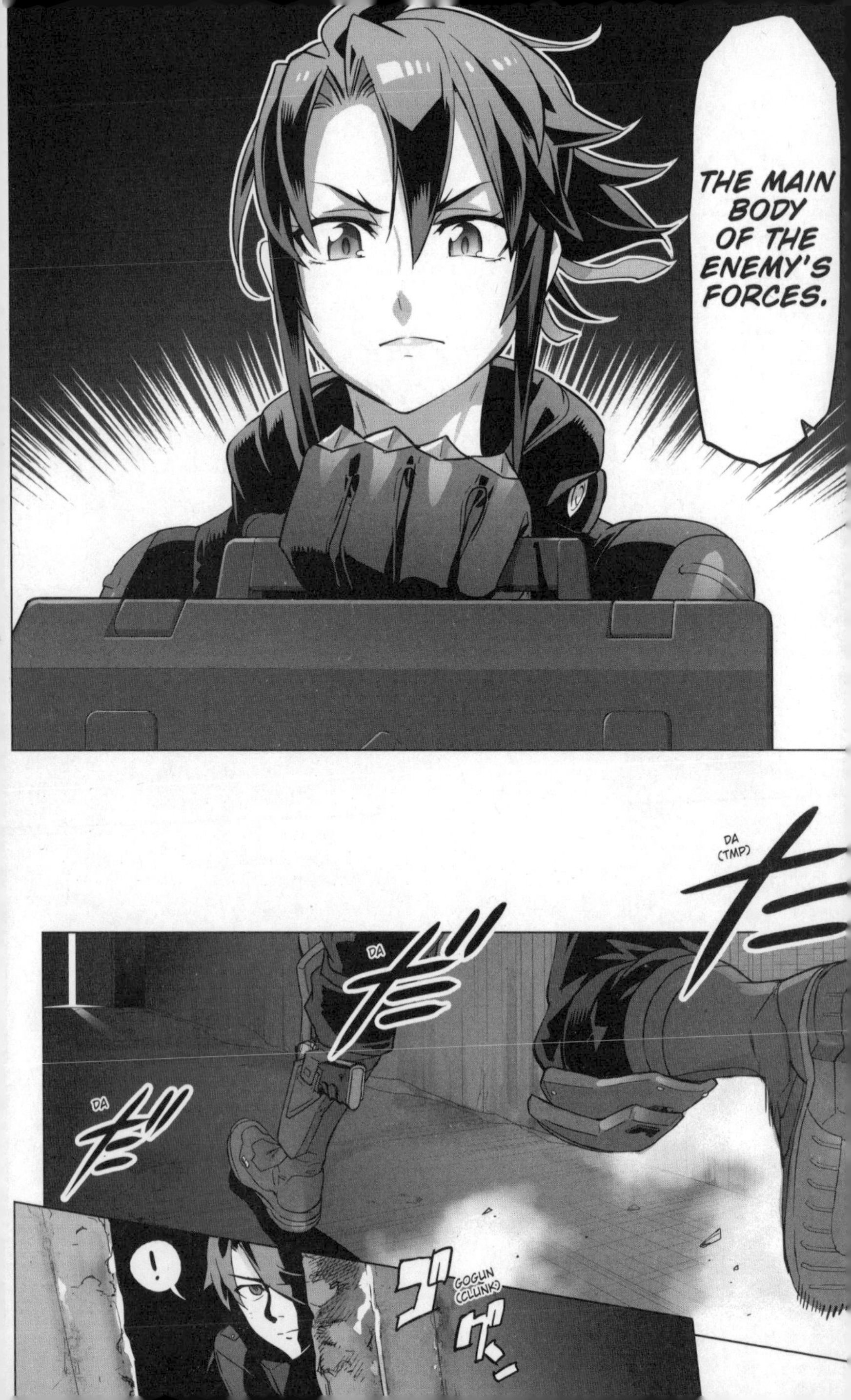
THE MAIN BODY OF THE ENEMY'S FORCES.
DA (TMP)
DA
DA
GOGUN (CLUNK)
!

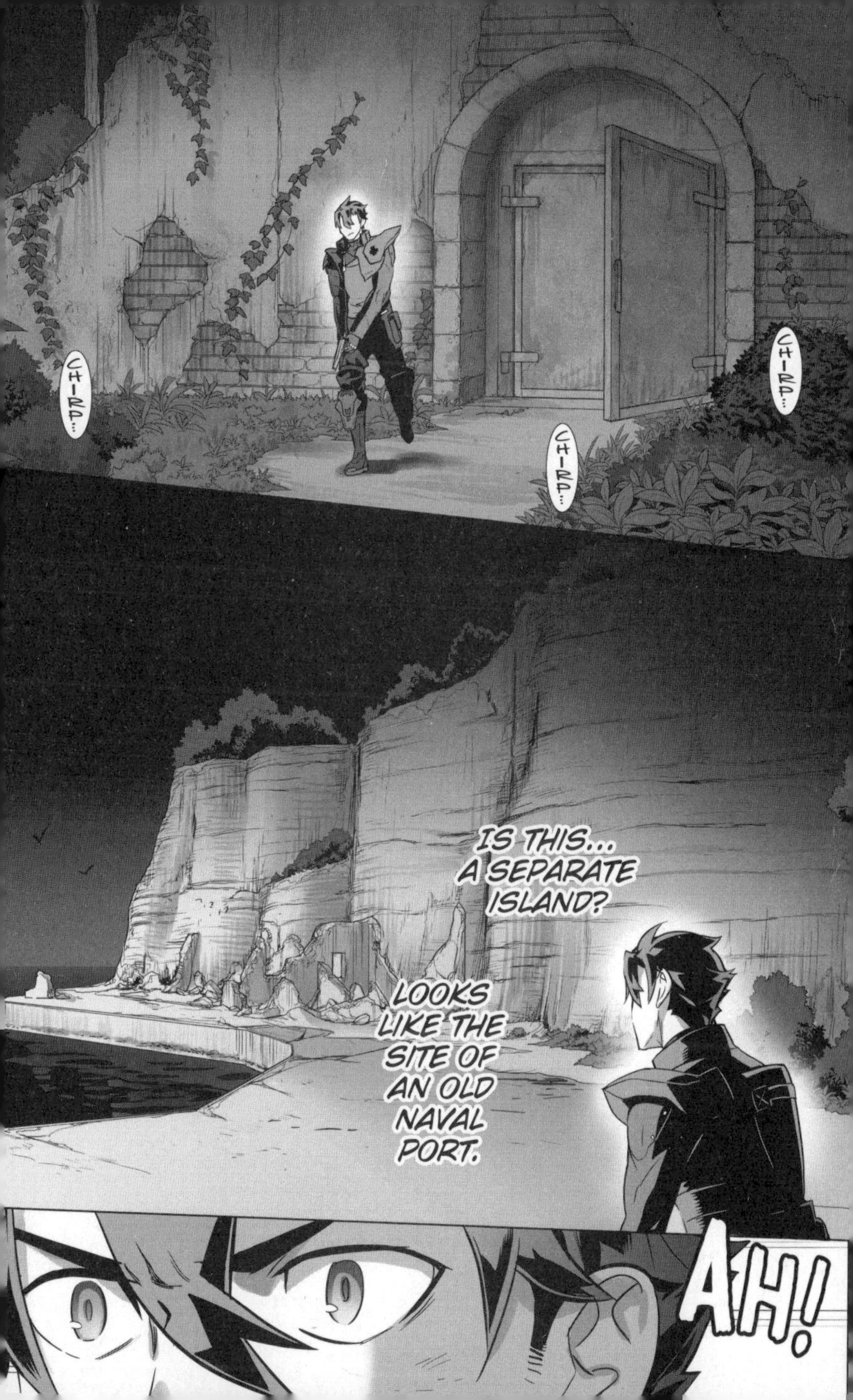
CHIRP...
CHIRP...
CHIRP...
IS THIS... A SEPARATE ISLAND?
LOOKS LIKE THE SITE OF AN OLD NAVAL PORT.
AH!

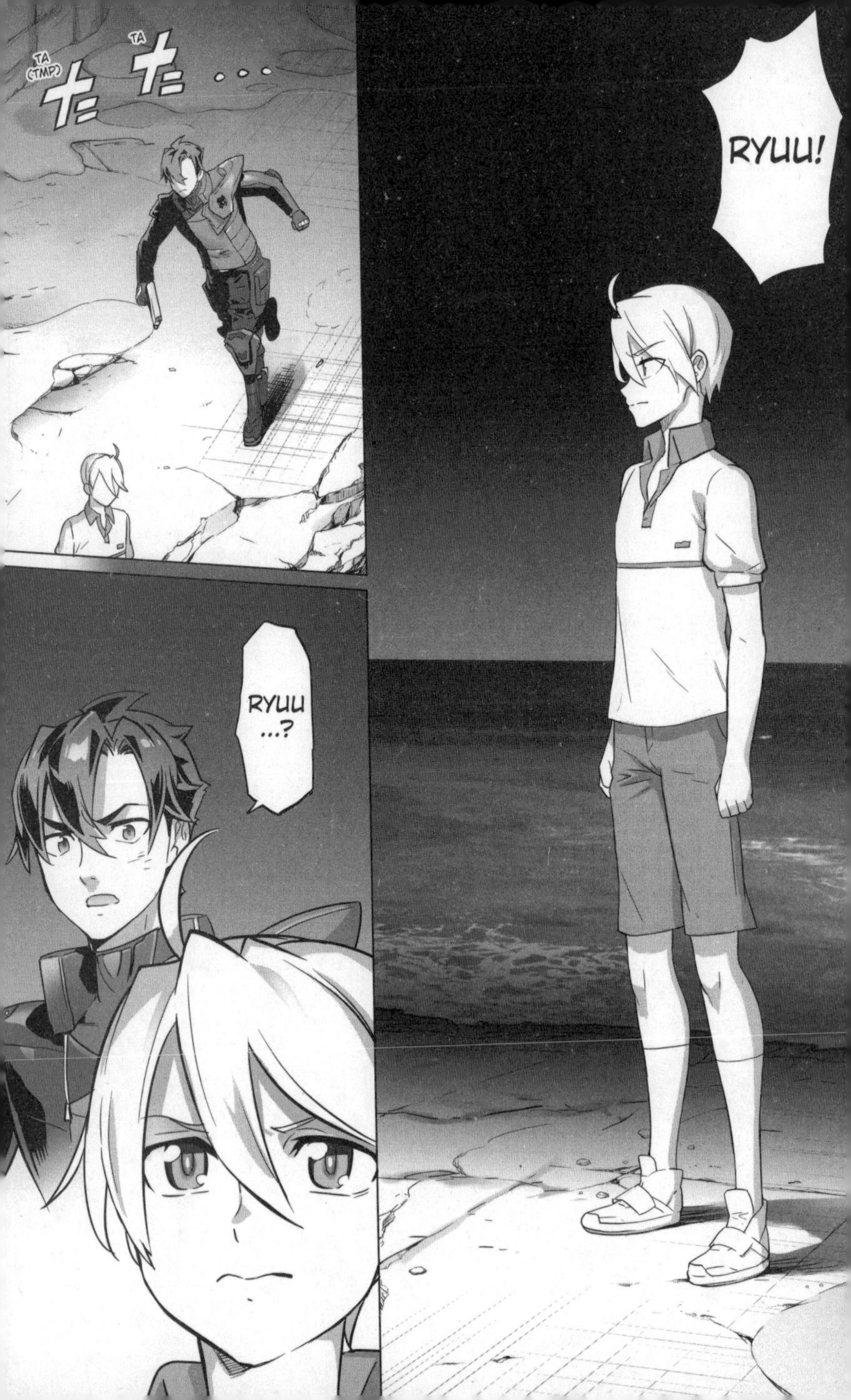
RYUU!
TA (TMP)
TA
...
RYUU ...?

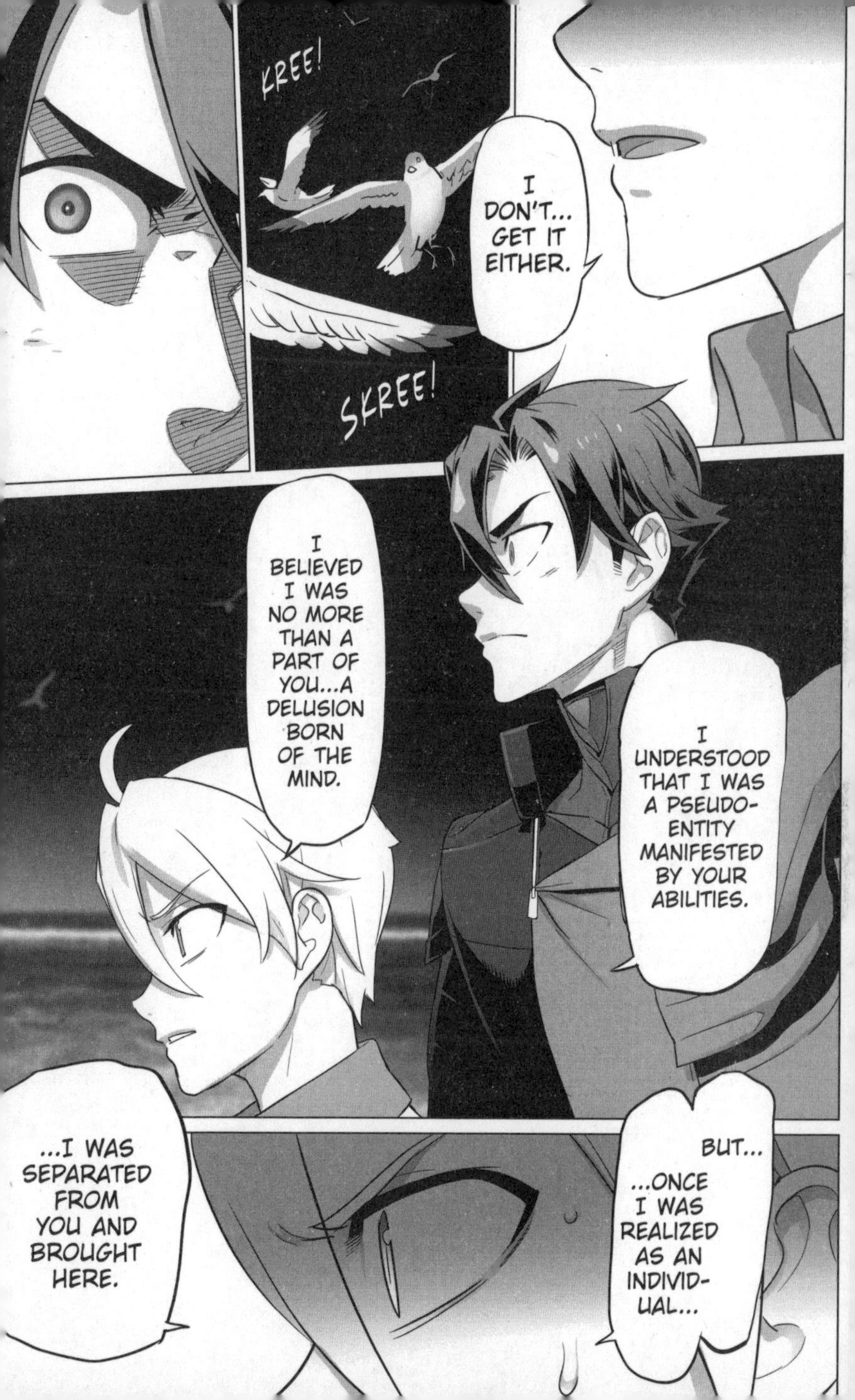
I DON'T... GET IT EITHER.
KREE!
SKREE!
I BELIEVED I WAS NO MORE THAN A PART OF YOU...A DELUSION BORN OF THE MIND.
I UNDERSTOOD THAT I WAS A PSEUDO-ENTITY MANIFESTED BY YOUR ABILITIES.
BUT...
...ONCE I WAS REALIZED AS AN INDIVID-UAL...
...I WAS SEPARATED FROM YOU AND BROUGHT HERE.

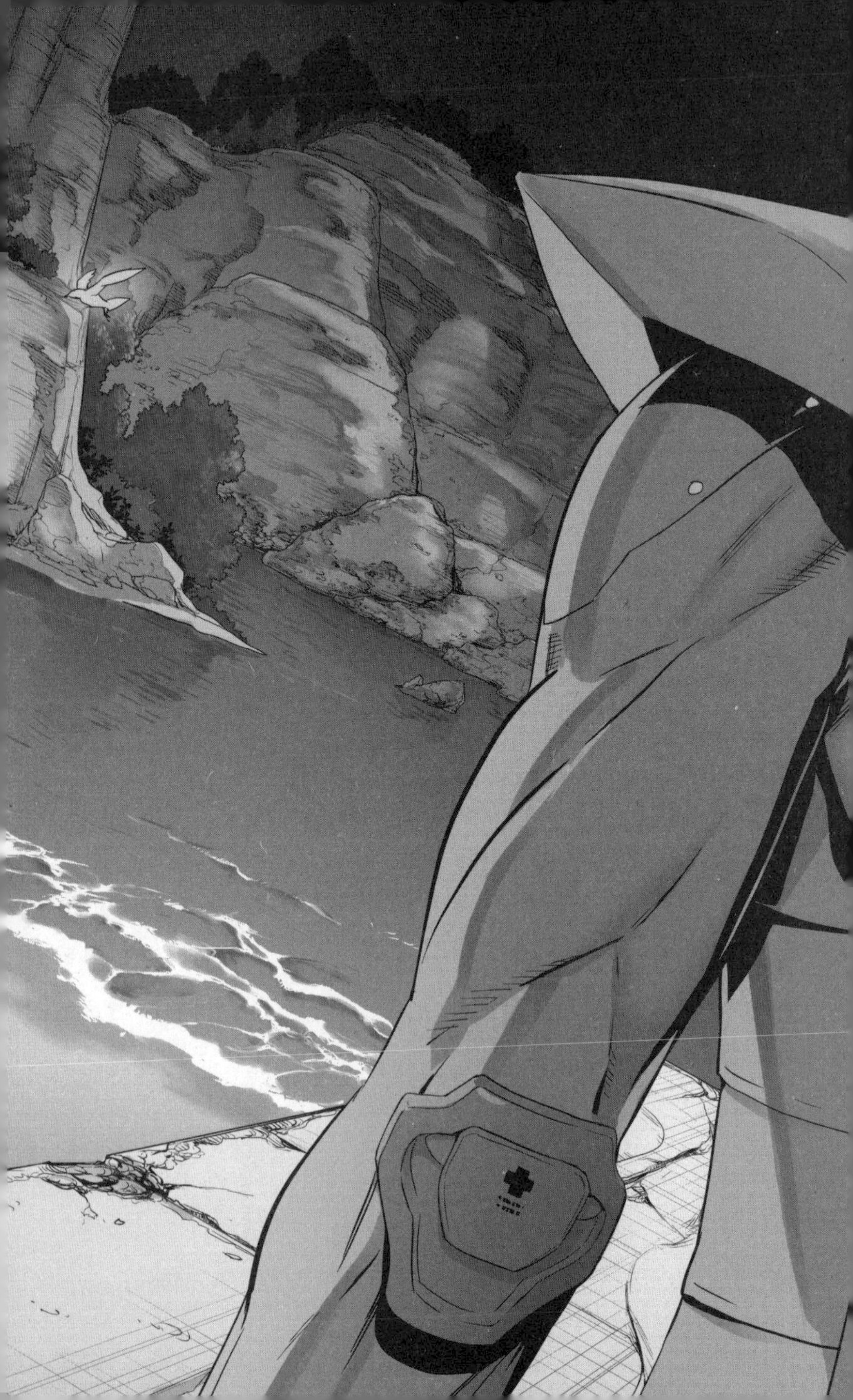

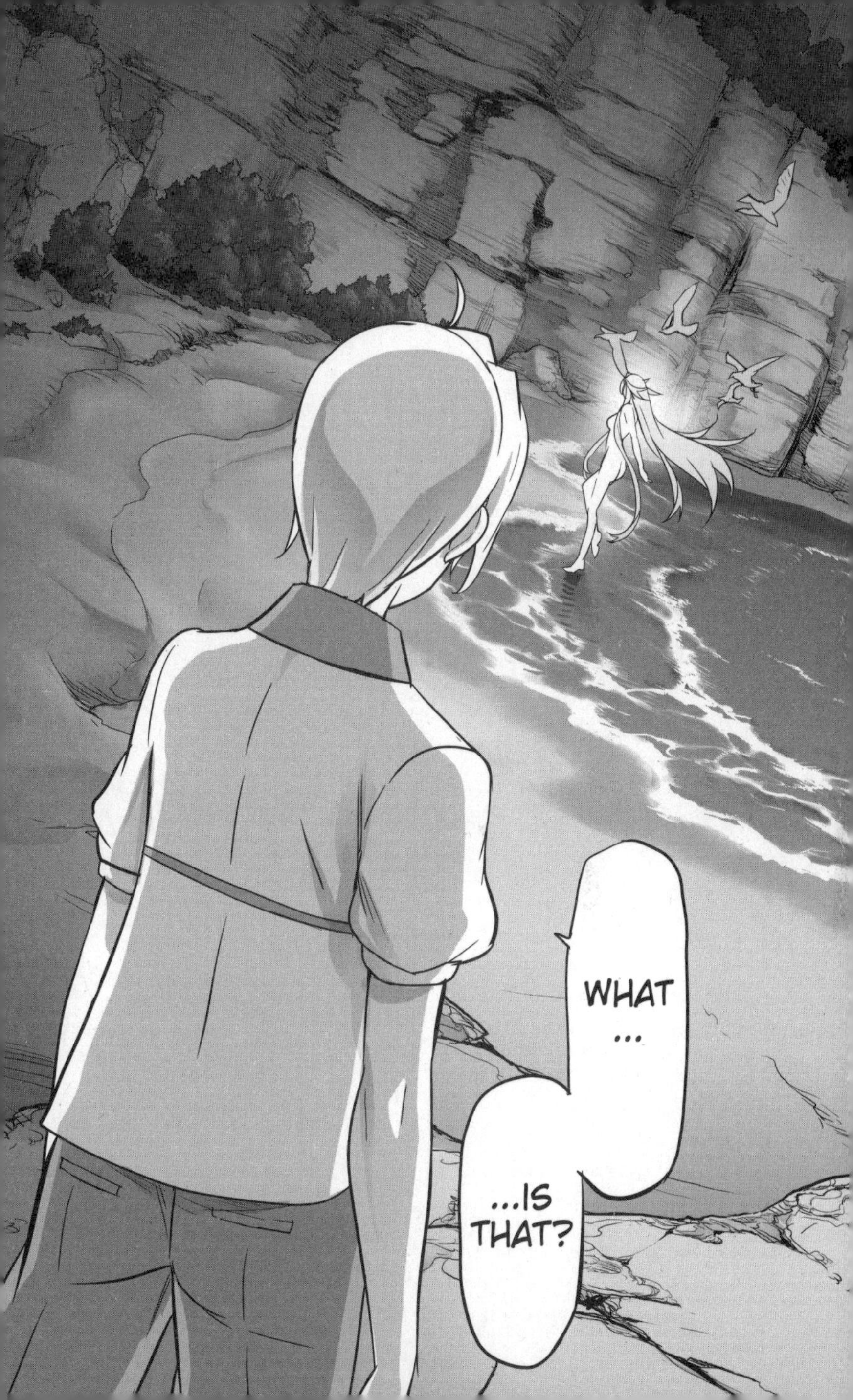
WHAT...
...IS THAT?

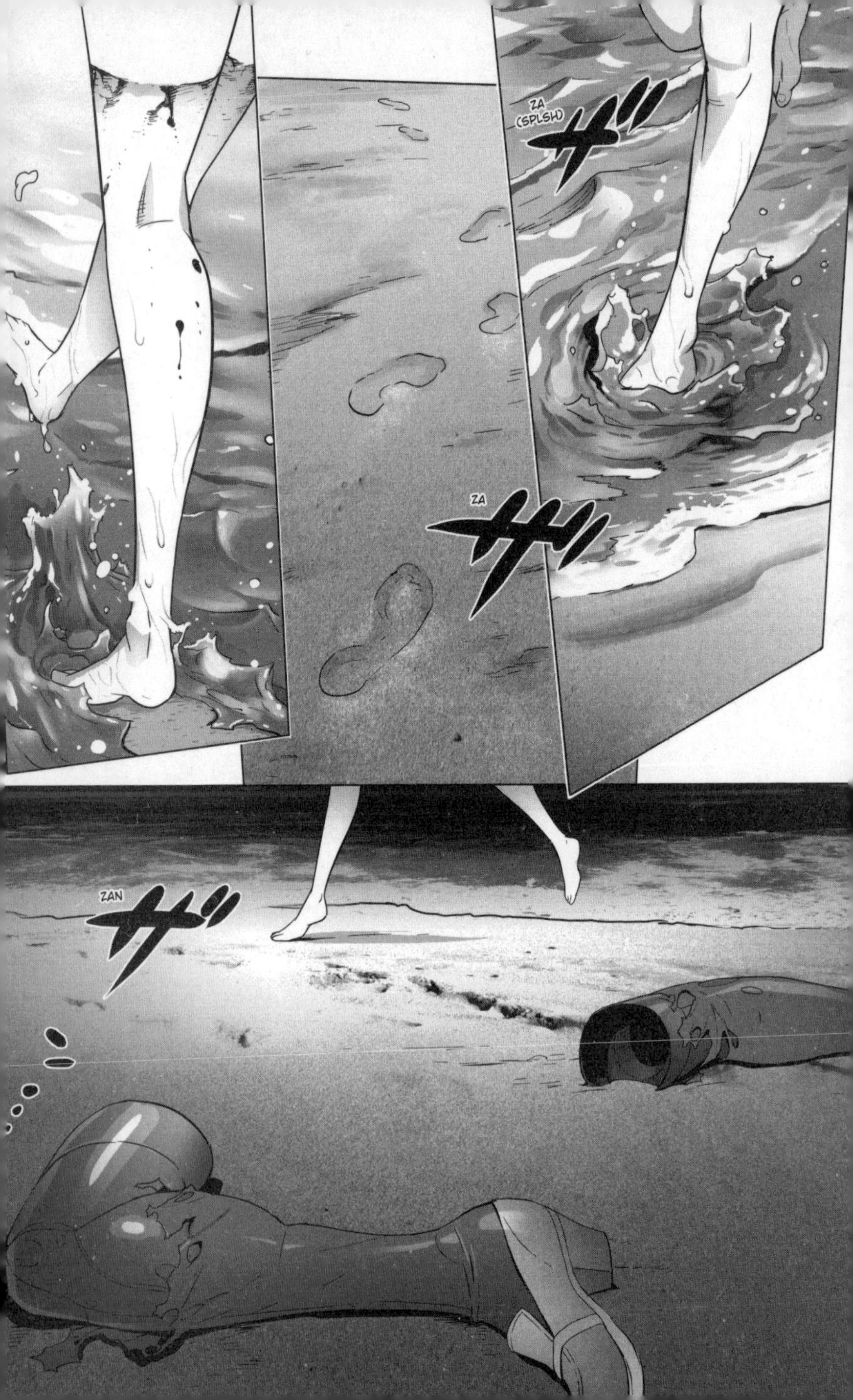
ZA (SPLSH)
ZA
ZAN

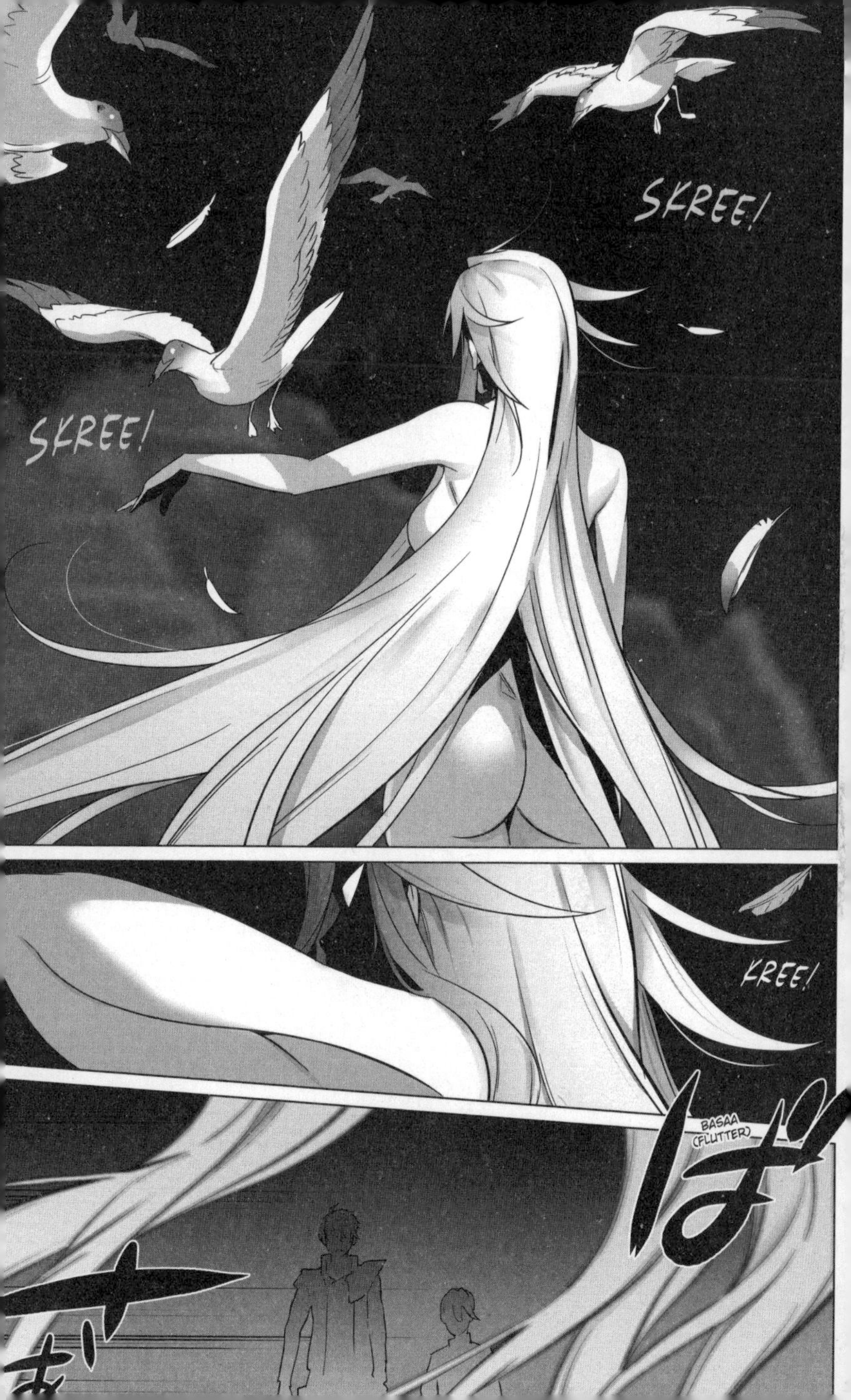
SKREE!
SKREE!
KREE!
BASAA (FLUTTER)

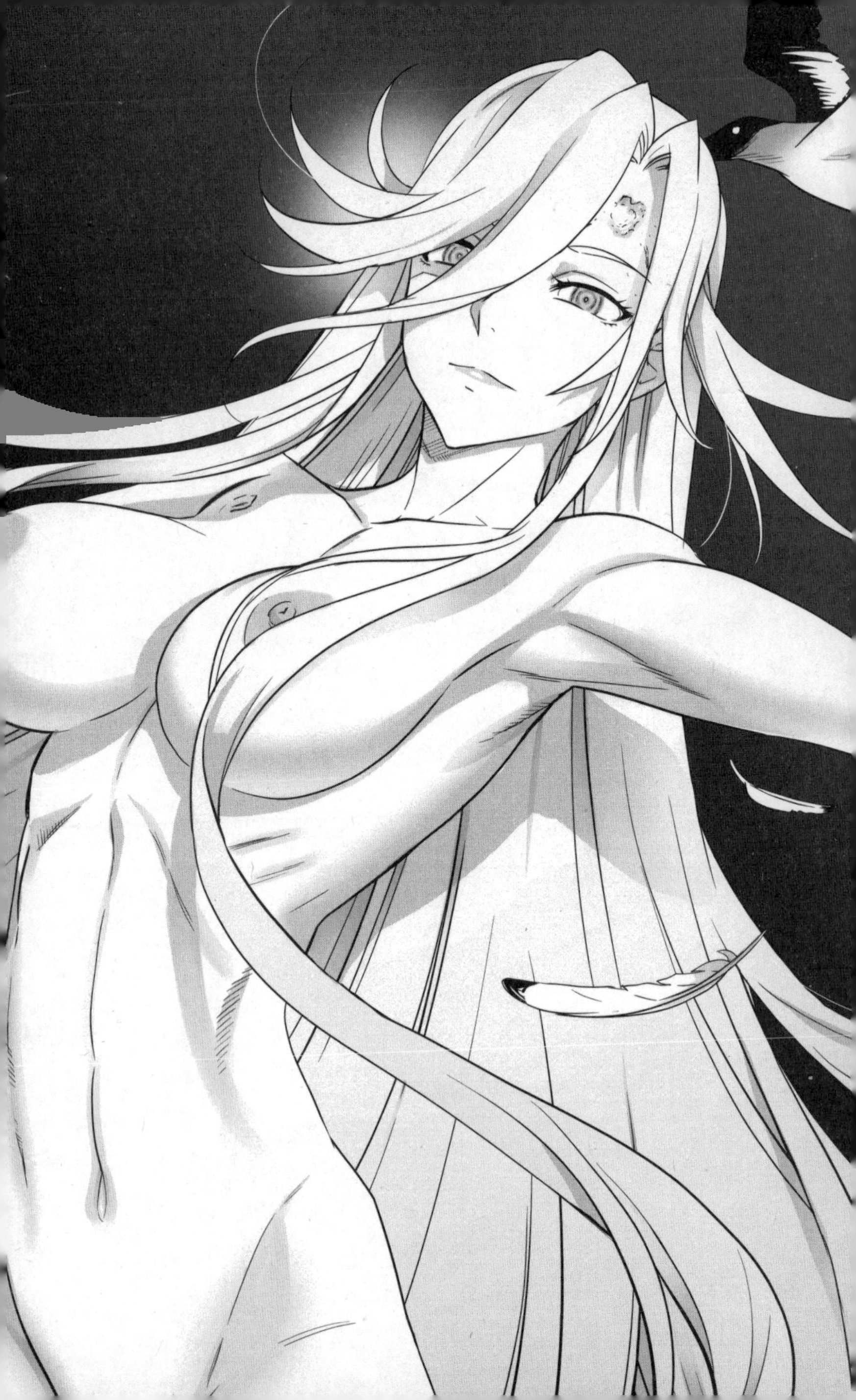

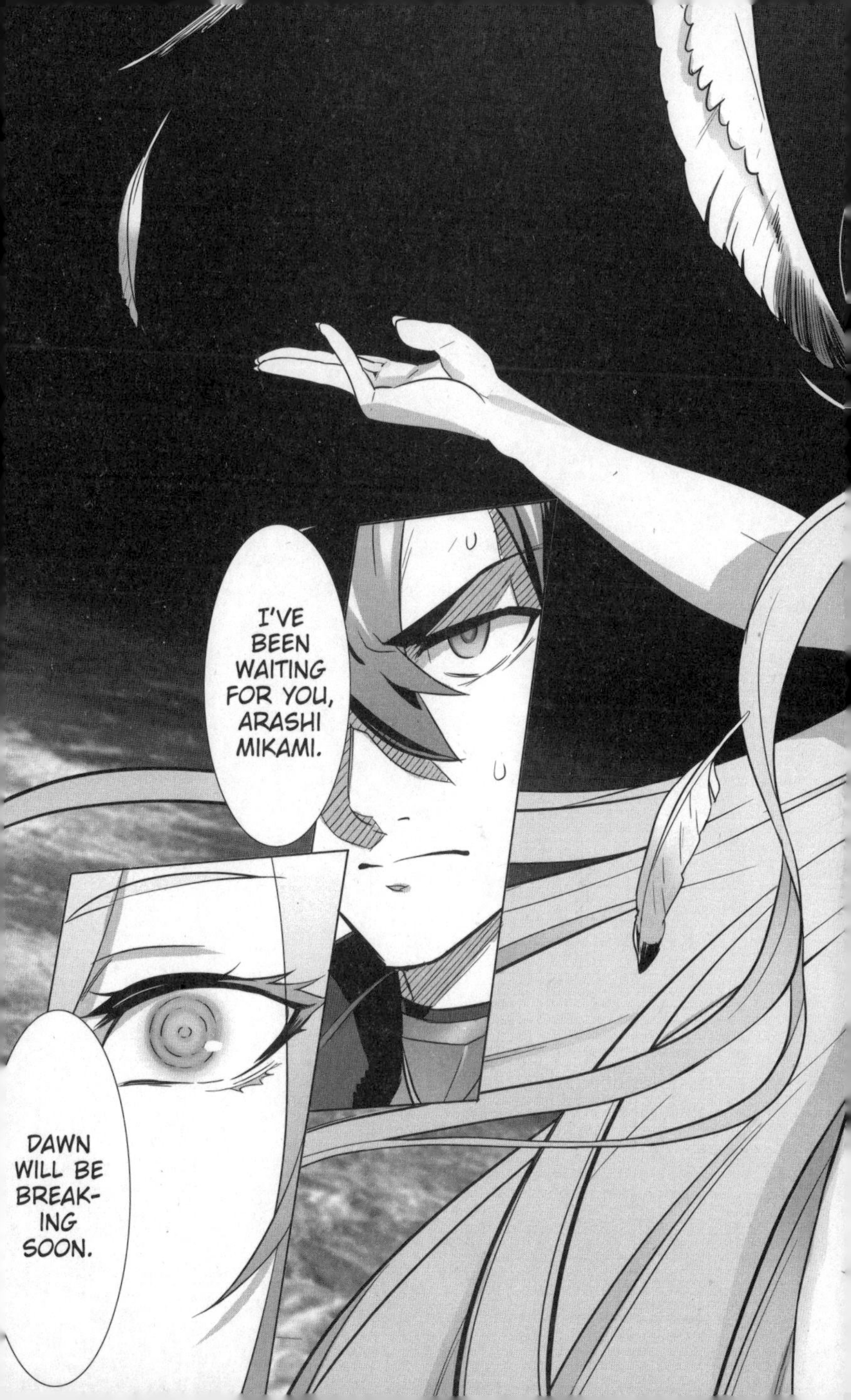
I'VE BEEN WAITING FOR YOU, ARASHI MIKAMI.
DAWN WILL BE BREAK-ING SOON.

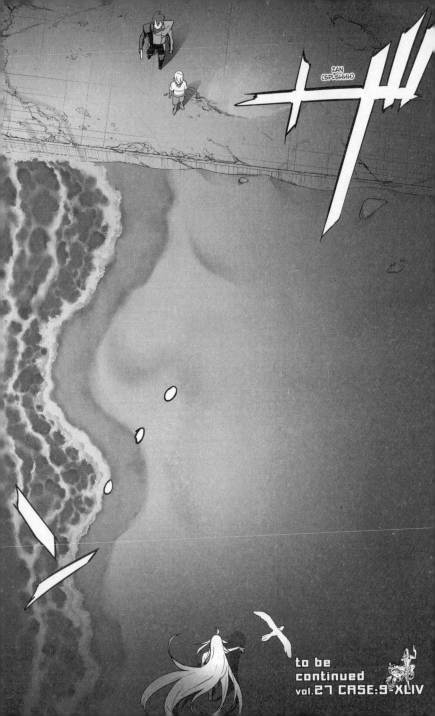

ZAN
(SPLSHHH)

to be
continued
vol.27 CASE:9-XLIV

TRIAGE X

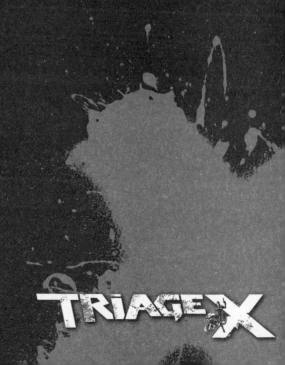

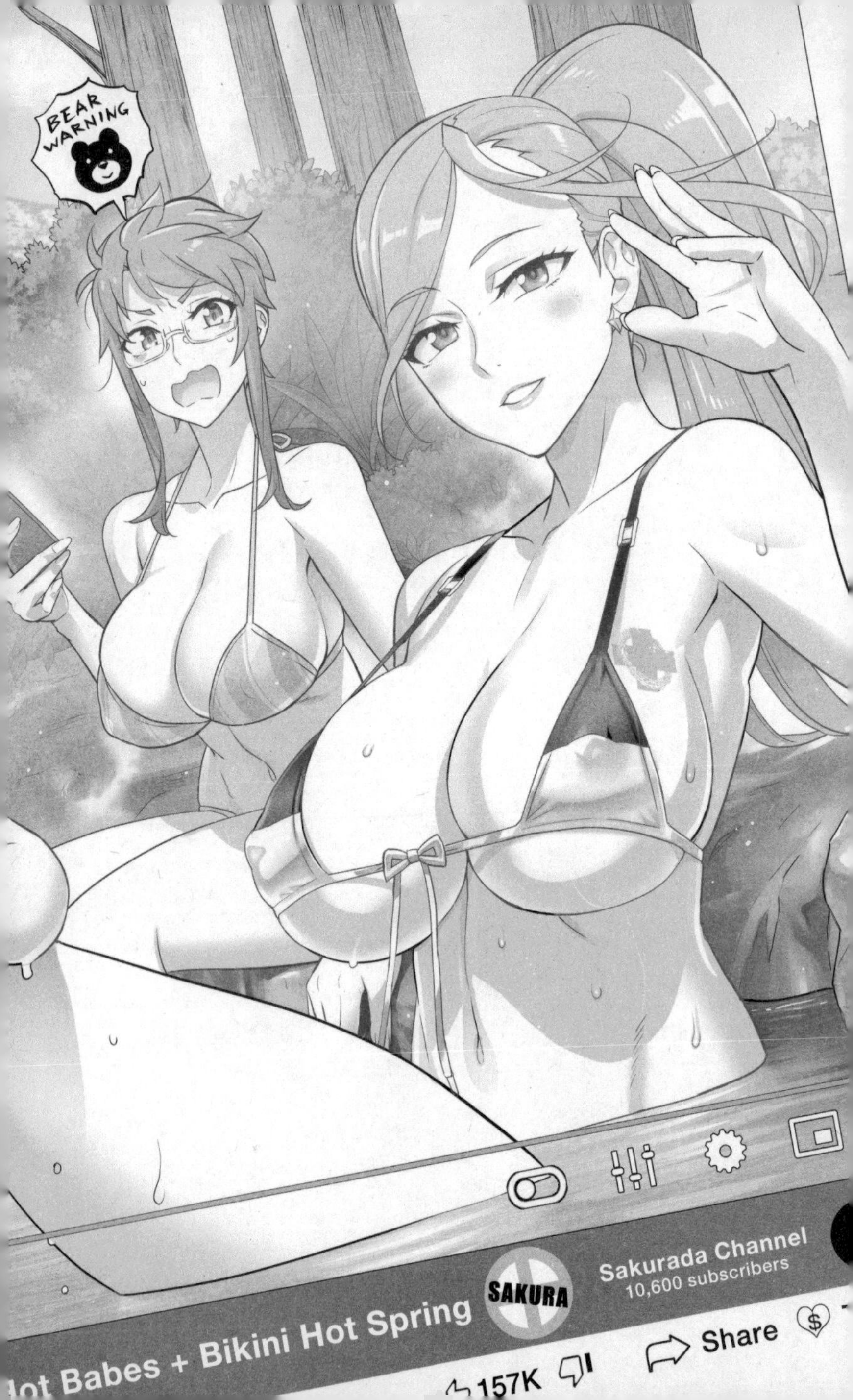
BEAR WARNING
Sakurada Channel
10,600 subscribers
SAKURA
ot Babes + Bikini Hot Spring
157K
Share

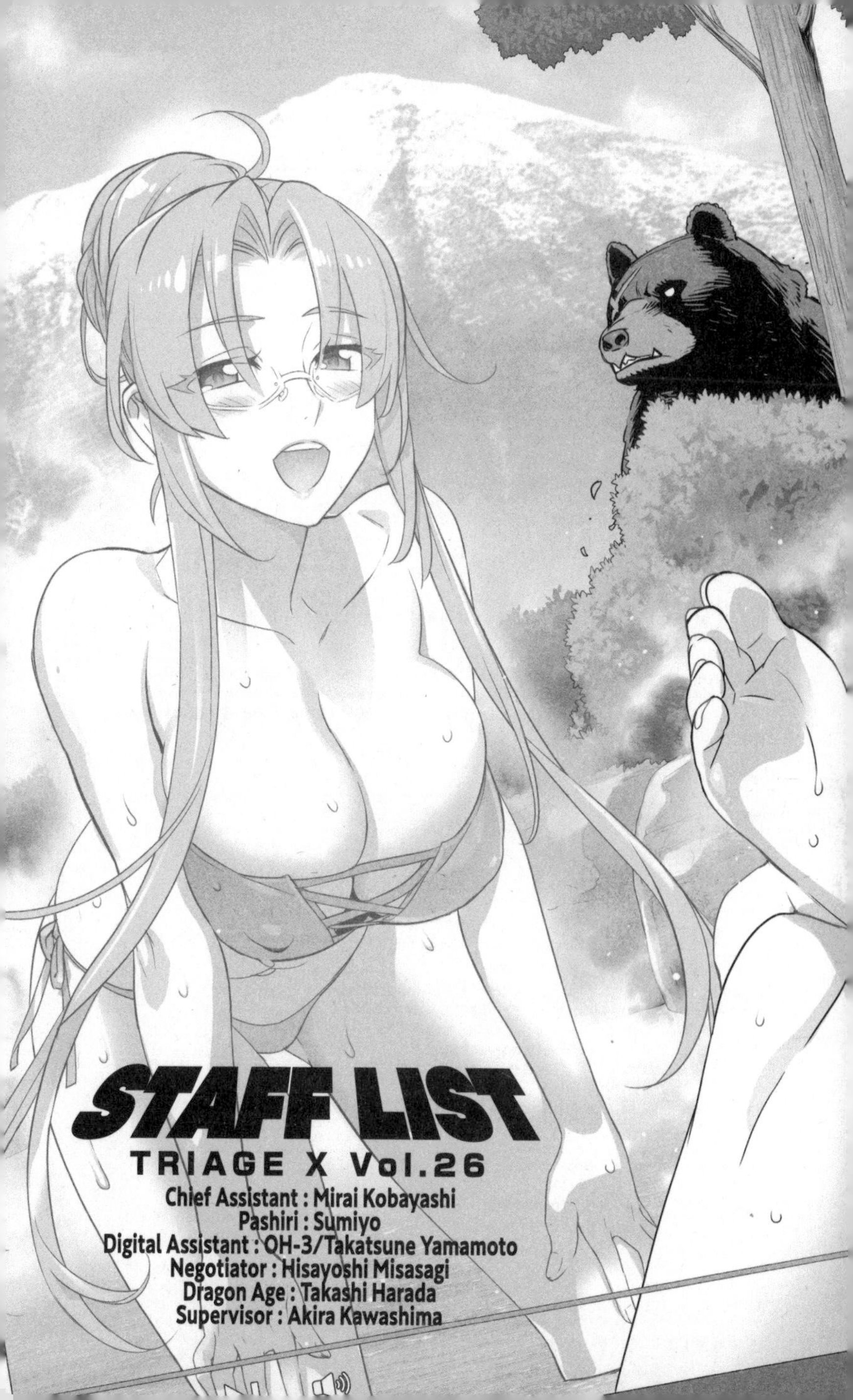

STAFF LIST

TRIAGE X Vol.26

Chief Assistant : Mirai Kobayashi
Pashiri : Sumiyo
Digital Assistant : OH-3/Takatsune Yamamoto
Negotiator : Hisayoshi Misasagi
Dragon Age : Takashi Harada
Supervisor : Akira Kawashima

TRIAGE X ㉖

SHOUJI SATO

Translation: Christine Dashiell

Lettering: Abigail Blackman

TRIAGE X Volume 26 © Shouji Sato 2023. First published in Japan in 2023 by KADOKAWA CORPORATION, Tokyo. English translation rights arranged with KADOKAWA CORPORATION, Tokyo, through TUTTLE-MORI AGENCY, INC., Tokyo.

English translation © 2023 by Yen Press, LLC

Yen Press
150 West 30th Street, 19th Floor
New York, NY 10001

Visit us at yenpress.com
facebook.com/yenpress
twitter.com/yenpress
yenpress.tumblr.com
instagram.com/yenpress

First Yen Press Edition: October 2023
Edited by Abigail Blackman & Yen Press Editorial: Carl Li
Designed by Yen Press Design: Eddy Mingki, Wendy Chan

Yen Press is an imprint of Yen Press, LLC.
The Yen Press name and logo are trademarks of Yen Press, LLC.

Library of Congress Control Number: 2015952593

ISBNs: 978-1-9753-7369-6 (paperback)
        978-1-9753-7370-2 (ebook)

10 9 8 7 6 5 4 3 2 1

WOR

Printed in the United States of America

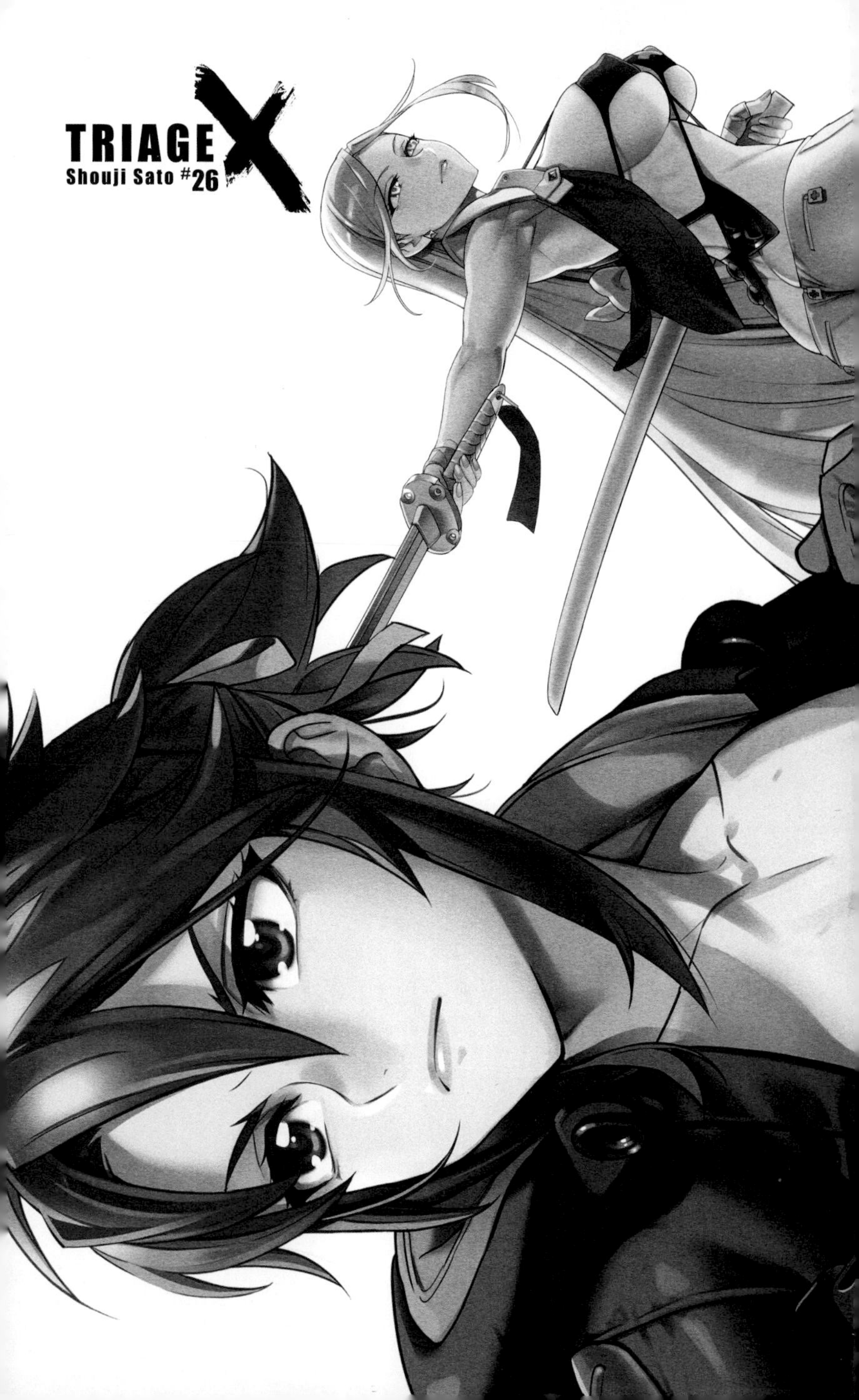
TRIAGE X
Shouji Sato #26

TRIAGE

CONTENTS

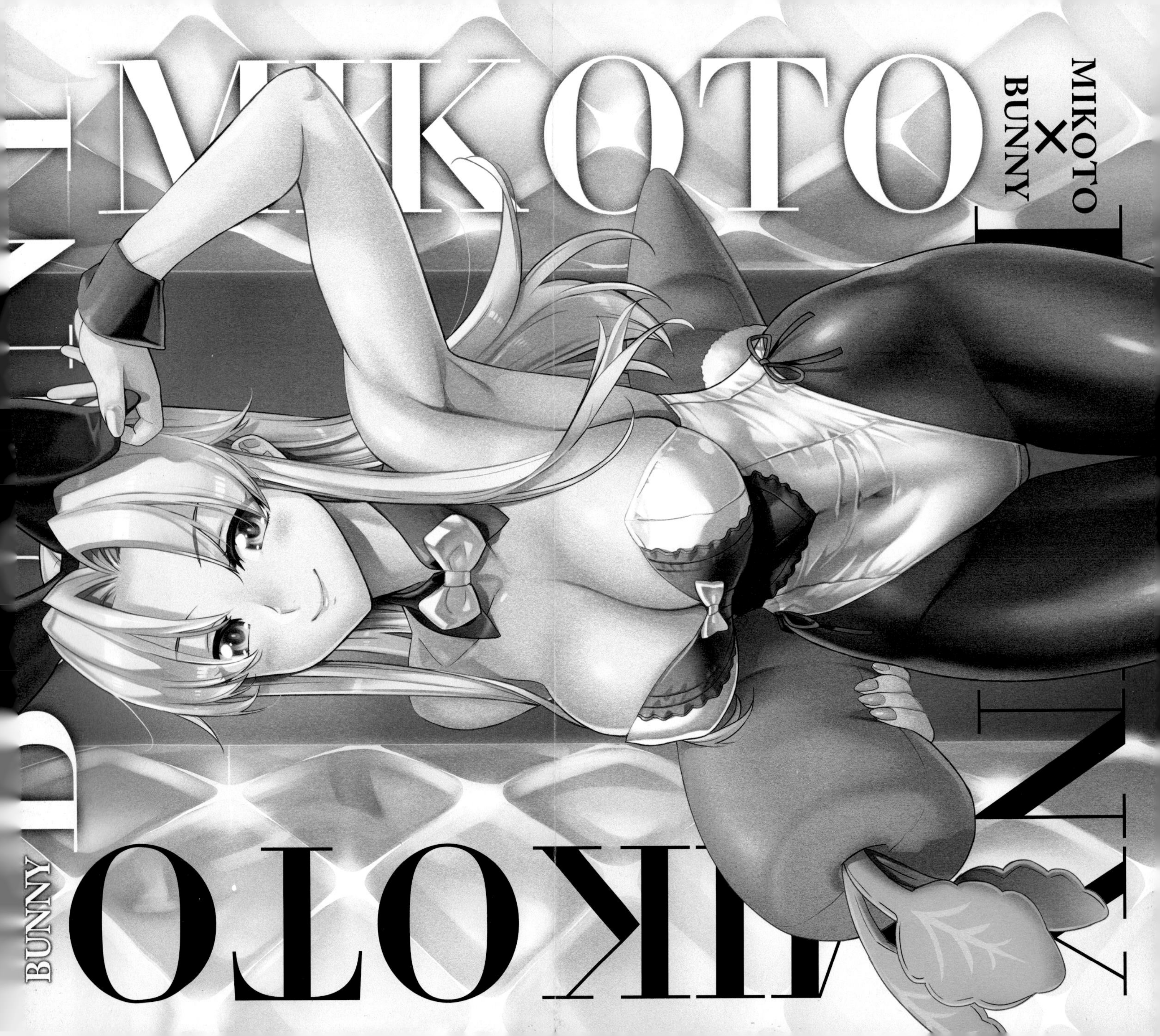
MIKOTO
MIKOTO × BUNNY
BUNNY
MIKOTO

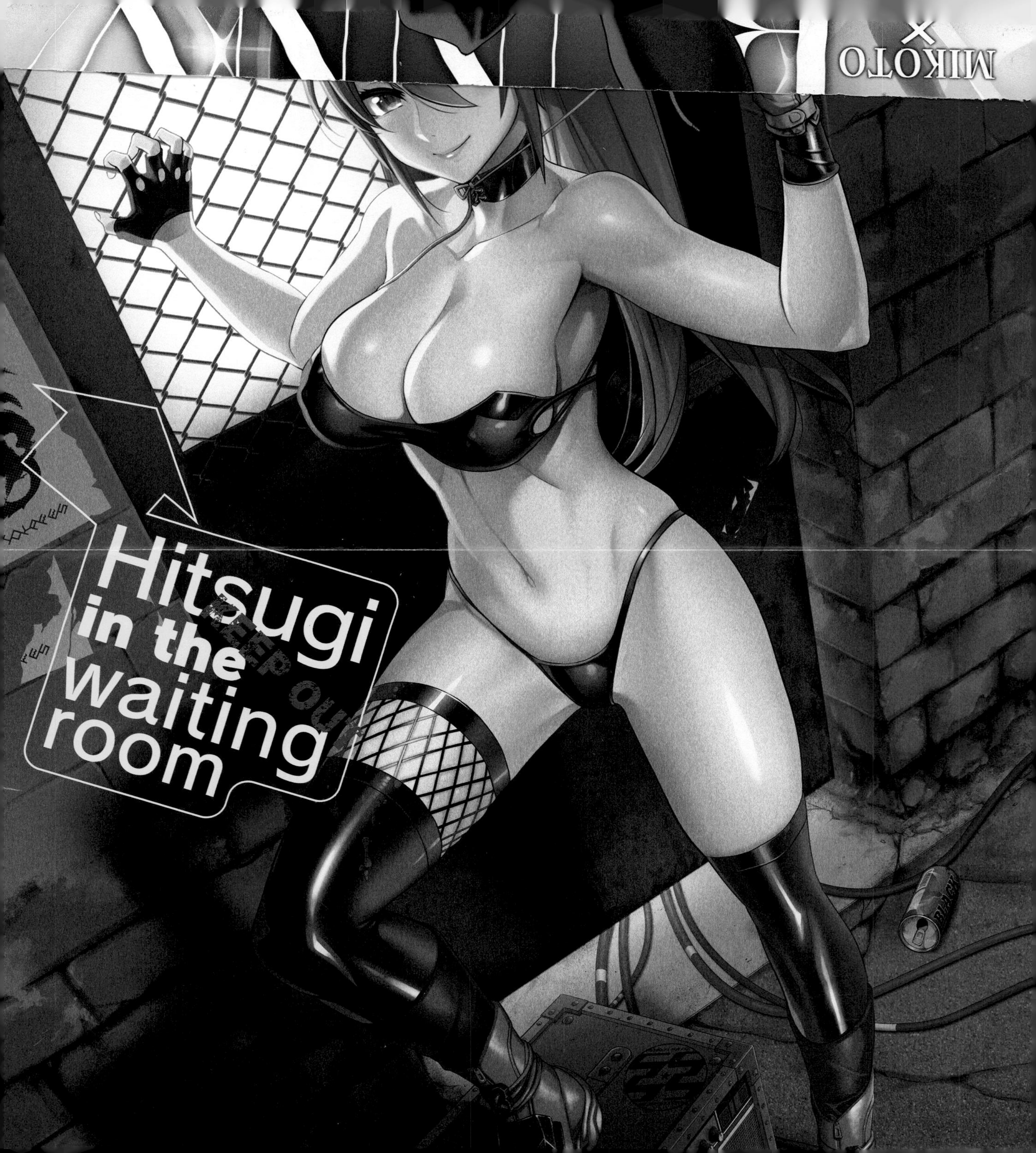
Hitsugi in the waiting room
BLACK